Garfinkel and Ethnomethodology

Garfinkel
and
Ethnomethodology

John Heritage

POLITY PRESS

© John Heritage, 1984

First published 1984 by
Polity Press in association with Blackwell Publishers Ltd.
Reprinted 1986, 1989, 1992, 1995, 1996

Editorial office:
Polity Press
65 Bridge Street, Cambridge CB2 1UR, UK

Marketing and production:
Blackwell Publishers Ltd
108 Cowley Road, Oxford OX4 1JF, UK

Published in the USA by
Blackwell Publishers Inc.
238 Main Street, Cambridge, MA 02142, USA

ISBN 0–7456–0060–3
ISBN 0–7456–0061–1 (pbk)

A CIP catalogue record for this book is available from the British Library and the Library of Congress.

Typset by Cambrian Typesetters, Frimley, Surrey
Printed and bound in Great Britain by Hartnolls Limited, Bodmin, Cornwall

Contents

Preface

Notwithstanding his world renown, Harold Garfinkel is a sociologist whose work is more known about than known. My own contact with his writings began when, quite by chance, I exercised my newly acquired rights as a graduate student to request the loan of a doctoral dissertation from the Widener Library at Harvard. The dissertation was entitled 'The Perception of the Other: A Study of Social Order' and had been written by Garfinkel some sixteen years previously. It contained a profound and arresting analysis of social action which quite transcended anything I had previously read in the field. Eager to locate more of Garfinkel's work, I quickly discovered that he had recently published a collection of papers entitled *Studies in Ethnomethodology*. My subsequent encounter with this volume was one of considerable shock. There seemed to be scarcely any connection between the Garfinkel of the dissertation and the new and puzzling sequence of studies. I had little idea of what to make of them and it was only after a considerable period that an understanding of the newer work could be co-ordinated with my knowledge of its background.

That initial puzzlement and the difficulties of understanding Garfinkel's work, which are still widely experienced today, have informed the writing of this book. In it, I have attempted to set Garfinkel's major theoretical contributions in the context of the traditional preoccupations of social theory and, through these continuities, to make the character of his thinking available to a wider audience. I am only too conscious of the pitfalls and difficulties inherent in this enterprise of making 'good sociological sense' of Garfinkel. The strains towards oversimplification and even downright revisionism which inhabit any expository work press all the more insistently on those who would expound truly innovative perspectives. The danger of traducing newly minted insights by rendering them in a more traditional conceptual coinage is an ever-present one. Nonetheless, the risks will have been worth running and this book will have served its purpose if it enables others to have more direct and productive contacts with the originals it represents.

In writing this book I have been more than fortunate in the encouragement and criticism which I have received from friends and colleagues who have read it in whole or in part. Margaret Archer, Max Atkinson, Robert Dingwall, Paul Drew, Anthony Giddens, David Greatbatch, Christian Heath, Martin Hollis, Mike Mulkay, William Outhwaite, Ian Procter and Rod Watson have generously helped in the task of eliminating weaknesses of substance and presentation and I am indebted to all of them. Two outstanding Warwick undergraduates, Peter Burnham and John Mattausch, did their best to reassure me that the text was reasonably accessible to student readers and I am grateful to them for their advice. My greatest debt is to my wife, who has been a constant source of encouragement and has survived the writing of this book with cheerfulness and patience.

Stratford upon Avon, June, 1984

The author and publisher are grateful to the following for permission to reproduce the figures: The Mary Evans Picture Library for figure 1, Basil Blackwell Publisher Ltd for figure 2, and Professor Richard Gregory for figure 3.

CHAPTER 1

Introduction

In studying a man's empirical work the questions asked will not merely be, what opinions did he hold about certain concrete phenomena, nor even, what has he in general contributed to our 'knowledge' of these phenomena? The primary questions will, rather, be, what theoretical reasons did he have for being interested in these particular problems rather than others, and what did the results of his investigation contribute to the solution of his theoretical problems?

Parsons, *The Structure of Social Action*

Any attempt to give an account of Garfinkel's work and the subsequent development of the ethnomethodological movement which he founded is immediately confronted with two formidable obstacles. There is, firstly, the character of the work itself. Garfinkel's entire published output has appeared in essay form and on a diversity of substantive topics. An essay on rationality rubs shoulders with an analysis of studies of intake decisions at a psychiatric clinic. Accounts of jury deliberations, the behaviour of a person seeking a sex-change operation, interpersonal conduct in a range of extraordinary, yet quasi-natural, experiments all jostle for attention, each in its own terms, seeming to lack any connecting theme. These studies are discussed in a difficult prose style in which dense thickets of words seem to resist the reader's best endeavours, only to yield, at the last, forceful and unexpected insights which somehow remain obstinately open-ended and difficult to place.

Then again there is the curious 'off-stage' role of theory. Although the writings convey an immediate sense of theoretical power, the theory itself is nowhere systematically stated, let alone used to integrate the various studies. Programmatic statements crop up, but they are formidably abstract and remain largely detached from traditional sociological reference points. The reader is thus confronted by a series of essays which, in their singularity and lack of compromise with conventional sociological sensibilities, both invite an engagement of an absolute kind whilst simultaneously resisting the assimilation of their perspectives and subject matter to any extant sociological framework. In both style and content the work is self-consciously revolutionary, demanding the abandonment of a range of widely held sociological assumptions before its message can be perceived fully.

The second obstacle lies in the reception accorded to Garfinkel's work during the past decade. The publication of *Studies in Ethnomethodology* in 1967 coincided with a period of widespread dissatisfaction with the prevailing orthodoxies of sociological theory and methodology. Parsonian systems theory, with its analytic subordination of the actor to an environment of functional requirements, had lost its appeal in a decade of libertarian social movements and political protest. These latter found theoretical expression within sociology in an upsurge of interest in frameworks which stressed the analytic primacy of the actor's point of view and the social construction of reality. A related critique, which spread into social psychology, stressed the weaknesses of social science methodologies which were based on a view of social actors as simply the passive bearers of sociological and psychological attributes. Common to both critiques was a renewed stress on the role of human agency in social life, a novel emphasis on the cognitive bases of action and a focus on the situation of action as a means of resolving previously intractable research dilemmas.

In this context a number of ethnomethodological tenets, pillaged from their carefully constructed frameworks, seemed to speak directly to the mood of the moment. The enduring ethnomethodological emphasis on the local, moment-by-moment determination of meaning in social contexts appeared, in itself, an important prophylactic against the mystifying consequences of 'grand theorizing' and 'abstracted empiricism', while the collateral focus on the contingency of meaning resonated happily with the humanistic overtones of theories which stressed the interpreted and constructed nature of social reality. By the same token, the ethnomethodological vocabulary of 'accounts' and 'accountability' seemed to many to give straightforward access to that most elusive phenomenon, the actor's definition of the situation. The dramatic oversimplifications embodied in these borrowings were facilitated during this period by the apparent alignment of several of the more significant empirical studies — such as Cicourel's and Kitsuse's *The Educational Decision Makers* (1963) and Cicourel's *The Social Organization of Juvenile Justice* (1968) — with the more readily understandable sociological approaches prominent at the time. The net result was an assimilation of a range of perspectives — symbolic interaction, labelling theory, the phenomenological analyses of Berger and Luckmann, and ethnomethodology — into a single category: the 'sociology of everyday life'. In this process, Garfinkel's fundamental and enduring analytical achievements were lost from sight at the very moment at which 'ethnomethodology' became a household word in sociology.

Unlike such famous contemporaries as Foucault or Habermas, Garfinkel's significance as a sociologist does not arise from the encyclopaedic range of his investigations nor from any attempt at large-scale theoretical synthesis. Rather it derives from his sustained attack on a narrow range of problems which have preoccupied him throughout an intellectual career spanning nearly forty years. These problems — the theory of action, the nature of intersubjectivity and the social constitution of knowledge — have been central areas of investigation throughout the history of the discipline and, in their various aspects, have persistently concerned its most distinguished practitioners. The positions adopted on these topics have been among the most distinctive hallmarks of the major schools of sociological theory. They are universally acknowledged as fundamental to the discipline.

Garfinkel's contribution has been a strikingly original re-analysis of these problems and a highly integrated treatment of their various implications for the conceptualization and analysis of fundamental aspects of social organization. This analysis, which has been widely influential across a range of social science disciplines, has emerged in a succession of papers in which Garfinkel has repeatedly returned to, and reworked, the foundational issues which have concerned him.

Like Husserl, Garfinkel has consistently sought to be a 'true beginner' and he has never attempted to follow Weber or Parsons in building outwards from his analysis of social action towards a large-scale systematic theory of social structure. Instead, he has persistently worked to secure and deepen the analyses of foundational social processes which he began as a doctoral student at Harvard in 1946.

By the mid-1950s, Garfinkel had coined the term which would subsequently make him famous. 'Ethnomethodology' was originally designed simply as a label to capture a range of phenomena associated with the use of mundane knowledge and reasoning procedures by ordinary members of society. The term, Garfinkel relates (Garfinkel 1974: 16), occurred to him as he was writing up a study of jury deliberations. The jurors, he found, were preoccupied with a variety of 'methodological' matters such as the distinction between 'fact' and 'opinion', between 'what we're entitled to say', 'what the evidence shows' and 'what can be demonstrated' (ibid.). The jurors worked with these kinds of distinctions seriously and methodically as part of a deliberative process which all of them knew to be highly consequential and through which they determined the reasonableness of particular evidences, demonstrations, conclusions and, ultimately, verdicts. These distinctions were handled in coherently organized and 'agree-able' ways and the jurors assumed and counted upon one another's abilities to use them, draw appropriate inferences from them and see the sense of them. Although the systematic use of the distinctions was an essential part of the jurors' tasks, Garfinkel found that the distinctions themselves were not made or employed by using a special 'juror's logic'. Quite the contrary, they were overwhelmingly made by reference to common-sense considerations that 'anyone could see'. As Garfinkel put it, 'a person is 95 per cent juror before he comes near the court ' (Garfinkel 1967d: 110). The term 'ethnomethodology' thus refers to the study of a particular subject matter: the body of common-sense knowledge and the range of procedures and considerations by means of which the ordinary members of society make sense of, find their way about in, and act on the circumstances in which they find themselves. The term was designed to be cognate with a number of related anthropological terms, such as ethnobotany and ethnomedicine, but its scope is not restricted to any particular domain of knowledge. In its open-ended reference to any kind of sense-making procedure, the term represents a signpost to a domain of uncharted dimensions rather than a staking out of a clearly delineated territory.

As the preceding discussion suggests, by the mid-1950s Garfinkel was already working in a terrain which was largely alien to the majority of sociologists. During this period every form of sociology simply took for granted and left out of consideration the key questions of the construction and recognition of social activities by the actors themselves. In this context, it fell to Garfinkel to point out that these questions are analytically primary to any theory of social action and ultimately to any form of sociological investigation. His achievement has been to show that a consideration of these issues can be made an integral part of the theory of action and that they can be addressed as productive research questions in concrete empirical investigations with significant analytic results.

Although these achievements can be simply stated, they are in fact the products of a complex reconceptualization of both the theory of action and the sociology of knowledge aimed at wresting each from its preoccupation with the phenomenon of error. In the theory of action this is manifested in the long-standing distinction between rational and (normatively determined) non-rational action as a fundamental theoretical axis. Garfinkel has consistently opposed the use of this distinction in the analysis of action, arguing that it is an irrelevant and misleading distraction from the most central features of the organization of social activity — its inherent intelligibility and accountability. An emphasis on these latter characteristics, however, places a new weight on the kinds of knowledge that the actor might be viewed as possessing or drawing upon in devising or recognizing conduct. Here the older neo-Kantian sociology of knowledge, with its parallel focus on the distinction between rationally founded knowledge on the one hand and error and ideology on the other, was simply insufficient to carry the burden. Hence Garfinkel drew extensively on Schutz's writings to develop a sociology of mundane knowledge-in-action and, in accomplishing this, then found it possible to proceed to an adequately grounded analysis of institutionalized conduct.

Finally, in both its positive recommendations for the study of common-sense knowledge and its rejection of analytical frameworks premised on the assumed, in-principle superiority of social science knowledge over its lay equivalents, Garfinkel's work also issues in a programme of study which focuses on the social constitution of knowledge. Here we encounter the obverse of Garfinkel's insistence that the analysis of action must take account of the actor's use of common-sense knowledge, namely, that the social constitution of knowledge cannot be analysed independently of the contexts of institutional activity in which it is generated and maintained. This position is most obviously asserted in Garfinkel's ' "Good" organizational reasons for "bad" clinic records' (Garfinkel, 1967f) and it has recently found exemplification in a range of detailed studies of organizational knowledge as it is produced and reproduced in the mundane work of scientists and professionals of various kinds (Garfinkel, forthcoming).

The full depth of the theoretical innovations through which Garfinkel has come to stress the profoundly reflexive relations between knowledge and action has tended to remain dimly perceived or badly misconstrued in the reception of his work. The unhappy result of this has been a widespread failure to appreciate the major advances in the analysis of knowledge and action which he has accomplished and which remain, partially submerged, in the particulars of his various studies. Accordingly, I have thought it right to begin this book with a fairly extensive account of the theory of action which Garfinkel encountered as a graduate student in the late 1940s and to discuss at some length his transformation of the main features of this theory. Subsequently, I have used this discussion of action as a basis from which to consider Garfinkel's analysis of institutionalized conduct and his treatment of the social organization of knowledge. Finally, it has proved valuable, if only as a background, in situating both the development of conversation analysis and of the more recent studies of organizational work which, in their different ways, have been strongly influenced by his teachings.

CHAPTER 2

A Parsonian Backdrop

In most available theories of social action and social structure rational actions are assigned residual status.

Garfinkel, *Studies in Ethnomethodology*

Garfinkel's career as a theorist effectively began when, in 1946, he enrolled as a doctoral student at Harvard University in the newly formed Department of Social Relations. The department was the recent product of an amalgamation of several social science disciplines (incorporating sociology, social anthropology, and social and clinical psychology) and had been expressly created in order to promote the development of integrated interdisciplinary research. A primary focus was to be social theory and, within five years, a group of faculty members was to produce a first interdisciplinary synthesis, *Towards a General Theory of Action*, which represented 'a kind of intellectual stocktaking of what underlay the social relations experiment' (Parsons 1970: 843).

This novel, even revolutionary, emphasis within the Harvard department on theory and, in particular, the theory of action was due largely to the influence of its first chairman, Talcott Parsons. During the previous decade Parsons had consistently advocated the significance of systematic theory construction in the social sciences in a largely empiricist intellectual climate which stressed the importance of piecemeal empirical research over against the claims of theoretical work. In *The Structure of Social Action* (1937) Parsons had insisted against this prevailing orthodoxy that *theoretical* development is the hallmark of science. No discipline, he argued, is simply created as an assemblage of 'raw facts'. On the contrary, empirical findings and the disciplines which are based on them are always and inevitably the products of theoretical interpretations of available evidence. In this context, the theorist has a vital and essential role to play. It is one of explicitly formulating, clarifying and developing the conceptual frameworks in terms of which evidence is evaluated, interpreted and integrated within a discipline's corpus of scientific fact.

Parsons coupled these claims with an extensive discussion which introduced American sociologists to a range of European theorists whose work was not widely appreciated at the time. Moreover he presented a powerful case for the latent convergence of the major theorists (Marshall, Pareto, Durkheim and Weber) on a single basic theoretical framework − the 'voluntaristic theory of action' − which made the actors' treatment of their circumstances in terms of subjectively held norms and values central to the analysis of social institutions. The effect of these claims was two-fold. They created a case for the significance of theory which was to become increasingly influential during the post-war period while, additionally, proposing a major site for theoretical development based on the voluntaristic theory itself.

It was these proposals which became central to the early development of the 'social relations experiment' at Harvard. The voluntaristic theory provided a coherent and viable focus for the department's initial endeavours, not least because the theory's emphasis on the normative aspects of conduct permitted a satisfactory intellectual division of labour among the constituent social science disciplines. Thus, in both its constitution and its objectives, the Department of Social Relations represented a radical departure from prevailing patterns of research in American sociology. Its novel and distinctive institutionalization of theoretical work as a legitimate form of sociological research in its own right proved a powerful attraction for a new post-war generation of graduate students and it was to this department, during its most richly innovative period, that Garfinkel came to participate in what Parsons later recalled (Parsons, 1970: 843) as a 'golden age' of graduate studies at Harvard.

Yet, although written under the supervision of Parsons and extensively occupied with his thought, the theoretical viewpoint of Garfinkel's dissertation was not derived from the 'structural functionalist' conceptual system then emerging through a stream of publications from the department. Instead, Garfinkel sought to dig still deeper into basic problems in the theory of action which had been raised, but incompletely dealt with, in *The Structure of Social Action*. In particular, he was dissatisfied with — and sought to remedy — the sketchy treatment of the actor's knowledge and understanding within the voluntaristic theory. Garfinkel summarized the differences between Parsons' achievements and his own interests in the opening paragraph of his dissertation:

> At least two important theoretical developments stem from the researches of Max Weber. One development, already well worked, seeks to arrive at a generalized social system by uniting a theory that treats the structuring of experience with another theory designed to answer the question, 'What is man?' Speaking loosely, a synthesis is attempted between the facts of social structure and the facts of personality. The other development, not yet adequately exploited, seeks a generalized social system built solely from the analysis of experience structures. (Garfinkel, 1952: 1)

The objective of the dissertation was 'to go as far as possible in exploring a theoretical vocabulary to transform [the second development] into a working scheme for the experimental investigation of the sociological phenomenon of social order' (ibid.). From the outset therefore, Garfinkel was in search of a theoretical framework which would directly catch at the procedures by which actors analyse their circumstances and devise and carry out courses of action. Such a framework would, in turn, result in an account of social activity which was more directly based on an analysis of the organization of experience itself. While the theoretical vocabulary to be used in this task was to be drawn from the phenomenological writings of Schutz and Gurwitsch, it would be used to analyse classical problems in the theory of action and to propose entirely novel avenues towards their solution. The differences between Parsons and his student would ultimately crystallize around the question of whether the actor's point of view, and its role in the organization of action, should be analysed and treated by means which were intrinsic to, or external to, the structure of the actor's experience. Although the distinction might seem to be a slender one, it entailed a transformation in the analysis of action no less complete in its consequences than the previous shift — from the utilitarian to the voluntaristic framework — canvassed by Parsons himself.

THE ACTION FRAME OF REFERENCE

One of the central claims of *The Structure of Social Action* is that all of the various social sciences essentially deal with systems of social action. The basic units of such systems, Parsons argued, are 'unit acts' which, in turn, are composed of the following irreducible elements:

(1) An *actor*, the agent of the act.

(2) An '*end*', a future state of affairs which the actor seeks to bring about by the act.

(3) A current situation within which the actor acts and which he or she seeks to transform by his or her action. The situation is analysable into two kinds of elements: the *conditions* of action over which the actor has no control and the means of action over which he or she does have control.

(4) A *mode of orientation*, comprising at least one selective standard, in terms of which the actor relates the end to the current situation.

These elements which, together, comprise the action frame of reference are, according to Parsons, 'the indispensable logical framework in which we describe and think about the phenomena of action' (Parsons, 1937: 733). Here Parsons made a specific analogy between the action frame of reference in the social sciences and the space-time framework formulated by Kant as the a priori basis of Newtonian mechanics. As he put it, without the irreducible framework of the action frame of reference, 'talk about action fails to make sense' (ibid. 732).

Two important consequences flow directly from this conceptualization of action. First, Parsons argued, action must necessarily be viewed as involving the use of effort over time. For an end is, by definition, a future state of affairs —

something which has yet to come about and which must be brought about by the overcoming of obstacles. In the course of overcoming the obstacles to an end (the conditional elements of situations), energy will be expended and time will elapse. In stressing this aspect of action, Parsons particularly sought to counteract the tendency which he identified in the German idealistic tradition to view action as simply an automatic 'emanation' of cultural ideals.

The second major consequence of this conception of action is that it necessarily involves a thoroughgoing analysis of the subjective point of view of the actor. It is, of course, axiomatic that an 'end', as a future state of affairs, can only presently exist 'in the mind' of the actor. Additionally however, the 'selective standards' by reference to which the actor relates aspects of the present situation to the end cannot be conceived as anything but subjective in character. Finally, since what will appear as the 'means' and the 'conditions' in the situation will depend both on the goal which the actor has in mind and the 'selective standards' which he or she brings to bear, the actor's conceptualization of the situation of action in terms of 'means' and 'conditions' will also be subjectively determined. In sum, the specification of each of the elements of the action frame of reference will inevitably involve some recourse to the subjective point of view of the actor. This stress on the subjective direction of human effort to overcome real world obstacles — Parsons' 'voluntaristic metaphysic' (Scott, 1963; Procter, 1978) — lies at the very heart of the Parsonian conception of action and gives rise to his most fundamental preoccupation: how to conceptualize and account for the fact that, rather than passively adapting to their external circumstances as they are originally encountered, human beings act positively (and sometimes at great cost) to transform recalcitrant environments in accordance with the dictates of subjectively held normative ideals.

Examined from the perspective of this conception of action, it is possible to review the various preceding accounts of action as involving different emphases or 'loadings' on the various terms of the action frame of reference. Thus within the utilitarianism of Hobbes and his intellectual successors (Parson, 1937: 89 *et seq.*) the ends of action were treated as random and no attempt was made to give an account of either their origins or interrelationships. The actor was treated as having a veridical grasp of the objective features of the situation which included the objectively given conditions of action, the range of available means for the achievement of ends and the full range of consequences of their use. Finally, the utilitarian theorist characteristically assumed that the sole selective standard governing the actor's choice of means to an end would be that of 'intrinsic rationality' in which ends are pursued 'by the means which, among those available to the actor, are intrinsically best adapted to the end for reasons understandable and verifiable by positive empirical science (ibid. 58). As Parsons viewed it, the utilitarian theory of action was acutely indeterminate on two counts. Firstly, it lacked any account of the ends of action and thus could shed no light either on how the individual could establish priorities among ends or, even more seriously, why the conflictual pursuit of ends should not result in a Hobbesian state of war. Secondly, in its reliance on a single selective standard of 'intrinsic rationality', the theory could only account for the actor's divergence from a rational choice of means by treating such divergences as the product of the actor's ignorance or error. These latter, like the ends of action, were treated as random in occurence (ibid. 65–6).

Subsequent positivistic variations on the utilitarian framework designed to remedy these defects, Parsons argued, simply resulted in the destruction of the action frame of reference altogether. The positivistic theory of action explained the formation of ends as a product of hereditary factors or environmental conditioning. Similarly, the actor's ignorance or error in departing from 'intrinsically rational' choices of means to ends were accounted for as products of the same factors. Thus, in each of the problematic areas, the actor's action was viewed as the conditioned product of biological make-up or environmental circumstances. The result was a violation of the fundamentals of the action frame of reference and, in particular, of the analytical independence of the 'ends' from the 'conditions' of action. The positivistic theory results in a view of action as a process of adaptation to the environment — a far cry from action as Parsons conceived it.

As he put it, 'there can in the last analysis be no such thing as a radically positivistic theory of action' (ibid. 762). To the extent that a theory of action is 'positivistic' in Parsons's terms, it is not a theory of 'action' at all.

At the opposite pole from the utilitarian and positivistic streams of social theory stood the German idealistic tradition. This viewpoint had, since Hegel, been preoccupied with the uniqueness, reflexivity and moral qualities of the human subject. Expressed in German historiography in particular, these preoccupations emerged in an emphasis on the uniqueness of historical events and cultural complexes, their resistance to positivistic methodological techniques and, above all, in the view that the social order pre-eminently expresses the moral commitment of its members to a set of cultural values. It is, of course, this value dimension of the social order which is ignored in positivistic accounts of social action and which has, at best, a residual status in utilitarian economic thought. However, the idealistic tradition, with its focus on the unique cultural complexes underlying particular societies, tended to develop a view of action which emphasized the significance of values to the exclusion of the real recalcitrant conditions which actions are designed to overcome. As a result, both individual actions and social structures appeared in these writings as simple 'expressions' of cultural values. The truth of the matter, as Parsons saw it, is that

> action must always be thought of as involving a state of tension between two different orders of elements, the normative and the conditional. As a process, action is, in fact, the process of alteration of the conditional elements in the direction of conformity with norms. Elimination of the normative aspect altogether eliminates the concept of action itself and leads to the radical positivistic position. Elimination of conditions, of the tension from that side, equally eliminates action and results in idealistic emanationism. Thus conditions may be conceived at one pole, ends and normative rules at the other, means and effort as the connecting links between them. (ibid. 732)

The task which emerges then is that of creating a body of social theory and empirical analysis which does not jettison one or another of the elements of the action frame of reference and which thus remains an analysis of 'social action'.

As Parsons had conceptualized it during the thirties, the key to this task could be developed from the convergent works of the European social theorists. The emerging voluntaristic theory of action, he argued, sharply reduces both the extent to which actions are to be explained as the products of means— ends efficient choices and the degree to which the actor's subjective point of view is to be likened to that of a scientific observer.

> The basic tenet of the voluntaristic theory is that neither positively nor negatively does the methodological schema of scientifically valid knowledge exhaust the significant subjective elements of action. Insofar as subjective elements fail to fit as elements of valid knowledge, the matter is not exhausted by the categories of ignorance or error, nor by the functional dependence of these elements on those capable of formulation in non-subjective terms, nor by elements random relative to these. Positively, a voluntaristic system involves elements of a normative character. (ibid. 81)

Effectively, the voluntaristic theory intervenes at each of the crucial problem areas encountered by utilitarian thought. Firstly, at the level of the choice of means, the voluntaristic theory embodies the proposal that normative standards other than those expressed in the rational application of scientifically valid knowledge may constitute the basis on which a course of action is chosen. Secondly, at the level of ends, the voluntaristic theory provides that the ends of action, far from being random, are the products of systems of ultimate values. Further, such systems of values, if held in common among the members of society, will constitute a factor contributing to the explanation of social organization and social integration.

In thus breaking out of the narrow restrictions of utilitarian thought, the voluntaristic theory seemed able to handle a much wider range of social actions than its predecessor. In particular, religious and other forms of 'value-rational' conduct – the classical territory of the *Geisteswissenschaften* – were opened up for scrutiny on a similar footing with the more instrumentally rational forms of conduct. Nor was this the only advance enabled by the voluntaristic theory. In particular, Parsons took from Durkheim not only the idea that social integration is the product of collective subscription to commonly held norms and values, but also the conception that such values could be 'internalized' and thus not merely limit egoistic tendencies but become constitutive in the formation of the objects of desire. Finally, the voluntaristic theory provided a conceptual scaffolding which, in giving due weight to the full range of subjective considerations in the organization of action, seemed capable of development into a thoroughgoing analysis of social action in the Weberian tradition.

Nonetheless, despite the fact that Parsons asserts that Weber's concept of action is 'closely similar' and 'substantially the same concept dealt with all through this study' (ibid. 640–2), the analysis of action which emerged from *The Structure of Social Action* and subsequent publications had little in common with Weber's emphasis on the meaningful character of action and the necessity of its analysis from the actor's point of view. This departure from the Weberian tradition resulted from two convergent trends in Parsons's thought: his substantive preoccupation with 'the problem of order' and his distinctive conception of social science.

THE SUBJECTIVE ELEMENTS AND THE PROBLEM OF ORDER

The most significant theoretical advance represented by the voluntaristic theory of action lay, for Parsons, in its contribution to resolving the Hobbesian 'problem of order'. Hobbes's proposal that the 'unloosed passions' would naturally result in endemic social conflict had remained unanswered in subsequent utilitarian writings. Locke's bland assumption of the natural identity of interests had merely evaded the problem and, in Parsons's judgement, any solution to the problem based solely upon the co-ordination of individual interests was insufficient. Even if one assumes an ideal initial situation in which interests interlock harmoniously, he asserted, social order will remain inherently problematic because the interlocking of interests is a brittle thing which comparatively slight alterations of conditions can shatter at vital points. A social order resting on interlocking of interests alone, and thus ultimately on sanctions, is hence hardly empirically possible . . . For, on the one hand the greater the need for sanctions, the weaker the ultimate force behind them; on the other, the conditions of human social life being what they are, alterations of sufficient magnitude to shatter such a brittle and unstable order can scarcely be avoided for very long. (ibid. 404–5)

According to Parsons the key to the Hobbesian problem lay in the analysis, convergently developed by Durkheim and Freud, of the internalization of norms. By this process, social actors would come to adopt value standards which would limit the range of ends they could aspire to and the means they could employ to achieve them. Given this outline solution, the task as Parsons saw it was to develop and systematize the theorem in application to institutional actions. The fulfilment of this task was Parsons's core contribution to the manifesto of the 'social relations experiment' at Harvard — *Towards a General Theory of Action*.

In this volume and its companion, *The Social System*, social actors were viewed as orienting to the environment along three dimensions in which they (1) discriminate the objects of the situation, (2) invest these objects with (positive or negative) cathectic significance and (3) evaluate possible courses of action in relation to them. All three of these dimensions of actor orientation are, in turn, influenced by culturally transmitted value orientations ('organized sets of rules or standards'|(Parsons et al, 1951: 60)) which are used to determine (1) the validity of cognitive judgements, (2) the appropriacy of cathectic attachments and (3) the choices of courses of conduct.

In order to depict how the internalized value standards integrate institutional activity, Parsons begins with an idealized situation in which:

(1) The actors share complementary role expectations.
(2) These expectations are themselves integrated with a more general value system which is also shared.

(3)   Both the specific role expectations and the wider values are internalized by the actors.

In such a situation — an idealized microcosm of any routine social circumstance from the exchange of a greeting in a corridor, or a mother's relationship with a child, to participation in a large-scale organization — the actors will co-operate with one another in a co-ordinated pattern of activity for three basic reasons. First, they will have become committed to the prescribed or expected course of action because each has internalized it as the appropriate or proper one; second, they have internalized other related values which may be threatened or strained by their failure to 'live up to' the demands of the present situation, causing painful internal conflicts or loss of self-esteem; and, third, they fear that others will punish them for not acting appropriately by frustrating their expectations and/or withdrawing love, approval or esteem from them. The 'double contingency' involved in this theorem of institutionalized action is such that any pattern of activity will tend to 'crystallize' and become self-stabilizing and self-equilibrating over time because any tendency (from any actor) to deviate from the standardized expectations will encounter sharply disadvantageous consequences.

The central theoretical significance of this account of institutionalized action is to limit substantially the importance of purely instrumental interests as motivating forces in conduct. Instead, the workings of the theorem of institutionalized action effectively provide that the actor will become positively motivated to co-operate with others and, in turn, the theorem underwrites the likelihood that actors will actually come to want to act in accordance with institutional necessities. As Parsons and Shils put it:

> institutionalization itself must be regarded as the fundamental integrative mechanism of social systems. It is through internalization of common patterns of value-orientation that a system of social interaction can be stabilized. Put in personality terms this means that there is an element of super-ego organization correlative with every role-orientation pattern of the individual in question. In every case, the internalization of a super-ego

element means motivation to accept the priority of collective over personal interests, within the appropriate limits and on the appropriate occasions. (Parson et al, 1951: 150)

This analysis was a *tour de force*. Suitably elaborated with an account, derived from Freud, of the psychological mechanisms of adjustment and defence (Parsons, 1951: 201–26) so as to admit more friction and slippage into the system, it enabled the explanatory role of the internalization of norms to be drawn deeply into the analysis of institutional processes. It greatly increased the extent to which institutions could be viewed as non-coercively maintained. Furthermore it suggested an inherent social psychological process through which a 'skin' of legitimacy would inevitably coalesce around, and sustain, stable interaction patterns even where the latter were initially established on a coercive basis. Finally, if the theory appeared at times to eliminate the possibility of conflict in social relations altogether (Wrong, 1961), the sceptic could always be reminded that the analysis was an ideal typical one and that, to the extent that the condition of full institutional-ization was not met at the empirical level, the system would either be maintained through the operation of non-normative factors (e.g. coercion) or would simply undergo change.

Parsons's use of the internalization formula to meet the motivational problems raised by the question of egoistic self-interest is well known and has been widely discussed. Yet in the welter of commentary, his emphasis on the *motivational* role of norms and values has scarcely been remarked upon. This emphasis was, of course, a natural one. Hobbes, after all, has generally been interpreted as posing his fateful problem as one concerning the motivational wellsprings of action and the internalization formula straightforwardly answered him in kind. Yet to address Hobbes in this way is plainly to treat norms and values, once internalized, as *causes* of action. And this treatment inexorably draws attention away from the 'logic' of action, that is, the interpretative bases on which actions are constructed and understood in terms which are meaningful to the actors involved. Starting from a framework which began with the subjective point of view of the actor, Parsons had arrived at an entirely *external* analysis of the norms and values which he treated as constraining and determining conduct. This development was fully consistent with his view of social science, to which we now briefly turn.

PARSONS'S SCIENCE OF SUBJECTIVITY

Although, in *The Structure of Social Action,* Parsons was concerned to reject positivistic analyses of social action in favour of the voluntaristic perspective, he did not extend this rejection of positivism to the methods or objectives of positive science. On the contrary, he committed himself at an early date to the view that 'there is a methodological core common to all empirical science, no matter what its concrete subject matter' (Parsons, 1936: 679). In Parsons's analysis, all sciences worthy of the name develop when discrete empirical observations are knitted together by abstract theoretical concepts and expressed as generalized analytical laws. Such laws do not, of course, spring fully armed from empirical observation. Rather they arise through an intervening process in which observations are increasingly formulated in abstract theoretical terms (which Parsons terms 'analytical elements') which then become the basis for analytical laws. For example, classical mechanics initially developed from piecemeal observations of falling bodies, balls rolling down inclined planes, the motion of pendulums and so on. These observations could not be integrated, let alone furnish the basis for the laws of gravitation, until they were expressed in terms of abstract concepts ('analytical elements') such as mass, acceleration, etc. In Parsons's discussion, conceptual abstraction from the concrete is thus an essential precondition for theoretical advance towards the generalized laws characteristic of natural science. Parsons is adamant that, although the social sciences deal with 'subjective' phenomena, they are not on this account to be excluded from the general pattern of scientific development. If it is to develop as a science capable of expressing results as generalized laws, sociology must first pass through this crucial phase of conceptual development in which 'analytical elements' — the sociological equivalents of concepts like mass and acceleration — are formulated and used as a means of expressing the results of sociological observation.

In developing the implications of this view for the construction of a sociological science, Parsons began by making a key distinction between what he termed 'unit' and 'element' analyses. Unit concepts, he stated (Parsons, 1937: 31–3), make reference to entities such as the actor's orientation which are concrete or, as in the case of ideal types, 'hypothetically concrete'. Sociological analysis with the use of unit concepts will give the investigator treatments of social activity in terms of the meanings with which the actors invest it. However such treatments, Parsons insists, will remain collections of discrete observations approximately equivalent to the results of isolated experiments jotted into the physicist's notebook. If they are to be knitted together with other, similarly discrete, observations so as to yield general laws, these particular concrete observations must be broken down into their underlying components — the 'analytical elements'. If this is accomplished, each 'unit' observation will be found to comprise 'a specific combination of the values of one or more analytical elements' (ibid. 748). As for the 'analytical elements' themselves, Parsons identified these as the basic coordinates of the value orientations which lay at the heart of the voluntaristic theory of action. He specified them in terms of the 'pattern variables' — a logically exhaustive system of orientational possibilities collectively constituting a closed metric whose combinations and permutations would prove capable of expressing every humanly meaningful value stance, whether individual, institutional or societal. Integrated with his analysis of the functional imperatives for the survival of social systems, the pattern variables would subsequently be employed in Parsons's comparative work on social systems and his analysis of social change.

Thus Parsons's project for a sociological science was one which, although formally rooted in the 'action frame of reference', effectively focused attention away from the analysis of social action *per se*. Observation of the latter — the province of 'unit' analysis — would certainly be a vital source of raw data, but a sociological science could only emerge when 'unit' observations were decomposed into their component ('vector') value elements and accounted for in terms of universal 'analytical laws' governing the combination of value elements in human affairs. The net result, as Schutz noted in his 1940 correspondence with Parsons (Grathoff, 1978), was a rapid and straightforward suspension of interest in what the actor concretely believes in and acts upon.

In sum, under the convergent pressures of his interest in the problem of order and his conception of the tasks of social science, Parsons's analysis of the 'actor's point of view' was one which was overwhelmingly geared to developing a *causal* model of the subjective elements in conduct in which the actor's concrete reasoning was treated as epiphenomenal. Included among these 'subjective elements' were the normative phenomena, familiar from *The Structure of Social Action*, of 'values', 'orientations' and 'attitudes', but also, subsequently, psychological phenomena such as 'complexes' which could not possibly be meaningful to the actor in any straightforward sense. All of these 'subjective elements', for reasons to be discussed shortly, were conceived as opaque to the actor to varying extents and it is only in limiting cases, Parsons argues, that the actor's 'theory of his action' adequately reflects the truly determinative 'subjective elements'. Only on rare occasions do the actors become transparent to themselves and grasp their own motivating forces.

Parsons's subsequent theoretical development from this position was one which involved increasing stress on psychological processes. The actor was increasingly seen as the 'bearer' of internalized value patterns — the 'facts of social structure' evolved in response to the functional imperatives — and was viewed as accomplishing this task by virtue of the 'facts of personality' — a set of psychological properties and processes which included the mechanisms of socialization. Thus, rather than opening up the question of the actors' understandings of their practical circumstances, the properties of their judgements, the conditions under which courses of action might be initiated or abandoned, the scope and occasions under which actors might revise some view of the situation and so forth (Garfinkel, 1952), Parsons's interest in the 'subjective' was narrowed to describing the *psychological* processes (for example, the mechanisms of adjustment and defence) through which the internalized values were sustained in the face of frustration and disappointment. In this context, the actor's thoughts and feelings were viewed as simply 'intervening variables' (Parsons et al, 1951: 64). Indeed there was no other place for them, for the bridge between the 'subjective elements' conceived as causal determinants of action and the 'actor's point of view' conceptualized as the focus of intelligibly organized conduct had collapsed without trace. Thus the overall trajectory of Parsons's theory of action, established in *The Structure of Social Action* and maintained throughout his career, was towards a treatment of action in terms of concepts which were almost wholly 'external' to the point of view of the actor. Action was to be analysed as the product of causal processes which, although operating 'in the minds' of the actors, were all but inaccessible to them and, hence, uncontrollable by them.

A TROUBLESOME RESIDUE: THE PROBLEM OF COGNITION

Thus far we have seen that the outcome of Parsons's treatment of the subjective point of view was an analysis which stressed the internalization of norms as causal dispositions to action. This analysis was consistent with Parsons's view of the nature of social science and was conditioned by his determination to deal with the 'motivational' questions raised by the Hobbesian discussion of egoism. However Parsons's emphasis on the 'motivational' aspects of the theory of action left open a series of problems which centre on the actors' *knowledge* of their circumstances. Although these problems are complex and interrelated, three major problematic areas can be outlined.

First, while sociologists may have developed satisfactory analyses of the actors' actions, they are nonetheless confronted by actors who can account for their actions by citing particular aspects of their circumstances as relevant to their decisions. In these accounts, actors commonly portray their actions as 'chosen' in the light of a range of considerations. A potential conflict thus arises between the causal and deterministic analyses of action developed by sociologists and the accounts of action developed in terms of self-subsistent reasons by the participants (Wilson, 1970; Hollis, 1977). This conflict does not simply involve difficulties in reconciling divergences between the sociologist's and the participants' substantive explanations of actions, nor even merely the problems of reconciling the alternative explanatory logics of the two types of account, though these problems are very considerable. There is also the problem that the actors treat one another's accounts as intelligible and as objects of reasoned evaluation involving justification, blame and all the issues of moral entitlement which are associated with actors' treatments of one another as agents. Moreover, actors treat such accounts as real by acting on them — in this way making them real in their consequences. These phenomena pose very difficult issues of reconciliation which have traditionally surfaced in the theory of action as the *problem of rationality*: the problem of what kind of significance to accord to actors' accounts of their reasons for action.

Second, the actors co-ordinate their actions in terms of putatively shared knowledge of their circumstances and, in many cases, shared knowledge of the range of considerations which may influence choices among courses of action. The theorist of action is thus faced with the *problem of intersubjectivity*: the problem of accounting for shared or mutual knowledge and understanding among actors.

Third, actors may from time to time subjectively apprehend and describe their actions as the products of 'strategic' choices in which they manipulate the normative grounds of activities for some ulterior purpose — 'finding an excuse' to avoid going to a party is an obvious and commonly experienced example. This raises a third major *problem of reflexivity*: the problem of the extent to which the theorist of action will allow that the actors have 'insight' into the normative background of their own actions.

Characteristically, Parsons is fully aware of these major problems, but, to anticipate the following discussion, we shall find that his handling of each of them is strongly shaped by his desire to accomodate them to his pre-existing explanatory framework which stresses the internalization of norms as causal determinants of action.

The Problem of Rationality

Parsons's approach to the nature of the actors' knowledge involves the ploy, characteristic within utilitarian and neo-Kantian approaches to the topic, of describing the extent to which the actors' knowledge of their circumstances overlaps with what is known with scientific certainty. This is more or less explicit in his definition of rational action:

> Action is rational in so far as it pursues ends possible within the conditions of the situation, and by means which, among those available to the actor, are intrinsically best adapted to the end for reasons understandable and verifiable by positive empirical science. (Parsons, 1937: 58)

Since this definition of rationality intrinsically involves a comparison between the actor's knowledge and the putatively complete and accurate knowledge possessed by the scientific observer, it will be obvious that questions concerning the rationality of action cannot, for Parsons, be divorced from questions concerning the theory of knowledge.

Parsons's approach to the theory of knowledge, which is developed within a broadly neo-Kantian framework, is that of 'analytic realism' in which 'it is maintained that at least some of the general concepts of science . . . adequately "grasp" aspects of the objective external world' (ibid. 730). This viewpoint, like others of a neo-Kantian stripe, starts from the assumption that the empirical world consists of externally given states of affairs whose existence and facticity are entirely independent of the ways in which they may be humanly known. Human beings will necessarily examine these states of affairs from a variety of particular perspectives which will be shaped by their theoretical and practical interests, but, provided that scientific methods and procedures are employed, objective knowledge of empirical states of affairs can and will be achieved by a process of 'successive approximation'. The resulting knowledge will not, of course, be complete and total. On the contrary, it will be incomplete because it has been produced in response to particular problems and in the light of particular interests. But this incompleteness of knowledge does not undermine its objectivity which is guaranteed by the intrinsic rationality of the scientific method. Finally, it is implicit within this framework that objective knowledge is useful knowledge, if only because those who have objective knowledge of their empirical circumstances are more likely to succeed in their projects than those who do not.

Given these assumptions of an externally given world and the positive value of objective knowledge of it, it follows that social actors too will find it both possible and desirable to acquire such knowledge – although, once again, the objective knowledge they acquire will be shaped by their practical interests. It is possible therefore, within the Parsonian frame of assumptions, that the actor's factual knowledge of a situation will approximate the scientific observer's and, if the actor's end is attainable and appropriate means are chosen, the actor's action will be 'intrinsically rational'. Here the actor guides an action by reference to knowledge which 'adequately expresses' its real empirical circumstances. This rational orientation of the actor to the situation cannot be the subject of further causal explanation without the threat of relativistic implications for the entire epistemological framework, and in these cases the actor's 'theory of his action' is treated as an adequate explanation for it.

However, where the actor's theory does not adequately express the circumstances, or where the actor's viewpoint is cast in terms which, however adequately or inadequately, reflect his or her sentiments or ultimate values, then the actor's concrete viewpoint is not of serious value or interest in explaining conduct (ibid. 270 *et seq.*). In these latter cases, we must make reference to internalized values or to the additional psychological processes comprising the remainder of the 'subjective elements' in order to account for the actor's actions. Thus Parsons's discussion of the role of rationality in the explanation of conduct accurately foreshadowed the now familiar distinction between rational action which is to be accounted for in terms of its self-subsistent grounds and non-rational action which is the legitimate object of causal explanation.

The net effect of this treatment of rationality is twofold. Firstly, it addresses the troublesome discrepancies between the theorist's and the actor's views of the actor's situation of action by providing that the actor's view of the circumstances will be permitted to stand only when it coincides with the theorist's view of the matter. With this move, the superior cognitive claims of science are upheld in the face of the actor's problematic tendencies to view the world differently. Secondly, the analysis putatively addresses the 'problem of error': the tendency for actors to persist in invalid or erroneous views of the world (and in non-rational courses of action) despite the fact that they would be more successful in their projects by correcting them. For the actor can be viewed as having 'internalized' invalid cognitive norms and as participating in systems of action within which such errors are institutionalized. And, at the limits of the argument, this institutionalized non-rationality can itself be accounted for in functional terms.

Overall, then, the Parsonian treatment of the problem of rationality is one which both preserves the superior cognitive claims of science and, at all points, emphasizes the role of institutionalization in the organization of action and hence the role of normative determination in conduct. However, in its insistence on a distinction between rational and non-rational action based on 'hard' methodological criteria, the theory routinely involves the portrayal and evaluation of the actor's actions from a (scientific) standpoint which is discrepant with, and *external* to, the situation of action as viewed by the actor. Moreover, the election of such a strict criterion of rationality effectively reduces to a vanishing point the significance which can be attached to the actor's interpretation of the circumstances. As Garfinkel puts it, generalizing the argument:

> because sociologists find with such overwhelming frequency that effective, persistent, and stable actions and social structures occur despite obvious discrepancies between the lay person's and the ideal scientist's knowledge and procedures, sociologists have found the rational properties that their definitions discriminated empirically uninteresting. They have preferred instead to study the features and conditions of non-rationality in human conduct. The result is that in most of the available theories of social action and social structure rational actions are assigned residual status. (Garfinkel, 1967h: 262–3)

Given, in turn, that the 'institutionalization theorem' is waiting in the wings to provide an external, causal account for the vast majority of the actor's actions, the net effect of this analysis is to further diminish the sociological significance of the actor's interpretation of his or her circumstances, although at the cost of treating the actor as a 'judgemental dope' (Garfinkel, 1967b: 68) who unthinkingly (and, as we shall see, unknowingly) 'acts out' the institutionalized directives of the culture. Thus, at the end of the day, the causal analysis of action runs in parallel with, but insulated from, the common-sense rationalities of the actors' judgements. The actors' analyses of their circumstances thus remain at best 'intervening variables' through which the 'hidden hand' of institutional process determines conduct. Pareto is thus finally turned on his head and the rational properties of action have become 'residues'.

The Problem of Intersubjectivity

In accounting for the intersubjectivity of knowledge, two basic avenues are open to the theorist operating within Parsonian assumptions. They closely correspond with the treatment of rationality already outlined.

An initial procedure for accounting for shared knowledge arises out of the conditions for gaining objective knowledge of the world. Given that, in Parsons's analysis, objective knowledge of the world can be acquired by the application of scientific procedures, it follows that those actors who implement such procedures will converge in their objective knowledge of 'the facts' of their circumstances. It will be apparent, however, that this account of intersubjective knowledge is a narrow one which can provide for the shared knowledge only of those actors who are engaged in scientifically founded courses of action. It cannot handle the sharing of knowledge in the remaining, and empirically predominant, cases of normatively determined institutionalized actions which Parsons had laboured to open up for sociological investigation. Plainly the sharing of knowledge in these other spheres requires a different analysis.

Parsons resolves this issue by a variant of his 'institutional-

egoism – the theory that one's self is the motivation end goal is one's action.

ization theorem'. Here, he proposes, common value standards will determine the nature and limits of knowable 'fact' within any given institutional framework. At the same time, common institutionalized standards of cathectic orientation will limit the divergences of 'interests' among actors and hence ensure that their objects of orientation will be viewed from common perspectival standpoints. Thus just as Parsons appealed to institutionalization to resolve the problem of egoism at the motivational level, so too he appeals to the same source to resolve the problem of solipsism. However it can be noticed that, just as the institutionalization theorem provided an 'external' and programmatic account of the integration of the actors' motivations and took no account of the internal 'logic' of action, so too it is here used to provide an 'external' and programmatic account of the shared nature of the actors' knowledge and no attempt is made to develop a 'logic' of cognitive judgements. In both cases, an argument is built only for an 'in principle' tendency towards integration and the discussion is terminated at this level of abstraction.

If a known-in-common world is to be the *locus* of interaction between actors, it is of course essential not merely for the actors to know this world in common but also to communicate about what they know. In Parsons's analysis, the institutionalization theorem is invoked once more to account for the facts of communication. Communication, Parsons argues, is guaranteed by a common system of symbols which are necessarily generalized from the particularities of single situations: 'When such a generalization occurs, and actions, gestures or symbols have more of less the same meaning for both ego and alter, we may speak of a common culture existing between them, through which their action is mediated' (Parsons et al, 1951: 105). The institutionalization of common meanings for symbols in advance of their use in particular situations is, in Parsons's analysis as in Mead's (1934), the basis upon which communication is possible. And, once again, with the 'in principle' point established, Parsons abandons the issue while leaving open the question of *how* sameness of meaning might be established or maintained in actual contexts of situations, or, indeed, how communicative interaction might proceed.

Solipsism
– the view/theory that the self is all that can be known
to exist.

In sum, Parsons's approach to the problem of intersubjectivity involves the assumption that any social situation will display a range of objective features which are available for scientific appraisal and description. Where these features are so appraised, 'objective', and hence intersubjective, knowledge will be generated as the product of the scientific method by all its users. In most institutional contexts however, the actors' appraisals of the situation will be non-scientific. In these instances, their appraisals will be guided by shared and institutionalized cognitive standards which will determine what the actors may perceive and know about the situation and, hence, guarantee a community of 'knowledge' which is contaminated to a greater or lesser degree by institutionalized error. Communication is governed by similar principles.

This whole 'in principle' analysis is underpinned by a 'correspondence' theory of truth in which the actors' knowledge is evaluated in terms of its agreement with the 'facts of the situation' as determined by the scientific observer. A parallel 'correspondence' theory of language is also invoked in which language is treated essentially as a set of names which can only have intersubjective meaning to the extent that correspondences between 'names' and 'things' (signs and referents) are already socially established and are adequately reproduced in acts of communication.

It is clear that this cursory and, as we shall see, inadequate treatment of the actor's knowledge and communication, while embodying a 'sociologized' version of the logical positivist treatments of epistemology and semantic analysis then in the ascendency, also speaks to Parsons's general lack of interest in the 'logic' or 'mechanics' of the actor's knowledge. Responding to Schutz's critical discussion of *The Structure of Social Action*, in which the latter had stressed the significance of investigating common-sense knowledge, Parsons wrote:

> Again and again, in reading your work, you make points which as they are stated sound perfectly plausible, but I am always compelled to ask the question 'What of it?' If I accept your statement in place of my own formulations which you criticize, what *difference* would it make in the interpretation of any one of

the empirical problems that run through the book, or in the formulation of the systematic structure of theory. (Grathoff, 1978: 67)

The paucity and conceptual emaciation of the treatment of cognition in the major Parsonian texts was the practical embodiment of this scepticism. And, more generally, it is clear that Parsons's treatment of cognition and language was merely intended as a 'long stop' analysis which was designed to round out and secure closure for his much fuller discussion of the 'motivational' questions which preoccupied him.

The Problem of Reflexivity

As we have already seen, Parsons proposes that it is only in cases of rational action that the actor's 'theory of his action' adequately reflects the real grounds of his action. Predominantly, the actor's actions are portrayed as driven by a variety of normative processes. Yet, in considering what the actors may know, know in common and communicate about within the Parsonian framework, it is still relevant to ask how much the actors are deemed to know about the normative underpinnings of their own conduct.

In addressing this question, Parsons allows that cultural values may be treated as objects to which the actor 'orients' and he similarly allows that the 'self' of the actor may be an object of the actor's orientation. However, he specifically *excludes* as objects of the actor's orientation *the cultural values which the actor has internalized* (Parsons et al., 1951: 103). To this extent, Parsons conceptualizes patterns of cultural values as operating to motivate the actors 'behind their backs'. Accordingly, the actors will tend to lack 'insight' into the normative underpinnings of their own actions. As Parsons puts it:

> There is a range of possible modes of orientation in the motivational sense to a value standard. Perhaps the most important distinction is between the attitude of 'expediency' at one pole, where conformity or non-conformity is a function of the instrumental interests of the actor, and at the other pole

the 'introjection' or internalization of the standard so that to
act in conformity with it becomes a need disposition in the
actor's own personality structure, relatively independently of
any instrumentally significant consequences of conformity.
The latter is to be regarded as the basic type of integration of
motivation with a normative pattern-structure of values.
(Parsons, 1951: 37)

Parsons justifies this proposal by reference to the two-fold
binding-in process through which value standards become
internalized. The nature of this process, as we have seen, is
such that the introjection of value standards is, effectively,
conditioned in the actors. Thus while Durkheim stressed that
it was essential for actors to have an attitude of 'respect'
towards the norms and values of the *conscience collective*,
Parsons does away with this element of conditionality in
favour of postulating a psychological process which ensures
that the actor cannot but act on the basis of internalized
values. One paradoxical consequence is that the actor,
equipped in this fashion, is conceptualized as incapable of
exercising a moral choice. The net effect however is, as
Garfinkel puts it, that the actors cannot 'see through' the
normative system in which they are, willy-nilly, enmeshed.
Deprived of this crucial element of 'reflexivity', the actors will
inevitably remain welded to any or all the institutionalized
systems of action with which they come into sustained
contact.

This theoretical rejection of the phenomena of reflexivity —
which is inevitable given Parsons's framework of assumptions
— serves as a convenient focus to draw together some of the
methodological and substantive themes in this discussion of
Parsons's writings. The reflexivity of the actor is denied within
the Parsonian framework by virtue of three related considerations. First, if the actors can and do treat the normative
foundations of their own conduct reflexively, then their own
normative orientations would have to be theoretically treated
as part of the *conditions* of their actions. A form of sociological
positivism would arise which would violate the basic terms of
the action frame of reference. For the actors would have to be
conceived as adjusting to the normative constraints of the

situation (including their own normative make-up) in much the same way as, in the earlier version of rationalistic positivism, they were conceived as adjusting to the constraints of the physical environment. In the process the 'voluntaristic metaphysic' — the idea of actors striving to alter their circumstances in the direction of normative ideals — would be lost as a central theme in the analysis of action.

Second, insofar as the actors can and do adopt a reflexive attitude to their normative environments, they can act manipulatively in relation to them. The reflexive actor, therefore, is one for whom the normative framework is not an analytically independent element capable of autonomous causal influence and the sources of normative conformity must, of necessity, be located elsewhere than in the mere 'existence' or 'internalization' of the normative framework.

Third, at the substantive level, actors who can manipulate their conduct in relation to a normative environment are those who can act strategically. At a stroke, the normative bulwark against the Hobbesian Machiavel is destroyed. In *The Structure of Social Action* Parsons contrasted a situation in which moral rules 'are lived up to from motives of moral obligation' with 'the motive of 'interest' which, looking upon the rules as essentially conditions of action, acts in terms of the comparative personal advantage of obedience or disobedience and acceptance of the sanctions which will have to be suffered' (Parsons, 1937: 404). In cases where the latter motive of 'interest' prevails, he adds, social structure becomes inherently fragile because, the interlocking of interests 'is a brittle thing which comparatively slight alterations of conditions can shatter at vital points' (ibid.).

In sum, if norms are not determinate *causes* of action, two consequences follow within a Parsonian framework of assumption. First, norms will be incapable of harnessing and constraining the forces of egoism, with social disintegration as the probable consequence. Second, a deterministic social science built upon the fundamentals of the action frame of reference cannot be achieved.

We have now come far enough to develop a dilemma for Parsons which, in many ways, is as pernicious as those which he developed for utilitarianism and positivism. We might term it the 'dilemma of reflexivity' and, formulating it in Garfinkel's words, propose it as the choice between

> allowing the actor's view and thereby allowing the individual as a source of change in the system with the risk of indeterminism, or risk a gain in determinism at the cost of turning the system into a table of organization that operates as a set of impersonal forces that shove the individual around here and there, while taking it as a matter of factual interest that he is correctly aware or not of what is happening to him. (Garfinkel, 1952: 145)

On the whole, Parsons's theoretical implementation of his preferred versions of internalization results in his opting for a 'table of organization' view as a way of conceptualizing the actor's orientations, knowledge and self-knowledge. For Parsons, as we have seen, the empirical existence of social order and the scientific imperatives of its analysis together render this outcome inescapable.

CONCLUSION

No serious appraisal of Parson's approach to the theory of action can fail to register either its massive archetectonic qualities or the relentlessly systematic ways in which the core assumptions of the Parsonian framework are driven to their analytical limits. In Parsons's hands, the full range of theoretical issues which an analysis of action must necessarily handle are raised with the utmost seriousness and treated with a quite extraordinary consistency. Parsons's work is indeed 'awesome for the penetrating depth and unfailing precision of its practical sociological reasoning' (Garfinkel, 1967: ix). Nevertheless, in reacting to the theories of his famous teacher, Garfinkel formed fundamental disagreements with almost every major aspect of Parsonian sociology.

Specifically, Garfinkel denied that the social scientific formulation of objectively rational courses of action under 'given' conditions could be a useful, or even workable, procedure for the empirical study of social action. Similarly, he denied that such formulations could be useful yardsticks by which to evaluate the rationality of actors' actions. He insisted too that the preoccupation with 'scientifically rational' conduct had drawn attention away from the 'reasonableness' of actions and, relatedly, given rise to an inappropriate emphasis on normative determinism. Moving into the substantive details of Parsonian theory, Garfinkel rejected the view that normative rules — no matter how detailed and specific or deeply 'internalized' — could in any way be determinative of conduct; that intersubjective knowledge is founded upon such rules or that intersubjective communication is founded upon prior agreements about what words 'mean'. Rather than treating the reflexive aspects of actors' orientations as an obstacle to the maintenance (and the explanation) of social order and attempting to marginalize them as empirical phenomena, Garfinkel argued that they are critical to the maintenance of social organization.

At the heart of these various methodological and substantive differences lies a still more fundamental one. For Garfinkel rejected absolutely the view that the ordinary judgements of mundane social actors can in any way, or under any circumstances, be treated as irrelevant or epiphenomenal in the analysis of social action or social organization. It is the Parsonian disregard for the entire common-sense world in which ordinary actors choose courses of action on the basis of detailed practical considerations and judgements which are intelligible and accountable to others, which ultimately constitutes the central focus and point of departure for Garfinkel's treatment of the theory of action.

While the rationale and consequences of this treatment will be the subject of the next few chapters, a concrete example may serve to demonstrate the distance between the Parsonian theory of action and the common-sense world which it addresses. Consider Garfinkel's study of the jury project once more:

> In the course of their deliberations, jurors sort alternative depictions made by lawyers, witnesses and jurors of what happened and why between the statuses of relevant and irrelevant, justifiable and unjustifiable, correct or incorrect grounds for the choice of verdict. When jurors address such matters as dates. speeds, the plaintiff's injury and the like,

what do the jurors' decisions specifically decide? In something like the jurors' own terms, and trying to capture the jurors' dialectic, jurors decide between what is fact and what is fancy; between what actually happened and what 'merely appeared' to happen; between what is put on and what is truth, regardless of detracting appearances; between what is credible and, very frequently for jurors, the opposite of credible, what is calculated and said by design. (Garfinkel, 1967: 105)

This discussion raises a number of difficulties for the Parsonian approach to action. In what possible sense could a social scientist establish a 'scientifically correct' verdict and use it as the basis to establish the elements of rationality and irrationality in the jurors' deliberations and judgements? In what sense could it be a useful or interesting procedure to attempt to specify the elements of normative determinism in the jurors' judgements and, in doing so, to discount jurors' accounts of the matter as either irrelevant to the scientific explanation of their conduct or, at best, intervening variables? In what way would it be useful to ignore the detailed and reflexive textures of jurors' deliberations when the jurors themselves evaluate one another's arguments in terms of that very texture? In what way does a normative deterministic theory of any of the courtroom participants' actions make contact with a social world in which all of them − judge, jury, lawyers, witnesses, plantiff and defendant − treat one another's actions as chosen and accountable and in which such treatment may be highly consequential for all concerned?

A similar range of difficulties invade quite mundane and 'quasi-rational' activities. For example, there is no 'scientifically rational' procedure for bargaining with a used car salesman of unknown characteristics. And, though rational strategies can be formulated for dealing with a salesman of known characteristics (Van Neumann and Morgenstern, 1952; Schelling, 1960), There is no scientifically rational procedure for determining those characteristics. Instead there is the same use of a range of procedures for differentiating appearance and reality, for example a 'final offer' from what is merely proposed as such, and so on.

In vast areas of social life, the theoretical choice is not between 'rational' and 'normatively determined' actions.

Rather mundane conduct is based on 'reasonable' considerations which are brought to bear in contexts of uncertainty
which, in turn, are absolutely resistant to scientific calculation.
In these domains, actions are evaluated and 'chosen' on the
basis of reasonable considerations and are evaluated *as* chosen
on a similar basis.

When set against these elementary observations, the
Parsonian framework assumes the characteristics of an
idealization which, although marvellously intricate, remains
almost entirely divorced from the gritty texture of reasonable
actions in terms of which the mundane world is constituted,
produced and reproduced. Garfinkel's proposal to develop a
'generalized social system built solely from the analysis of
experience structures' thus represented a direct attack on the
very domain which Parsons had omitted from consideration:
the realm of approximate judgements and reasonable grounds
which constitutes the common-sense world.

He commenced his task with two basic assumptions in
hand. First, if the construction and recognition of human
actions and social circumstances is a contingent task for actors
who work at it in terms of 'reasonable approximation', the role
of theory in the new analysis will be different from the old.
Specifically, the task of theory will not be to determine what
some set of social circumstances and events consist of in
advance of the actors' actions, and then to evaluate and
explain the latter in terms of their rational and/or normatively
determined characteristics. Rather it will be to directly
analyse the construction and recognition of these circumstances and events as they are played out 'frame by frame'
through the actors' actions. Second, the construction and
recognition of developing events by actors will, in some way,
be 'methodical' if only because human action is, in general,
intelligible and orderly. The task is possible because the order
is there. The questions are: what kind of order is it? and how
does it work?

To pursue this task, however, Garfinkel required a substantially new set of conceptual tools. These he took and adapted
from phenomenological philosophy which was, during the
immediate post-war period, the only available major source of
insights into the organization of experience.

CHAPTER 3

The Phenomenological Input

The surest symptom of impending change in a theoretical system is increasingly general interest in the residual categories.
Parsons, *The Structure of Social Action*

Of the many considerations which may have contributed to Garfinkel's recourse to phenomenological concepts in his approach to the analysis of mundane cognition, the following stand out as immediately suggestive. As already noted, the phenomenological movement, which represented the sole systematic assault on the problem of cognition in an intellectual climate hostile to cognitive analysis, was the primary repository of conceptualization and debate relevant to his interests. Moreover, at a local level, Harvard together with neighbouring universities in the Boston area contained a number of scholars with phenomenological commitments. Marvin Farber, whose monumental study *The Foundation of Phenomenology* was published in 1943 and who had founded the International Phenomenological Society and its journal *Philosophy and Phenomenological Research*, had done much to stimulate interest in phenomenological work on the eastern seaboard of the United States during the early forties. In Boston itself, Aron Gurwitsch became an important intellectual guide and one who had close connections with phenomenological researchers who had gathered around Alfred Schutz at the New School for Social Research in New York.

Additionally, members of the Department of Psychology at Harvard had fortunately 'cognitive' interests. In particular, an important series of experiments by Bruner and his associates (see, for example, Bruner and Postman, 1949) was demonstrating the role of subjects' expectations in structuring perception and cognition. Related work by Asch (1951) was showing that social pressure could exert a significant influence on these expectations. The experimental aspects of Garfinkel's Ph.D. research were aimed at demonstrating the methods and and limits of subjects' attempts to reconcile experiential discrepancies and they alsoincorporated the useof incongruity and of social pressure, both of which were becoming prominent in experimental procedures current in cognitive research at Harvard and elsewhere.

Thus in the Harvard of the late 1940s, Garfinkel found an intellectual atmosphere which was consonant both with his interests in cognition and with the expression of those interests in phenomenological terms. Most importantly of all, however, he found in Schutz's writings, then emerging at a steady rate, and in discussion with Gurwitsch a body of sociological theory which, in addition to being occupied with the problem of cognition, entered it at exactly the most troubled point of Parsons's treatment – the problematic relationship between scientific knowledge and mundane cognition. For, in his analysis of the methodological foundations of sociology, Schutz developed a stance towards the nature of meaningful action which dealt directly with the themes of the actor's knowledge, its intersubjective character and the nature of its sociological analysis.

THE PHENOMENOLOGICAL PERSPECTIVE:
A BRIEF INTRODUCTION

The initial impetus for phenomenology arose out of the crisis in mathematics (and, to a lesser extent, in physics) which developed towards the end of the nineteenth century. Edmund Husserl, its founder, trained as a mathematician, and his programme for phenomenology as a rigorous deductive science of subjectivity reflects this training. The mathematical world encountered by Husserl had recently lost some of its most basic and foundational certainties. In particular the development of non-Euclidean geometries during the first half of the nineteenth century had severely challenged the comfortable belief that mathematics simply studies the properties of the real world. Subsequently, during the last quarter of the century, the effort pioneered by Frege and Russell to place number theory on a strict logical foundation ran into problems (in the theory of types) which were subsequently demonstrated by Gödel to be insurmountable. Thus the same basic problem, uncertainties in the foundations of mathematics, which would drive Russell and later Wittgenstein from mathematics to philosophy, drove Husserl in the same direction ten years earlier.

Husserl began by attempting to derive the basic propositions of number theory from psychological principles in a procedure whose circularity was strongly criticized by Frege. Subsequently Husserl rejected psychological reductionism in all its forms in an argument set out in his *Logical Investigations* (1970a). The second half of this study presented phenomenological studies describing ideal types of experience corresponding to logical laws, the aim being to describe the experiential substratum of our knowledge of logical entities.

In this and all his later studies, Husserl proceeded on the assumption that there exists a parallelism or correlation between the object of an act of cognition on the one hand and an associated subjective structure pertaining to the act on the other. In the case of perceiving a cat, for example, there must be some set of subjective structures by virtue of which (1) the object of the perception is recognized as a 'cat' and (2) its perception is grasped as a 'perception' (rather than, for example, a recollection or hallucination). Without the relevant subjective structures, instances of 'cats' would remain unrecognized and the subject would be unable to determine whether he or she was perceiving, recollecting or hallucinating an object. Finally, Husserl was insistent that these subjective structures are not passively called into play by sensory experience but are active in the *constitution* of the objects of experience. The role of consciousness in actively constituting its intended objects is easily demonstrated by gestalt figures such as Rubin's (Figure 1)which can be seen, alternatively, as a pair of faces or as a vase. What differs between these alternative 'seeings' is not the sensory information presented by the figure. This remains constant. Rather the difference lies in the way in which the figure is attended to and what is constituted of its sensory presentation.

As we have already seen, Husserl developed this 'correlational' viewpoint as a means of access to problems in the

Figure 1 (Source: The Mary Evans Picture Library)

foundations of mathematics. He wanted to investigate the constitutive processes involved in our experiences of mathematical and logical entities such as geometrical figures and prime numbers. These are, of course, entities which we experience but, unlike the cat of the previous example, they are the ideal objects of theoretical disciplines. From the very outset then, in developing his phenomenology of experience, Husserl was not simply concerned with describing how we experience the objects of the external world, but rather with giving an account of how we encounter any object of experience whether concrete or ideal, and whether perceived, remembered, imagined, theorized, dreamed, or otherwise experienced. In approaching these various modes of experience, he insisted on a purely descriptive orientation. The objects of experience and the subjective structures through which they are given to consciousness were to be described as faithfully as possible and not explained away by reference to psychological forces. Then Husserl adopted a view of the constitutive role of consciousness as 'primordial' and treated the description of consciousness and its operations as foundational in relation to psychological and epistemological reflection.

In approaching this constitutive subjective realm, Husserl made a fundamental distinction between the 'natural attitude' and the phenomenological reductions of that attitude. Husserl used the term 'natural attitude' to characterize the framework in terms of which we mundanely perceive, interpret and act on the world in which we find ourselves. Fundamentally governed by pragmatic considerations, the natural attitude involves the suspension of doubt (Schutz, 1962e: 229) that things might not be as they appear or that past experience may not be a valid guide to present and future experience. In the natural attitude, the perceiver simply believes that 'as he sees things, so they are'; the cognizer simply assumes, until he has counter-evidence, that his understanding of his circumstances is adequate, and the actor likewise assumes that actions which were successful in previous similar conditions will be successful in the present situation.

The reverse of the natural attitude is radical 'Cartesian doubt' which sceptically denies the objectivity of perception, the adequacy of knowledge or the utility of past experience. This kind of doubt is not involved in the phenomenological reduction. Instead, in the latter, the investigator *suspends* his or her belief in, for example, the objective existence of the objects of perception in order to examine *how* they are experienced as objectively existent. Thus, in the natural attitude, one simply 'sees a chair'. After performing the phenomenological reduction, it is possible to analyse 'the chair as it appears to me' as an element in my stream of experience (Schutz, 1962d: 106). The reduction does not involve any scepticism or doubt about the existence of the chair; it is merely a device with which to explore the subjective correlates of 'experiencing the chair as existent'.

With the phenomenological reduction accomplished, the phenomenologist can proceed to the question 'how is the chair perceived?'; through what set of subjective structures and operations is 'the chair as it appears to me' constituted in consciousness? The answer is that 'the chair as it appears to me' is the product of a complex series of unconscious and automatic ('prepredicative') operations in which the present perception of the chair is referred to a variety of previous experiences of it viewed from different angles, to other experiences of chairs and of solid objects in general. For example, 'the chair as it appears to me' will inevitably have a perspectival appearance in which some of its parts will be obscured from view. Thus in identifying the sensory presentation before me as a 'chair', I will tend to fill in the presently invisible parts. For example, viewing what I presently see as the 'back' of the chair, its presently invisible front legs and seat are called into play or 'appresented' as part of the process in which I identify the object before me as 'a chair'. The identification of an object from a perspectival sensory presentation is thus always a 'constructive' process even if, within the natural attitude, the nature of this process is entirely obscured from consciousness.

It will further be apparent from this analysis that as I change my position in relation to the chair, for example by walking up to it or around it, its sensory presentations will also undergo change. It is only insofar as this succession of sensory presentations can be integrated within a continuously updated 'synthesis of identification' that 'this chair' can continue to exist for me as an identical self-same object (rather than a series of different objects). And, of course, it is by virtue of similar constitutive activities that a sequence of varied sensory presentations can be identified as, for example, 'this galloping horse'.

In sum, the phenomenologist makes a strong distinction between, on the one hand, a sensory presentation and, on the other, an intended object constituted of the sensory presentation. From a phenomenological perspective, all objects of consciousness whether referred to the real world (as in the case of my chair) or to one or another ideal world (as in the case of the prime number seven) exist as the products of constitutive acts of consciousness. As such they stand as unities of meaning which are established in their moments of recognition. Within this framework, the expression 'object' means no more than 'constituted-as-a-unity-of-meaning', while the term 'real object' means 'constituted-as-a-unity-of-meaning' with reference, *inter alia*, to standard time and place.

Finally, in describing the objects of consciousness, the

phenomenologist distinguishes between the 'inner' and 'outer' horizons of the object. Returning to my chair, we have already encountered its 'inner horizon'. Perceiving its back, I called into play its unseen seat and front legs which, with all their particularities, form its 'inner horizon'. However, perceiving some scratches on the chair, I may refer the chair-with-its-scratches to my recollection of the once-pristine-chair and its history of minor accidents, to the recollection of my buying it, the discomfort I experience when sitting on it and so on. All these aspects and the many other experiences to which I might refer my present experience of the chair form its 'outer horizon'. All objects, both real and ideal, have these horizonal features and it is through them, with all their entanglements, that human experience is connected.

PARTINGS OF THE WAYS

With the above, highly simplified, account of the phenomenological approach to mundane object constitution behind us, it is now possible to glimpse a variety of possible directions which phenomenological research can take.

A first direction would be to continue in the way sketched in the preceding paragraphs. Such a programme of research into mundane perception, cognition, memory, etc., properly carried out, results in a phenomenological psychology (Schutz, 1962d: 115). It is represented by the work of several major figures in phenomenology including Merleau-Ponty (1962, 1964), Gurwitsch (1964, 1966) and, to a lesser extent, Schutz himself (1970). As Schutz noted (1962d: 116), this work converges strongly with that of the American pragmatist philosophers such as William James (1950) and George Herbert Mead (1934), gestalt psychology and it may be added, subsequent developments in cognitive psychology (e.g. Bruner, 1974, Gregory, 1974b and computationally sophisticated work such as Marr, 1982).

A second, philosophically radical, direction for phenomenology was taken by Husserl himself. His aim, it will be recalled, was to establish an indubitable foundation for all human knowledge through a consideration of its constitution

in subjective acts of consciousness. Since objects are constituted as unities of meaning in consciousness in ways which
transcend the sensory signals in which they are based, Husserl
looked to consciousness itself as the foundation of knowledge
and sought, in the transcendental operations of pure consciousness, the foundations of intersubjectivity.

The rejection of this radical Husserlian programme is
fundamental to the third, existential, development of Husserl's
philosophical initiative by Sartre and Merleau-Ponty. In their
different ways, the existentialists placed renewed stress on the
correlation between consciousness and its objects which had
been Husserl's initial starting point and they combined this
with an emphasis on the contingent, contexted and 'interested'
nature of the encounters between the human subject and the
world. They also reinforced the view, expressed in Husserl's
last writings (Husserl, 1970b), that all human reflection is
grounded in the *Lebenswelt*, the mundane world of lived
experience already existing as a product of the unreflecting
cognitions of ordinary actors.

It is this same *Lebenswelt* which is also the starting point for
Schutz's phenomenological sociology. For Schutz, the *Lebenswelt* is a world of mundane events and institutions which the
ordinary members of society constitute and reconstitute
without ever necessarily becoming aware of the fact. This
mundane world is both the unnoticed ground on which social
science is founded and, in many respects, its unnoticed object
of investigation. Throughout his work, Schutz used a range of
phenomenological concepts to describe the fundamental
features of the social world as it is constituted and oriented to
by ordinary actors going about their daily business. Although,
like Parsons's, this work was almost entirely theoretical,
Schutz's observations and insights effectively transformed the
bases on which a theory of action could be constructed. For he
focused on the very area of analysis which Parsons omitted from
consideration: the knowledgeable character of actors' activities.

SCHUTZ AND THE *VERSTEHENDE* BASIS OF SOCIAL SCIENCE

Schutz's approach to social theory developed in the aftermath of the great nineteenth-century German debates on the nature and methodology of the social sciences. Like Weber, he sought to reconcile the apparently competing claims of science and subjectivity in this domain. His first major study, *The Phenomenology of the Social World* (1967, first published in 1932), was an attempt to develop Weber's methodological synthesis of these competing claims by deepening the analysis of the meaning structures underlying the social world by the use of phenomenological concepts. In this and all his subsequent work, Schutz insisted that the social world is, in the first instance, experientially interpreted by its members as meaningful and intelligible in terms of social categories and constructs. This did not imply for Schutz that the social world cannot be studied scientifically, but it did indicate the special subject matter and constraints with which a scientific understanding of the social world must come to terms.

Following his move to the United States in 1940, Schutz was again caught up in contemporary debates on the methodology of the social sciences. These represented a renewal of earlier arguments concerning the distinctive nature of the social sciences and were inspired by the rise of an aggressive new form of positivism developed by Carnap and the Vienna Circle. The neo-positivists – Hempel, Nagel, Neurath and others – followed Carnap in asserting that the methodological procedures of science are unitary regardless of their domain of application; that the goal of science is the explanation of individual phenomena by reference to general laws and that scientific statements must be testable by reference to publicly observable events. All three of these propositions were projected in ways which were hostile to the *verstehende* approach to social science. The neo-positivists argued that societies can be regarded as a set of 'brute facts' or regularities. The latter exist quite independently of how they are interpreted and oriented to by social participants and should properly be explained by reference to general laws. This approach embodies a simple refusal to acknowledge the significance of *verstehende* interpretation, both in social life and in social science, in favour of a purely external treatment of social facts. In neither social life, nor its sociological analysis, are the processes of subjective interpretation of any importance. This position, in turn, is justified by claims that, in any case, we can never know what others are thinking or experiencing in any 'testable' sense and that the process of *Verstehen* is unobservable in ordinary actors and 'private' and uncontrollable among social scientific observers. The net result is that, at best, *Verstehen* can be regarded as a heuristic device (Abel, 1948) in which empathetic intuition is used as a means of generating hypotheses for more rigorous and objective social scientific testing.

Schutz responded to these neo-positivist arguments in a paper 'Concept and theory formation in the social sciences' (1962b) which, although courteously phrased, was withering in its implications. In it, he stressed three major theses. First, he distinguished between the natural and the social sciences on the basis that the latter are dealing with events and relationships which are 'pre-interpreted' and, as such, already meaningful to the actors involved. Second, he argued that *verstehende* processes are the central procedures through which the world is meaningfully interpreted by ordinary social participants, and third that, properly understood, *Verstehen* is an indispensable method of the social sciences.

The Natural and the Social Sciences

The starting point for Schutz's defence of *Verstehen* is the meaningful nature of the social world. As he puts it:

> The world of nature, as explored by the natural scientist, does not 'mean' anything to molecules, atoms and electrons. But the observational field of the social scientist – social reality – has a specific meaning and relevance structure for the human beings living, acting, and thinking within it. By a series of common-sense constructs they have pre-selected and pre-interpreted this world which they experience as the reality of their daily lives. It is these thought objects of theirs which determine their behaviour by motivating it. (Schutz, 1962b: 59)

Since social theory fundamentally deals with this domain of meaningful experience and action, the sociologist's appraisal of the social world cannot be based solely on its overt or 'external' features stripped of all interpretation without an intolerable loss of information. For example, an overt behaviour (for example, a tribal pageant captured on film) cannot be analysed without the understanding that what is going on is a war dance, a barter trade or the reception of a friendly ambassador (ibid. 54). Moreover, the emphasis on overt, observable behaviour overlooks both 'negative actions' (i.e. the intentional refraining from action) and those beliefs and convictions which go beyond the sensory realm but which are collectively defined as real and are real in their consequences (ibid.). Finally, Schutz argues (in a position replicated by Apel (1972, 1967) some twenty years later) that scientific activity itself is permeated with *verstehende* relations. As he puts it in an ironic passage:

> The postulate of describing and explaining human behaviour in terms of controllable sensory observation stops short before the description and explanation of the process by which scientist B controls and verifies the observational findings of scientist A and the conclusions drawn by him. In order to do so, B has to know what A had observed, what the goal of his inquiry is, why he thought the observed fact worthy of being observed, i.e. relevant to the scientific problem at hand, etc. This knowledge is commonly called understanding. (ibid. 53)

Thus, all forms of naturalism and logical empiricism simply presuppose 'intersubjectivity, interaction, intercommunication and language . . . as the unclarified foundation of these theories' (ibid.). In sum, any attempt to characterize, let alone explain, the social world as a set of external and meaningless 'goings on' will inevitably result in an impoverishment – amounting to the destruction – of the facts to be explained. For social events are, in the first place, oriented to and interpreted as meaningful by and for those who participate in them or in any way (including scientifically) attend to them.

Verstehen *in the Social World*

Whatever the neo-positivists may have believed about the role of *Verstehen* in science or social science, it is quite inescapable that *verstehende* processes permeate social life. Schutz treats it as axiomatic that the social world is not regarded as an arena of merely 'external' and unintelligible happenings which await causal explanation, but is through and through interpreted as infused with subjective meaning and intention:

> The social world is experienced from the outset as a meaningful one. The Other's body is not experienced as an organism but as a fellow-man, its overt behaviour not as an occurence in the space–time of the outer world, but as our fellow-man's action. We normally 'know' what the Other does, for what reason he does it, why he does it at this particular time and in these particular circumstances. That means that we experience our fellow-man's action in terms of his motives and goals. (Schutz, 1962b: 55–6)

And this process of interpretation in terms of imputed meanings, motives, hopes and fears transcends the vivid reality of face-to-face encounters and personal acquaintance:

> If I read an editorial stating that France fears the re-armament of Germany, I know perfectly well what this statement means without knowing the editorialist and even without knowing a Frenchman or a German, let alone without observing their overt behaviour. (ibid. 55).

Similarly, this process of interpretation is extended to inanimate, but humanly constructed, artefacts:

> A tool, for example, is not experienced as a thing in the outer world (which of course it is also) but in terms of the purpose for which it was designed by more or less anonymous fellow-men and its possible use by others. (ibid. 56)

The pervasive interpretation of the events and artefacts of the social world in terms of subjectively intended meaning is powerful evidence that *Verstehen* is not, in the first instance, a special social scientific method, but rather 'the particular experiential form in which common-sense thinking takes cognizance of the socio-cultural world' (ibid.).

What is involved in this process of mundane *Verstehen*? Plainly it is not simply a matter of observing overt 'behaviours' since, in the first place, *Verstehen* involves the interpretation of such behaviours as *actions* by the imputation of goals, motives, intents, etc. Neither, however, does *Verstehen* involve the attempt to grasp the other's actual experiences by means of 'empathetic identification' (ibid.). From the outset of his career, Schutz denied the possibility that either social participants or social scientists could gain immediate access to what another 'concrete actor "really" experiences' (Parsons, in Grathoff, 1978: 88). The full particularity of the subjective meaning of another's acts is, Schutz insisted, 'essentially inaccessible to every other individual' (1967: 99) and is 'at best a limiting concept' (ibid. 98). Rather mundane *Verstehen* proceeds through the application of learned common-sense constructs to actions, events and their contexts (1962b). These constructs (1962a) are of typical motives, typical identities, or typical actions given particular typical circumstances or antecedent actions. It involves a 'making out' of 'what's going on here' from the where and when and who of the activity and from what would be typical or reasonable for that where, when and who. The type constructs used in these procedures are, Schutz asserts (ibid.; Schutz and Luckmann, 1974) varyingly precise, specific, detailed, familiar and vague. They are entertained as shared 'for all practical purposes' and 'until demonstrated otherwise'. When set against the intimate knowledge which others have of the meaning of their actions, these constructs inevitably 'fall short' of complete understanding (1962a: 24). Moreover their application is never certain and always involves an element of 'risk' that misunderstanding will take place. Yet, 'in spite of all these inadequacies, common-sense knowledge of everyday life is sufficient for coming to terms with fellow-men, cultural objects, social institutions – in brief, with social reality' (Schutz, 1962b: 55).

Schutz goes on to argue that common-sense knowledge is adequate as a vehicle for *Verstehen* because common-sense constructs are shared and in various ways socialized. We shall return to these arguments in the next section. He also concludes that their use in *verstehende* processes is not, in any sense, a private, unobservable or uncontrollable business, either in social science or in social life. If it were, the mundane intelligibility of social life would simply collapse and it would be difficult to account, for example, for 'the discussion by a trial jury of whether the defendant had shown "pre-meditated malice" or "intent" in killing a person, whether he was capable of knowing the consequences of his deed, etc.' (ibid.). With these observations, Schutz takes up a position which is strikingly convergent – in attitude and atmosphere, if not in specific argumentation – with the later Wittgenstein's strictures against the privacy of language and of 'other minds'.

Verstehen *as a Social Scientific Method*

If the social world is a matrix of activity which is interpreted by its participants with the use of intersubjectively available constructs which 'determine their behaviour, define the goal of their action, the means available for attaining them – in brief, which help them to find their bearings within their natural and socio-cultural environment' (Schutz, 1962a: 6), then it follows that the social scientist cannot afford to ignore the role and influence of these constructs in human action. A social scientific theory which does so, Schutz asserts,

> loses its basic foundations, namely its reference to the social world of everyday life and experience. The safeguarding of the subjective point of view is the only but sufficient guarantee that the world of social reality will not be replaced by a fictional non-existing world constructed by the scientific observer. (Schutz, 1964a: 8)

Fortunately, the social scientist *qua* member of society has intimate access to these common-sense constructs as they are used and acted upon. Moreover the community of social scientists can exert collective controls over interpretative processes in just the ways that jurors, or other members of society, can cross-check one another's interpretations of social events. Thus the social scientist is, *ab initio*, in a position to engage in publicly controllable interpretative investigations.

However, Schutz asserts, the aims and attitudes of social scientists' interpretations differ from those of ordinary actors insofar as the former are distanced from practical engagement with 'here and now' decisions and actions in the social world. From this position, the social scientist can construct typified models of social activity. This involves the creation of 'second order constructs'. The social scientist, in modelling actors' actions, is essentially engaged in developing models of the actors' constructs of the social world, their judgemental processes and their consequent actions under varying conditions. Schutz asserts that much social scientific activity – for example, model building in economics, political science and sociology – proceeds wittingly or unwittingly along these lines. However there remain a range of social scientific problems (including methodological problems) which require more detailed foundational work on the basic processes through which intersubjective understanding itself is maintained. These processes also turn out to be critical for the analysis of social action and the foundations of social organization and it is to these issues that we now turn.

A TYPIFIED WORLD

The starting point for Schutz's analysis of mundane knowledge is his delineation of its *typicality*. Here Schutz follows Husserl in arguing that an experiencing consciousness is inherently a typifying one. The constructs in terms of which an 'object' of some kind is constituted of a set of sensory presentations are themselves the 'sedimented' products of past activities of comparing and contrasting out of which mundane typifications arise. A major consequence of this process of typification is that every experience of the actor occurs within 'a horizon of familiarity and pre-acquaintanceship' (1962a: 7) which is furnished through a presently unquestioned (though, Schutz insists, always questionable) stock of knowledge at hand. Even the utterly novel and unfamiliar is grasped as such against this pre-established background of normality and typicality.

The stock of knowledge at hand minimally comprises (1) type constructs of objects (e.g. 'mountains', 'trees', 'animals', 'fellow men') and (2) typified 'recipe knowledge' concerning the 'how to do it' of all kinds of courses of action. Both kinds of knowledge inherently anticipate the future: the actor pragmatically assumes that knowledge which proved adequate up to the present will continue to do so in the future. Finally, most of the actor's stock of knowledge at hand is treated as contingently valid or 'valid until counter-evidence appears'. In the latter event, relevant aspects of the stock of knowledge will undergo revision.

In drawing upon type constructs to organize their mundane experiences of objects, actors in the 'natural attitude' simply assume that 'as they see things, so they are'. For example actors do not, in the normal run of events, 'consult' their knowledge of types in such a way that, finding for example that a newly observed 'Irish Wolfhound' conforms with a knowledge of 'typical dogs', they proclaim their knowledge of the latter to be confirmed. This would be to 'intellectualize' social actors and indeed to suggest that, like a scientist, they are constantly engaged in testing out the adequacy of their constructs. This is not the case. Rather, actors simply *see* objects 'in their mode of typicality'. Their 'employment' of the constructs is largely unreflecting and pragmatic. Indeed, preoccupied with acting on the world in the 'here and now', they cannot afford to reflect on the adequacy of their type constructs and will only do so if the world starts to run counter to expectations. Thus the actors' type constructs are the (revisable) yardsticks in terms of which their experience of the world is organized and upon which they rely in order to make sense of a world in which they must act. Finally, while most of the actors' constructs are contingent and revisable, their use (and revision) occurs against a background of fundamental and axiomatic experiential constructs: for example, that 'the world consists of more or less circumscribed objects . . . among which we move, which resist us and upon which we may act' (ibid.). These characteristic assumptions of the natural attitude arise out of the actors' earliest experiences in the manipulation of objects. Other, similarly fundamental, assumptions – that the world existed before the actor was born and will continue to do so after his or her death, that the movements of others are animated by goals, intentions, etc. – arise in the course of the actor's experiences of the social world.

As to the type constructs themselves, Schutz asserts that they may be varyingly and variously detailed, specific, familiar and precise. All of these terms, however, are relative. By their very nature, type constructs *abstract* from the concrete uniqueness of objects and events and they therefore bear an inherently approximate, adjustable and 'elastic' relation to the objects they typify. Thus in their abstraction from, and application to, unique configurations, type constructs bear a relationship to concrete particulars which is, in 'absolute' terms, vague. Type constructs have to be 'applied' and in their 'application' the unique specificity of objects and events is irretrievably lost (ibid. 21).

Thus the precision, specificity, etc. of type constructs is a *relative* one and is judged relative to other type constructs which might have been employed given the actor's practical purposes. 'Rover' can be viewed as an animal, a vertebrate, a mammal, a dog, an Irish Setter, my friend and companion of the last seven years and so on (ibid.). Moreover the relative precision etc. of these typifications is necessarily contextual and can be determined *only* in relation to the actor's practical purposes. The construct 'dog' may be sufficient for the actor's purposes as he or she reviews the shelves of tins in a supermarket with a view to buying Rover's dinner. It will not be sufficient when the actor tries to enter Rover in a dog show. Thus, Schutz argues, the actor can typify 'Rover' in many ways and these typifications will be invoked and used in accordance with his or her current practical purposes and relevancies (Schutz, 1970). All of these assertions about type constructs apply equally to their vernacular expression in natural language which Schutz characterizes as 'the typifying medium *par excellence*' and as 'a treasure house of ready made pre-constituted types and characteristics' (Schutz, 1962a: 14). In sum, the type constructs with which the actors navigate the natural and social worlds and with which they communicate through natural language are inherently approximate, open-ended and revisable. They may undergo change, elaboration or qualification at any moment subject to local contingencies. Their development and use is shaped by the practical experiences and relevancies which arise in the course of the actors' engagement with the world around them.

Finally, Schutz notes that few of the type constructs constituting the actors' knowledge of the world originate within personal experience. While certain basic constructs arise prior to the acquisition of language and serve as the foundation for its acquisition (Schutz and Luckmann, 1974: 233–5), these constructs are rapidly and overwhelmingly 'socialized' through the development of increasingly complex communicational skills (ibid. 261 *et seq.*). This development, in turn, permits the acquisition of further, socially derived, constructs from parents, teachers, etc. which are 'language carried'. All of these 'socialized' acquisitions involve and require intersubjectivity and it is to Schutz's treatment of this problem which we now turn.

THE PROBLEM OF INTERSUBJECTIVITY

Schutz's treatment of the problem of intersubjectivity is a subtle and profound one. Like the later Wittgenstein's, it is premissed on the abandonment of the search for any pristine 'fail-safe' technique through which intersubjectivity could be said to be assured or guaranteed. Instead, from his earliest writings (Schutz, 1967: 98 *et seq.*), Schutz treats the problem as a mundane one and explicitly rejects Husserl's attempt at a transcendental derivation of intersubjectivity (Schutz, 1966a). Thus, rather than treating intersubjectivity as an essentially philosophical problem for which a determinate in-principle solution must be found, Schutz treats its achievement and maintenance as a *practical* 'problem' which is routinely 'solved' by social actors in the course of their dealings with one another.

The 'problem of intersubjectivity' can be posed as the following question: how can two or more actors share common experiences of the natural and social world and, relatedly, how can they communicate about them? Schutz's answer to this problem is to state categorically that human beings can never have *identical* experiences of anything, but that this is irrelevant because they continuously *assume* that their experiences of the world are similar and *act* as if their experiences were identical-for-all-practical-purposes. A parallel argument is developed in relation to linguistic communication.

We have already encountered Schutz's insistence that the full particularity of the subjective experience of the other is 'essentially inaccessible to every other individual' (1967: 99).

Moreover, mundane actors also 'know' that the 'same' objects, as encountered by each of them, are encountered differently and for two reasons. Firstly, the two actors are physically located in different places and thus see different aspects and configurations of objects. Similarly, given their different positions relative to a domain of objects, some objects can be seen, heard and manipulated by A and not by B and vice versa. Secondly, each actor comes upon the domain of objects with different practical purposes in hand and knows that, 'motivationally speaking' they may be viewing the domain of objects in differently 'interested' ways. It will be obvious that these differences could, in principle, destroy any possibility of truly intersubjective knowledge. In practice, this simply does not happen. Instead, the actors routinely perform two basic idealizations which Schutz refers to as 'the general thesis of reciprocal perspectives'. These two idealizations are:

(1) *The idealization of the interchangeability of standpoints*: I take it for granted – and assume my fellow man does the same – that if I change places with him so that his 'here' becomes mine, I shall be at the same distance from things and see them with the same typicality as he actually does; moreover, the same things would be in my reach which are actually in his . . .

(2) *The idealization of the congruency of the system of relevances*: Until counter-evidence I take it for granted – and assume that my fellow man does the same – that the differences in perspective originating in our unique biographical situations are irrelevant for the purpose at hand of either of us and that he and I, that 'We' assume that both of us have selected and interpreted the actually or potentially common objects and their features in an identical manner or at least an 'empirically identical' manner, i.e. one sufficient for all practical purposes. (Schutz, 1962a: 11–12)

This proposal of Schutz's is an absolutely crucial one. It is through the operation of these two assumptions that a 'common world' which transcends the actors' private experiential worlds can be established. For example, it is only via these idealizations that 'we both see the "same" flying bird in spite of the difference of our spatial position, sex, age, and the fact that you want to shoot it and I just to enjoy it' (Schutz, 1962f: 316). Further, it is only insofar as these idealizations can be consistently sustained that an intersubjectively shared 'stock of knowledge' can be established and maintained and language can perform its typifying functions (cf. ibid. 321–3, 327–9). In this context, it is worth noting that primitive versions of these idealizations must antedate the acquisition of language and be grounded in conjoint activities of 'looking' and 'pointing out' and in shared activities with objects (Bruner, 1975a, 1975b, 1976, 1977, 1984).

In sum, within the natural attitude of common-sense thought and action, a 'common world' is maintained by virtue of the fact that the actors treat ordinary objects, actions and events under two partially contradictory assumptions. On the one hand, the actors assume from the outset that they share a common world. On the other, they know that the world displays a perspectival appearance in the two senses outlined above. It is through a continuous process of adjustment – expressed in the two idealizations – that the actors succeed in resolving the discrepancies in their perspectives which could otherwise throw doubt on the shared nature of their perceptions and cognitions. It is essential to note, in this context, that Schutz here proposes that intersubjective knowledge, as a product of these idealizations, is derived solely from the fact that the *actors* sustain the idealizations *and has no other 'external' guarantee than this maintenance.*

Moreover, through the postulation of these idealizations, Schutz insists that the achievement and management of an intersubjectively constituted social reality is through and through an affair which remains with the actors. Thus although Schutz's various descriptions of shared stocks of typified knowledge, the typifying function of language, etc. may seem to invoke an effectively Parsonian appeal to the 'common culture' as the bedrock of intersubjectivity, such an appeal is instantly and absolutely qualified by his assertion that the common culture exists and continues to exist subject, on every occasion, to the maintenance of the general thesis of reciprocal perspectives. Further, though the general thesis is presupposed and taken for granted, it is only maintained, Schutz emphasizes, until counter-evidence provokes revision, change or abandonment. Its maintenance is, in short, absolutely contingent.

Intersubjectivity, however, is not confined to the achievement of a shared apprehension of the external world. And the sociological 'problem of intersubjectivity' is not limited to the analysis of this achievement. There is also the problem of 'other· minds': the question of how the actors grasp the subjective meanings of one another's actions. Included in this rather amorphous category of 'subjective meanings' are the other's goals, intentions and motivations together with their affective colourings – the desires, hopes, fears and anxieties with which these goals and motivations are invested.

Schutz begins his treatment of the sociological problem of 'other minds' by noting that the actor in the natural attitude does not need to prove (or have it proved) that the other's actions are animated by goals and intentions. Rather the actor starts out with the unquestioned assumption that this is the case. Thus the actor's task is not the 'philosophical' one of justifying a belief in 'other minds', but the empirical task of specifying their 'contents' – the goals, intentions, etc. – which are operative on any given occasion. Schutz gives two complementary accounts of how the actor goes about this task.

First, in the course of socialization the actor acquires a range of constructs referring to typical actions performed under typical circumstances by typical actors. To adapt an example which Schutz often used, the child learns that there are men called 'ticket collectors' who stand at the end of platforms in railway stations and take passengers' tickets as they file past. The child may also gradually learn that when a passenger fails to present a ticket, the ticket collector will seek to prevent him from leaving the platform and, more generally, will 'take steps' about it. A large proportion of routine social activity, Schutz suggests, is organized through similar typified constructs. The latter are established on a taken-for-granted basis and they are valuable as a resource for navigating the social world because 'the pattern of typified constructs is frequently institutionalized as a standard of behaviour, warranted by traditional and habitual mores and sometimes by specific means of so-called social control, such as the legal order' (Schutz, 1962a: 19). These type constructs are characteristically anonymous in that they make no reference to the other's personal intentions, goals, hopes or fears nor even, in many cases, to the 'organizational rationale' of his or her actions. In the transaction of handing over and receiving a train ticket, both parties anonymize themselves by 'living up to' their institutional roles of passenger and ticket collector and no more than that.

Plainly more than this is happening in the more intimate, face-to-face relations which the actor enters into and these latter are the focus of Schutz's second, complementary, account of 'other minds'. Here the actors relate to one another in terms of constructs which are much more familiar, detailed and specific. Moreover these constructs are varyingly infused with the sedimented emotional colourings which derive from the actors' biographical experience. Additionally, in face-to-face contact with intimates, the other's actions are interpreted in the light of gestures, mannerisms, bodily comportment and facial expressions – all of which are treated as 'indications of subjectively meaningful processes' (Schutz, 1964b: 26). In sum:

> In the face-to-face situation I have immediate experience of my fellow-man. But as I confront my fellow-man, I bring into each concrete situation a stock of pre-constituted knowledge which includes a network of typifications of human individuals in general, of typical human motivations, goals, and action patterns. It also includes knowledge of expressive and interpretative schemes, of objective sign systems and, in particular, of the vernacular language. I have more specific information about particular kinds and groups of men, of their motivations and actions. If I formerly had direct experience of this particular fellow-man now confronting me, I may, of course, fall back on the highly specialized information sedimented in these experiences. In the on-going experiences of the We-relation I check and revise my previous knowledge about my partner and accumulate new knowledge about him. Thereby my general stock of knowledge also undergoes a continuous modification. My experience of a fellow-man in the We-relation thus stands in a multiple context of meaning: it is experience of a human being, it is experience of a typical actor on the social scene, it is experience of this particular fellow-man, and it is experience of this particular fellow-man in this particular situation, Here and Now. (ibid. 29–30).

In every face-to-face contact, typified constructs of varying familiarity, specificity and detail are brought to bear. Mutual understanding is ultimately dependent upon the co-ordinated use of these frameworks of common constructs. The congruence of these constructs is continuously adjusted in face-to-face interaction in the light of whether the other's actions confirm, or fail to confirm, the anticipations of the actor on which his or her own conduct is based (ibid.). In the absence of these opportunities for adjustment, the more remote relationships with contemporaries are less certain. They are based only on the possibility 'that the reciprocally ascribed typifying schemes (and corresponding expectations) will be used congruently by the partners' (ibid. 54). When I write to my bank manager, I have to hope that my justification of my need for a loan will square with the kinds of considerations which he will treat as adequate grounds for granting it. And my likelihood of success will depend on the *initial* adequacy of my constructs of his criteria of decision-making: there is no opportunity for me to revise my argument on seeing him frown.

In concluding this discussion of Schutz's treatment of intersubjectivity, it is useful to recall that, throughout his writings, Schutz is preoccupied with the overlapping boundaries and, in a certain sense, the tension between what is properly 'subjective' on the one hand and the realm of the intersubjective (or potentially intersubjective) on the other. Here Schutz sought in particular to distinguish between the *irremediably* private and unavailable aspects of experience and the *contingently* unavailable aspects of the other's subjective intentions, plans, etc.

With respect to the irremediably private, Schutz stresses that even though much of the actor's experience is constituted in terms of socialized and publicly communicable constructs, in the last analysis each actor remains biographically unique. Individuals, and only individuals, have access to the 'local' and particular shadings of experience which impregnate their constructs of the natural and social world. This much is private, inaccessible to an observer, and inexpressible in a public language. For these reasons, this experience is not available within the society and cannot be a datum of sociology. Schutz's attitude to this fact is cheerfully agnostic: what *is* available to sociology is the fact that the actors, despite their non-identical experiences and despite their lack of access to the full particularity of one another's experiences, can nevertheless proceed on the basis that their experiences are 'identical for all practical purposes'. Persistently conducting themselves on this assumption, a world of shared experience – extruded, as it were, through language – is brought into being.

This first sense of the 'inaccessibility of the subjective' is to be contrasted with a second situation of 'contingent inaccessibility'. Schutz defines action as 'conduct based on a preconceived project' (1962a: 19). And, basing himself on this definition, he treats the subjective meaning of an actor's action as the project, conceived by the actor in advance of the action, which the action is designed to implement. (A number of difficulties arise in the use of this definition, although they need not concern us here.) It follows then that *initially* only the actor knows the meaning of his or her action, i.e. the project or series of projects within which some present action is embedded: 'only the actor knows "when his action starts and where it ends" ' (ibid. 24). The task of fellow-actors, therefore, is necessarily one of *inferring* from a fragment of the other's conduct and its context what the other's project is, or is likely to be. Thus any fellow-actor's inferences about what some other is 'up to' are inevitably contingent and tend to be subject to revision and adjustment 'after the event', i.e. after some next phase of activity has elapsed.

It follows that the relation between the actor's understanding of his or her own actions on the one hand and the 'observing' co-interactant's understandings on the other – the 'private' and the 'public' – is one of contingent overlap. The meaning of the actor's action is potentially accessible, but the observer's understanding is not thereby guaranteed to be correct. Moreover, it is a situation in which, in principle if not in practice, the actor is always 'one jump ahead' of the observer. Now it is normally the case that the 'observing' co-actor cannot wait for the actor's action to have fully run its course before deciding 'what the actor was up to'. This is a luxury available only to historians and social scientists. In the social world, the prevailing situation is one in which the 'observer' must respond to the actor's action before the latter's entire course of action (and its underlying 'project') has been fully disclosed. The 'observing' and interpreting co-actor must thus 'take chances' in responding on the basis of an interpretation of the other's action which may yet turn out to be incorrect because all the facts were not, at that point, available. This circumstance has important ramifications for Schutz's treatment of rational action, to which we now turn.

THE PROBLEM OF RATIONALITY

In a late essay, Simmel wrote: 'We are all like the chess player in this regard. If he did not know, to a certain extent, what the consequences of a certain move would be, the game would be impossible; but it would also be impossible if this foresight extended indefinitely' (Simmel, 1971: 352). Schutz would have agreed. His discussion of rational action is permeated by an awareness of the essential and irremediable incompleteness of the actor's knowledge in any concrete situation of action. This incompleteness is of several types and derives both from the nature of the actor's knowledge and interests and from the conditions under which intersubjective understanding of 'other minds' is possible. The consequences of taking this incompleteness seriously is that, although Schutz is prepared to accept a view of rational action as involving, *inter alia*, a process of considered choice among goals and among means for achieving them, his analysis suggests that any further attempt to use a systematic distinction between rational and non-rational action for the kinds of theoretical purposes sought after by Parsons will prove largely vacuous.

Schutz's discussion of common-sense knowledge of the world is one which repeatedly stresses its pragmatic character. Common-sense knowledge is built up *ad hoc*, as a product of practical, 'interested' engagement with the world. In building up this knowledge,

we are guided neither by methodological considerations nor by any conceptual scheme of means-end relations, nor by any idea of values we have to realize. Our practical interest alone, as it arises in a certain situation of our life, and as it will be modified by the change in the situation which is just on the point of occurring, is the only relevant principle in the building up of the perspective structure in which our social world appears to us in daily life. (Schutz, 1964c: 72)

The practical interests which we acquire 'just living along', as Schutz puts it, and which motivate the acquisition of common-sense knowledge, also promote its 'patchiness'. In a revealing metaphor, Schutz often compared the actor's knowledge of society, its organized ways and practices and its institutional life with our ordinary knowledge of the geography of a city. We know the streets near our homes with great intimacy. We also have a highly detailed working knowledge of other areas, for example, downtown shopping districts or the area around our place of work. We have a good knowledge of the routes through the city which we regularly use. Yet there are other areas of the city of which we have only the sketchiest knowledge and these will tend to be the areas in which we have little interest and never visit. By the same token, the actors know their own 'local' social worlds in fine detail. Beyond this lie the decreasingly relevant and increasingly anonymous areas of social life which are understood with only the minimum specification and clarity necessary for each actor's practical purposes. This stratification of the actor's knowledge is largely pragmatic: it is based on an economy of effort. The actor may not 'need to know' or 'have time to find out' how the telephone, or the automobile, or the law of contract, or the National Insurance system 'works'. And the actor also knows that there are 'experts' in these matters who can be consulted if a problem should arise. Thus the actor navigates the social world using a patchwork of 'recipe knowledge' in which

clear and distinct experiences are intermingled with vague conjectures; suppositions and prejudices cross well-proven evidences; motives, means and ends, as well as causes and effects, are strung together without clear understanding of their real connections. There are everywhere gaps, intermissions, discontinuities. Apparently there is a kind of organization by habits, rules and principles which we regularly apply with success. But the origin of our habits is almost beyond our control; the rules we apply are rules of thumb and their validity has never been verified. (ibid. 72–3)

Turning now to rational action, Schutz argues that rational choice is characterized by the actor's knowledge of at least the following about an end and the means for achieving it:

(a) Knowledge of the place of the end to be realized within the framework of the plans of the actor.
(b) Knowledge of its interrelations with other ends and its compatibility or incompatibility with them.
(c) Knowledge of the desirable and undesirable consequences which may arise as by-products of the realization of the main end.
(d) Knowledge of the different chains of means which . . . are suitable for the accomplishment of this end, regardless of whether the actor has control over all or several of their elements.
(e) Knowledge of the interference of such means with other ends or other chains of means including all their secondary effects and incidental consequences.
(f) Knowledge of the accessibility of those means for the actor. (ibid. 79–80)

It will be obvious that these criteria are not met even in such a highly 'rationalized' decision as that of buying a car. How many people assess the costs of car ownership against the costs of public transport, or renting a car on occasion? How many compute the 'opportunity costs' of car purchase in terms of the tying up of funds or income? How many evaluate the relative costs of a fixed interest loan at 'today's high rates', against a variable interest loan which could become more costly as a result of such a remote possibility as the election of a tax-cutting American president? What is involved in the choice between a model renowned for its reliability and a different make against which the salesman will make a 'very good' offer for your current model? Or when someone in the family wants a 'metallic' paint finish and it is observed that such paints are 'difficult to match' in the event of a scrape? How does the actor assess a 'good road report' from an automobile magazine against a neighbour's advice 'never to buy an Italian car' – when the former carries a great deal of car advertising and the latter was wounded at the battle of Anzio? Is there any calculus for balancing these choices, or even for assessing their validity with the advantage of hindsight? Above all, is it even worth taking the time and trouble to work them out? And, of course, the criteria are even less applicable to other kinds of decisions, for example, to accept a particular job offer, to take a week off work with a plea of sickness, to go to a supermarket or telephone a friend. Finally, the actor may, confronted with the necessity of making an 'on the spot' decision, be unable to take the time to compute the various possibilities even though he or she regards such computation as desirable.

Moreover, Schutz points out, the calculus becomes even more complex and indeterminate in the case of social actions. For here,

> if I project a rational action which requires an interlocking of my and the Other's motives of action to be carried out . . . I must, by a curious mirror-effect, have sufficient knowledge of what he, the Other, knows . . . and this knowledge of his is supposed to include sufficient acquaintance with what I know. This is a condition of *ideally* rational interaction because without such mutual knowledge I could not 'rationally' project the attainment of my goal by means of the Other's co-operation or reaction. Moreover such mutual knowledge has to be clear and distinct; merely a more or less empty expectation of the Other's behaviour is not sufficient.(Schutz, 1962a: 31–2)

Going back to that car-salesman, I need to know not only 'how badly' he needs to make the sale but also his assessment of 'how badly' I want to buy. And I need to be able to compute this in 'real time' for it is in the 'frame-by-frame' moments of interaction that the salesman and I are making our assessments and taking up positions. Thus when we consider actions designed to influence other people, we find that the conditions for rational action are only met when we know how our own actions may be interpreted and misinterpreted, the other's reactions and their motivations, his or her plans, means, alternatives, etc. and the full range of the other's stock of knowledge (Schutz, 1964c: 80). Given these considerations and the range of contingencies to which they give rise, it will be obvious that the ideal of rational action undertaken with full clarity and foreknowledge becomes irrelevant as either an ideal or a yardstick for the assessment of actual conduct. Instead, we are left with a situation in which

> nowhere have we a guarantee of the reliability of all these assumptions by which we are governed. On the other hand, these experiences and rules are sufficient to us for mastering life. As we normally have to act and not to reflect in order to satisfy the demands of the moment, which it is our task to master, we are not interested in the 'quest for certainty'. We are satisfied if we have a fair chance of realizing our purposes, and this chance, so we like to think, we have if we set in motion the same mechanism of habits, rules and principles which formerly stood the test and which still stand the test. Our knowledge in daily life is not without hypotheses, inductions and predictions, but they all have the character of the approximate and the typical. (ibid.)

Finally, if the actor's stock of knowledge is stored in the form of typifications, it will be *essentially* incomplete. For typified knowledge is, by its very nature, indeterminate and revisable. It is open-ended; it requires application to the concrete particulars of situations and, as Schutz puts it, 'carries along an open horizon of undetermined content'. Thus Schutz comments, 'the consistency of this system of knowledge is not that of natural *laws*, but that of *typical* sequences and relations' (ibid.), and, in a parallel discussion, he concludes that, at the common-sense level, 'actions are at best partially rational and that rationality has many degrees' (1962a: 33). With this discussion, Schutz effectively demolishes any attempt to construct a model of 'scientifically rational' conduct as a standard by which concrete courses of action may be measured. Instead, he recommends the investigation and scientific description of whatever the actors within a domain of social reality find intelligible, together with the criteria of choice, evaluation, etc. which are applied within that domain. The only alternative would be to start from the assumption that, because social activities do not exhibit the features of 'scientific rationality', they must lack the coherence of recognizably 'reasonable' action. Schutz will have no truck with this latter alternative. To begin in this way would be to become detached, from the outset, not merely from the specific social reality of the phenomena under investigation, but also from the fundamental organizational properties of the common-sense world in which 'reasonable actions' have their 'reasonable' logics, grounds, evaluations and accountability. And, if these grounds do not participate in the frictionless universe of the purely rational, they are not to be discounted from sociological consideration on such a flimsy pretext.

CONCLUSION

The entire corpus of Schutz's writings reflects his fundamental belief that 'the sciences that would interpret and explain human action and thought must begin with a description of the foundational structures of what is pre-scientific, the reality which seems self-evident to men remaining within the natural attitude' (Schutz and Luckmann, 1974: 3). This uncompromisingly interpretative approach to social science with its emphasis on the intersubjective structuring of the actor's cognitive universe was, and remains, a powerful force for the expansion of sociological horizons. In the remaining paragraphs of this chapter, some attempt will be made to draw up a balance sheet of the main areas of advance and to set into relief those aspects in which the advance was incomplete.

First, it is relevant to notice that the Schutzian actor inhabits a vastly expanded cognitive universe. In contrast to the Parsonian actor who orients only to an empirically situational world of objects which he can know with varying degrees of approximation to scientific accuracy, the Schutzian actor has a greatly enriched 'inner life'. In addition to the 'real world' of perception and cognition, the latter can imagine, remember, dream and theorize and, moreover, do all these with respect to both empirical and ideal objects. These domains of consciousness and their objects, Schutz recommends (1962e), have a meaningful reality and an experiential 'logic' or structure which is not simply 'empirically inadequate' or reducible to a residual stratum of non-logical sentiments or attitudes. It is precisely this latter treatment, proposed by Parsons, which threatens to reduce the world of 'reasonable judgements' to a mere epiphenomenal by-product of 'internalization'. While it may be granted that the Schutzian viewpoint reveals an immense variety of 'object worlds' and of modes of attending to them, to sweep them all away as non-rational residues precludes a huge variety of investigations into such matters as

> the ways in which these objects are constituted, the rules that govern the tests that the experiencer uses of whether he has seen correctly, the tests that he considers legitimate ones for the accuracy of his judgements, the conditions under which he can experience a discrepancy between expectations and events, the consequences of such surprises, the socially legitimate methods for resolving such discrepancies, the rules that govern his judgemental behaviour, the devices by which he establishes and maintains the relevance of events for each other – all these show different characteristics as one compares worlds and the modes of attending them that are particular to each of these worlds. (Garfinkel, 1952: 98–9)

Schutz recommends a direct frontal assault on a range of universes of meaning – including the realms of religious experience, art, science, mathematics and music – and which should comprise, *inter alia*, investigations of *how* the objects of these various universes of meaning are constituted and communicated (Schutz, 1962e, 1962f, 1964d).

In making these recommendations, Schutz accomplished a particular liberation of the sociological imagination whose subterranean impact is only now receiving wider appreciation. This liberation is from the straightjacket of what Bloor (1976) has called the 'sociology of error' which arises whenever the attempt is made to grant an absolutely privileged status to social scientific constructs of social reality. Parsons adopts this latter position and, as we have seen, it results in fundamental difficulties in reconciling the basic discontinuities proposed to exist between the rational knowledge which the actor may, to a greater or lesser extent, share with the scientist and the remainder of the actor's non-rational constructs and orientations.

These proposed discontinuities generate a variety of problems. One concerns the justification of the rationality of social scientific methods and results in the face of the fact that the actor somehow 'knows different' and acts accordingly. A pervasive response to this situation is simply to declare, as Parsons does, in favour of the cognitive superiority of science. The cost of this declaration, however, in the context of the sociology of action is that sharply divergent treatments must be given to the rational (and hence 'self-explanatory') aspects of the actor's action on the one hand, and those which the theorist judges non-rational on the other. Only the latter are held to be relevantly subject to sociological explanation, if only because the admission that rational constructs are relevantly explained by social science would have relativistic implications for the entire enterprise.

A related problem arises when the theorist comes to consider how the actor can continue to act effectively, even 'successfully', and certainly comfortably given that, in the theorist's privileged view, he orients the world so inadequately (Garfinkel, 1952: 115–18). This problem has motivated immense theoretical effort. Accounts of how the actor can cheerfully persist in his erroneous ways have ranged from invocations of the Freudian mechanisms of defence, through the functionality – for the 'society' as a whole or some subsection of its members – of the 'community of myth' enjoyed by the actors, to the 'various structural arrangements and operations . . . whereby the members knowingly or not protect each other from the actual consequences of their errors' (ibid.). None of these theoretical moves, of course, are illegitimate. But it is relevant to notice that they are systematically required as 'secondary elaborations' in defence of the privileged status of social scientists' empirical judgements. And, in turn, preoccupation with the 'problem of error' and its resolution tends to deflect attention away from the systematic study of the actors' actual knowledge, the properties of their judgements, their procedures for assessing outcomes, etc.

The framework of assumptions embodied in the 'sociology of error', paradoxically, becomes most prominent where it is most obstructive – in the sociology of knowledge and culture –

where it engenders deeply ironic characterizations of, *inter alia*, religious beliefs and 'ideological' constructs of all kinds. Moreover since, through the assumptions of the 'sociology of error', domains of socially organized knowledge must first be declared cognitively defective before they can be legitimately investigated, a number of important fields become effectively closed to sociological investigation. Most notable among these are, firstly, domains where knowledge is – from the standpoint of sociology – effectively incontrovertible (Bloor, 1976). Such domains include 'core science' and mathematics: there is no neo-Kantian sociology of astrophysics or microbiology or of tensors or Feynman diagrams. Moreover, secondly, there is no neo-Kantian sociology of knowledge domains which do not embody cognitive claims as such – e.g. music – or of domains which are deeply diffuse in their cognitive claims as in the cases of art and language. The development of these domains is profoundly inhibited by the assumptions of the 'sociology of error' and such development is hardly possible without shedding these assumptions.

As we have seen, Schutz's analysis of the rationalities of everyday conduct undermines the fundamental assumption which generates the 'sociology of error' – the assumed hard and fast distinction between rational and non-rational knowledge and conduct. In so doing, he invites social scientists to examine the structures of self-evident constructs in each domain of social reality without prejudice. This does not mean, he insists, that social scientists should abandon a scientific commitment to gaining clear, logically organized knowledge of the domain in question. Still less does it imply that social scientists must endorse the domain of constructs under investigation with some kind of scientific imprimatur. Yet neither does scientific investigation, with its proper goals of fuller knowledge which is clearly and logically articulated, necessarily suggest that the actor's point of view is, if only by comparison, defective. In many ways, the social scientist's goals are peculiar and of historically recent origin. The objective of clear, logically organized knowledge of the social world which is independent of particular observers and the fluctuations of their circumstances is a special one which demands that observers check and recheck their observations.

Neither the goal nor the means are available to practical actors who must make 'snap' judgements and act on them despite the fact that they cannot fully determine the consequences of their actions. The social scientists' gains in clarity and logical structuring of their chosen materials can only be achieved through the opportunity for reflection and the reworking of data, and this, in turn, is only possible by virtue of a detachment from the situation whose elements they attempt to depict. Such opportunities are not available to the actor and the different properties of the actor's constructs are responsive to the quite different constraints of practical action, to which, indeed, the social scientist also becomes subject on stepping out of the office.

Finally, in this brief and selective stock-taking of Schutz's achievements, it is important to recall his stress on the contingency of intersubjective understanding. The background to this proposal is, of course, his emphasis on the differentiated and particularized viewpoints and relevances which inform individual conduct. However this pervasive emphasis is balanced by the corresponding recognition that intersubjective knowledge, communicative interaction and co-ordinated conduct are only possible insofar as, somehow, these various differences are suspended in the practical conduct of action and interaction. It is important to note in this context that, although these issues can have 'Hobbesian' overtones, Schutz's arguments are not presented as a 'solution' to the Hobbesian 'problem of order'. Schutz is not, in this sense, a consensus theorist. Rather his arguments are *anterior* to the issue of co-operation versus conflict. At the end of the day, conflict, just as much as co-operation, can only be conducted within an overarching frame of intelligibility and it is the maintenance of this overarching frame which is the central object of Schutz's theoretical investigations. For Schutz, the *cognitive* 'problem of order' is necessarily prior to the more traditional sociological question first raised by Hobbes.

This cognitive 'problem of order' is effectively deleted by Parsons with his proposal that knowledge and language are unproblematically shared by virtue of their institutionalization and internalization. For Schutz, by contrast, shared understanding is inevitably contingent. The ramifications of this proposal are extremely general. As Garfinkel summarizes it:

> The problem that Schutz addresses . . . is simple but potent: granted a world that actor and observer may know together, with whatever colorings of doubt, hesitancy, certainty, typicality, uniqueness, publicity, privacy, orderliness, confusion, determinateness or indeterminateness, repetition or singularity, and with whatever accents of immanence or transcendence to thought – granted all this. What are the conditions by way of the structuring of experiences and only of the structuring of experiences under which an experiencer experiences an order that shows these faces? (Garfinkel, 1952: 113)

And as these ramifications are general, so too the form of investigation must assume an equivalent breadth. *Whatever* the intersubjective knowledge and understanding is that is achieved and *however* it is achieved become legitimate topics of investigation as to their 'what' and 'how'. With this realization, we reach the threshold of ethnomethodology. For the investigations inspired by the Schutzian framework will be directed at the question of

> how men, isolated yet simultaneously in an odd communion, go about the business of constructing, testing, maintaining, altering, validating, questioning, defining an order *together*. (ibid. 114)

And, to repeat, the investigation of these topics will have completely transcended the question of the actors' 'rationality' in the sense developed by Parsons. For Schutz's discussion of the latter has already cut the social scientist off from invoking the external yardstick of the 'scientific rationalities' as a device with which to measure, estimate or assess the rationales of 'reasonable actions'.

If all the preceding observations represent gains deriving from Schutz's theoretical researches, a number of serious doubts still remain. First, it is by no means obvious, especially given the abstract quality of much of Schutz's theorizing, where the social scientist who has learned the Schutzian lessons is to proceed from here. Schutz's work seems to lead us along quite reasonably and carefully until we quite abruptly find ourselves at the edge of a precipice with all traditional guidelines shorn away and no clearcut means of going forward.

Moreover, although Schutz emphasizes that social scientists are obliged to seek fully rational models of action and to represent their elements with full clarity and logical articulation, his substantive theory stresses the tangled, discontinuous and underdetermined character of the network of typifications which the actors draw upon in dealing with their everyday environments. What is the relationship between this network with its imprecisions, discontinuities and opacities on the one hand and the clear, logically articulated models of action with which social scientists hope to emerge at the end of their labours? If this tangled network of thought-objects determines the conduct of actors which is to be explained, and it is vague and incomplete, then surely the *verstehende* sociologist who seeks to represent this knowledge with full clarity and logical articulation runs the risk of violating the actor's point of view by overrationalizing it. Schutz himself insisted (1962a, 1962b), citing psychoanalysis as his example, that rationalized models can be constructed of systems of constructs displaying the above-mentioned features, but plainly this can be done only with very great care, and Schutz nowhere fully demonstrates what the result would look like in practice. Additionally, there is the related question of just how these indeterminate systems of constructs can be subjected to methodologically controlled procedures of investigation.

In short, investigations of common-sense constructs as they are depicted by Schutz would seem, a priori, to come dangerously close to researching and illegitimately clarifying phenomena which are too tenuous, disorganized and arbitrary to support a systematic research programme. Faced with these problems – the lack of any 'ready made' research methodology or even self-evident research objectives and the absence of any guarantee that findings could prove significant – it is not surprising that many who may have found Schutz's theoretical work convincing have, nonetheless, been disinclined to engage in research based directly on Schutzian assumptions.

A second source of anxiety arises from the comparatively static character of Schutz's treatment of the phenomena of action. In a famous remark, W. F. Whyte commented of Parsons's action theory: 'there is a stage, there is a set, but the actors do not move.' A similar remark could not, in all fairness, be applied to Schutz for whom, indeed, the time perspectives of the actor and the pragmatic, action-oriented character of the actor's knowledge are paramount. Nonetheless, the theoretical situation in Schutzian sociology is not unlike 'Grandmother's Footsteps'. The actor is fully equipped for action, but somehow fails to act within the gaze of the theorist. Within Schutz's theoretical gaze the actors are caught in the frozen postures of actions-in-the-course-of-completion; 'cinema' however is never quite achieved.

Finally, and most troublesomely, Schutzian sociology is overwhelmingly a sociology of co-operation in which the actors, in their efforts to sustain a common world, suspend their differences of perspective and interest. The 'tough-minded' response to this portrayal runs to the effect that, while co-operation may indeed motivate such suspensions, conflicts of interest may constitute the crucial impetus to undercut common understandings and to undermine the 'small print' of the non-contractual elements of contract. And indeed a network of common typifications *per se* cannot guarantee a social order. In eighteenth-century warfare, for example, it was generally accepted that the capture of a capital city constituted victory. Yet the Russians secured victory over Napoleon by the simple expedient of refusing to comply with this traditional 'common understanding' when the latter entered Moscow. The whole texture of Schutz's intersubjective world, the critic argues, is overwhelmingly cast within a co-operative framework in which the chessboard of meaning is never wilfully overturned by the person in the losing position. What is it, then, that secures the ordinary agent's motivated compliance with the prescriptions and conventions of the common-sense world? Parsons provided for this compliance with his analysis of the internalization of norms as needs dispositions. In Schutzian sociology, there appears to be no parallel source of normative constraint. Somehow, the world of mundane typifications must be demonstrated to exert itself not only on the cognitions of actors but also on their actions and interactions if it is to address the Hobbesian dimension of the problem of organization in conduct.

It was Garfinkel's subsequent task to demonstrate both the researchability and the constraining power of a world organized according to Schutzian principles, since only in this way could 'a generalized social system built solely from the analysis of experience structures' become a credible possibility. His achievement was to demonstrate that this could be done. The demonstration was accomplished by catching at the nature of social action in the full flow of its movement and examining the properties of its constituent moving elements.

CHAPTER 4

The Morality of Cognition

It seems that rational social interaction becomes impracticable even among consociates. And yet we receive reasonable answers to reasonable questions, our commands are carried out, we perform in factories and laboratories and offices highly 'rationalized' activities, we play chess together, briefly, we come conveniently to terms with our fellow-men. How is this possible?

Schutz, ·*Collected Papers, Vol. 1*

In the previous chapters, two basic approches to the nature of social action and social organization have been outlined. In Parsons's analysis, social actions are alternatively characterized either (1) as rational actions with their self-subsistent grounds, or (2) as non-rational actions with their mainsprings in institutionalized norms of conduct which are varyingly opaque to their bearers. Within this analysis, social organization — the persistence of stable patterns of activity — is viewed as the product of the internalization of normative patterns as need-dispositions. Through this process, Parsons proposed, social actors come to want to do what the institutionalized normative patterns require them to do. A reconciliation is thus achieved between 'the facts of social structure' and 'the facts of personality' and a 'motivational' solution to the Hobbesian problem of order is achieved.

In the Schutzian analysis, social actions are not distinguished in terms of their rationality. Instead actors are viewed as devising courses of action on the basis of partially formulated 'recipe knowledge'. In the process, the actors find ways of assimilating the conditions and outcomes of their actions to the various socially standardized typifications in terms of which they concertedly attempt to co-ordinate their conduct. Within this analysis, social organization is viewed as a product of the co-ordinated 'accomodative work' (Garfinkel,

1963: 187) through which the actors establish, maintain, reproduce, restore and alter temporally extended courses of action. The Hobbesian problem of order, so central to Parsons's thinking, is not addressed as such by Schutz.

The two perspectives might be summarily contrasted by observing that Parsons treats the organization of action as maintained largely through the operation of externally and internally constraining 'moral' rules, while taking little or no interest in the properties of the actors' common-sense judgements. Schutz, on the contrary, is preoccupied with these latter properties, but takes little interest in the 'moral' force with which common-sense judgements are invested.

It thus fell to Garfinkel to effect an integration of the 'moral' with the 'cognitive'. This he accomplished through a series of ingenious experiments and with brilliant interpretations of their results. His conclusions are intellectually compelling and they permit us to remove the scare quotation marks from the term 'moral'; for they are consistent with the mundane actors' treatment of one another's actions as the chosen products of knowledgeable agents. It is this view of action treated as the product of accountable moral choice which, in turn, Garfinkel places at the centre of his analysis of social organization.

Accordingly, the next two chapters will be occupied with an outline of some of Garfinkel's central observations on the nature of action and its interpretation. In the present chapter, we will examine some of the ways in which Garfinkel researched, and ultimately transformed, the Schutzian framework. In the following chapter, some applications of this analysis to actions and their contexts will be discussed. Anticipating the thrust of both chapters, we will find that his work can be usefully viewed as the product of the consistent pursuit of a single question: how do social actors come to know, and know in common, what they are doing and the circumstances in which they are doing it? Garfinkel is insistent that it is this question, side-stepped by Parsons and renewed by Schutz's researches, which lies at the centre of any attempt to account for the nature of social organization and social order. In the interests of maintaining as much clarity as possible, we begin with a brief résumé of some of Schutz's central proposals about the properties of social action.

First, Schutz indicates that the analyst of action cannot properly avoid the use of 'second order constructs' — an analytic apparatus which deals with the actor's framework of knowledge and renders it as clearly and distinctly as possible. However, second, the analytic apparatus will embody the recognition that pragmatic actors, operating within the natural attitude, rely on this knowledge and will assume its validity until they are compelled to question it. The actors' attitude will not be, and cannot be expected to be, like that of a scientist who, ideally at least, is concerned with questioning the validity of knowledge. Thus the actors are taken to assume that 'as they see things, so they are', that objects remain the same despite changes in their appearances, that events have 'normal patterns' and 'usual causes' of occurrence that can be relied upon.

Next, Schutz proposes that the actors' knowledge will be held in typified form and that, regardless of its extent and detail, it will nonetheless admit of exceptions and contain much that is indeterminate and indistinct. Even the goals and projects which inform the actors' actions may remain only partially clarified or incompletely formulated. These same features may also characterize the actors' grasp of the means available to realize their projects. The conduct of activity, therefore, is likely to be a step-by-step affair in which the actors' view of goals and means will normally undergo progressive clarification and 'firming up' during the actual temporal course of action. Finally, Schutz suggests that actors engaged in co-ordinated actions with others will assume the socially standardized and shared nature of their knowledge and will seek actively, if unconsciously, to sustain it. They will accomplish this by maintaining the 'reciprocity of perspectives' — subject only to the provision that they assume that knowledge arising from their own particular biographical circumstances will be available to others only to a limited extent which is, partially at least, under the autonomous control of each individual.

As we have seen, these considerations generate a cognitive 'problem of order' for Schutzian theory which is prior to the more familiar Hobbesian formulation. This problem is not intuitively available to the ordinary actor in the natural attitude, who is actively, if unconsciously, engaged in 'assuming it away'. However Schutz notes that this active maintenance of a 'world in common' is sustained only in the absence of counter-evidence. In this hypothesized contingency of the reciprocity of perspectives, Garfinkel found the clue to its researchability. As he remarks:

> In accounting for the persistence and continuity of the features of concerted actions, sociologists commonly select some set of stable features of an organization of activities and ask for the variables that contribute to their stability. An alternative procedure would appear to be more economical: to start with a system with stable features and ask what can be done to make for trouble. The operations that one would have to perform in order to produce and sustain anomic features of perceived environments and disorganized interaction should tell us something about how social structures are ordinarily and routinely being maintained. (Garfinkel, 1963: 187)

The substance of his approach was the famous series of 'breaching experiments' (Garfinkel 1952, 1963, 1967).

The simplest of these experiments were conducted with the game of ticktacktoe (Garfinkel, 1963: 201–6) — a game similar to (British) 'noughts and crosses'. Here the experimenters (E) were instructed to ask the subjects (S) to make the first move. After this, the E erased the S's mark, moved it to another cell and made his own mark while avoiding making any indication that what he was doing was unusual. In 253 experimental trials, 95 per cent of subjects reacted to this action in some way and over 75 per cent of subjects objected to it or demanded some kind some kind of explanation for it. Those subjects who simply assumed that some new game was in progress (for example by copying the experimenter's move), or who assumed that the experimenter was playing a practical joke, or trying out a new method of play, and who therefore abandoned 'ticktacktoe' as an interpretative framework for understanding these events showed little disturbance. By contrast, those who continued to assume that a game of ticktacktoe was still in progress and tried to make sense of the anomalous events in terms of this assumption showed most disturbance. These findings held firm independently of the S's age, the degree of acquaintance between S and E, and the fact that Ss and Es were of the same or different sex.

The 'ticktacktoe' experiment yielded two significant conclusions (ibid. 206). First, behaviours which were at variance with the basic rules of the game 'immediately motivated attempts to normalize the discrepancy, i.e. to treat the observed behaviour as an instance of a legally possible event'. Second, senselessness and disturbance was increased if the subject attempted to normalize the discrepancy while retaining an unaltered view of the 'rules of the game'.

Despite these interesting conclusions, Garfinkel was wary of attempting to extrapolate these results to 'real life' situations, and for a number of reasons (ibid. 206–9). Games, he suggested, have a peculiar time structure such that, throughout a game's events, the participants know what it will take for the game to be complete. Again, success or failure is accomplished *within* the events of a game and is not subject to later developments (or re-evaluations) *outside* the parameters of the game itself. Games are fully 'public' in that their events are defined in terms of consensually understood 'basic rules'. Moreover, they are defined 'over against' everyday life, such that to 'leave' or 'finish' the game is to 'return to' the world of everyday life. Perhaps most importantly, the basic rules of a game, e.g. chess, are independent of the 'state of the game' or the strategies operated by the players. They are not altered by, or over, the actual course of play. There is practically perfect correspondence between the basic rules as normative descriptions of game conduct and actually occurring game conduct. (And, although the 'basic rules' do not cover every aspect of the player's comportment — think here of the famous chess game in the film *The Thomas Crowne Affair* or the notorious Fischer–Spassky championship — they do define. game constitutive events.) Finally, the basic rules define rational, realistic and understandable game activities.

It is this role of the basic rules in the constitution of game relevant events which made the 'ticktacktoe' breaches comparatively easy to engineer. But equally, since this role — together with the other characteristics of games — is not replicated in the world of daily life, further experiments which were more difficult to devise (ibid. 217–19) would have to be developed.

In the best known of the latter (reported in Garfinkel, 1963: 220–35 and Garfinkel, 1967b: 40–44), students were instructed to 'engage an acquaintance or friend in an ordinary conversation and, without indicating that what the experimenter was saying was in any way out of the ordinary, to insist that the person clarify the sense of his commonplace remarks' (Garfinkel, 1963:221). Some of the reported results are reproduced below (Garfinkel, 1963: 221–2):

Case 1: The subject was telling the experimenter, a member of the subject's car pool, about having had a flat tire while going to work the previous day.
> S: I had a flat tire.
> E: What do you mean, you had a flat tire?
> She appeared momentarily stunned. Then she answered in a hostile way: 'What do you mean? What do you mean? A flat tire is a flat tire. That is what I meant. Nothing special. What a crazy question!'

Case 3: On Friday night my husband and I were watching television. My husband remarked that he was tired. I asked, 'How are you tired? Physically, mentally, or just ¡bored?'
> S: I don't know, I guess physically, mainly.
> E: You mean that your muscles ache, or your bones?
> S: I guess so. Don't be so technical.
> (After more watching)
> S: All these old movies have the same kind of old iron bedstead in them.
> E: What do you mean? Do you mean all old movies, or some of them, or just the ones you have seen?
> S: What's the matter with you? You know what I mean.
> E: I wish you would be more specific.
> S: You know what I mean! Drop dead!

Case 6: The victim waved his hand cheerily.
> S: How are you?
> E: How am I in regard to what? My health, my finance, my school work, my peace of mind, my . . .
> S: (Red in the face and suddenly out of control.) Look! I was just trying to be polite. Frankly, I don't give a damn how you are.

In these cases, Garfinkel proposes, the student experimenters had successfully breached one of the idealizations making up Schutz's 'general thesis of reciprocal perspectives', namely the idealization of the congruency of relevances. According to this idealization, it will be recalled, the actors assume that differences arising from their unique biographical circumstances are irrelevant for the purposes at hand of each and that they have 'selected and interpreted the actually or potentially common objects and their features in an identical manner or at least an "empirically identical" manner, i.e. one sufficient for all practical purposes' (Schutz, 1962a: 12). In each of the above cases, the subjects had expected that the experimenters would, by drawing upon background knowledge of 'what everybody knows', supply a sense to their remarks that was 'empirically identical' with the sense intended by the Ss. The S thus assumed, in each case, that both parties knew 'what he is talking about without any requirement of a check-out' (Garfinkel, 1963: 220). In each case, the S took for granted that the E would supply whatever unstated understandings would be required in order to make recognizable sense of his talk. This requirement, as we shall see, pervades all interaction. As Garfinkel extensively demonstrated in his 'conversation clarification experiment' (Garfinkel, 1967b: 38–41), in any two-party conversation, 'much that is being talked about is not mentioned, although each expects that the adequate sense of the matter being talked about is settled' (Garfinkel, 1963: 221).

It is noticeable that the Es' breaches of this requirement resulted in interactional breakdowns which were extraordinarily rapid and complete and, as such, surprising in their extent even to Garfinkel himself (ibid. 198). Moreover it is noticeable that, in most cases, the Es' breaches were very rapidly and powerfully sanctioned. Thus in cases 1 and 6 above, the Ss assumed postures of 'righteous hostility' after only a single breaching move from the E and, in the second part of case 3, after two such moves. In all the other cases reported, the Ss made strenuous efforts to restore the situation of reciprocity and ended up either proposing or demanding explanations for the E's conduct. In each case, the S treated the intelligible character of his own talk as something to which he was morally entitled and, correspondingly, treated the breaching move as illegitimate, deserving of sanction and requiring explanation. The experiment thus indicated that maintaining the 'reciprocity of perspectives' (as one of the presuppositions of the attitude of daily life) is not merely a cognitive task, but one which each actor 'trusts' that the other will accomplish as a matter of moral necessity. As Garfinkel subsequently put it, summarizing the observations of his 1963 paper, 'the term "trust" is used there to refer to a person's compliance with the expectancies of the attitude of daily life as a morality' (1967b: 50). With just this evidence behind us, such compliance already appears to be the object of spectacular moral constraints.

In only one instance reported by Garfinkel were the above consequences of breaching incompletely realized. This instance was reported as case 8 in Garfinkel (1963: 222–3) (but not reprinted in Garfinkel 1967b). In it, the subject of the experiment was successful in transforming the sense of the 'breaching moves' by interpreting them as part of a different order of possibilities – a game or a childish joke. Moreover the subject in this case was successful in eliciting a sequence of activities from the E which were consistent with, and confirmatory of, his election of this new order of possibilities (see the protocol of case 8). The potentially anomic features of the interaction with the associated elements of moral outrage, which began to surface in the early parts of the interaction, were thereby attenuated and ultimately cut short. The evidence of case 8 confirmed the earlier findings from the 'ticktacktoe' experiment, namely that the S's election of an alternative framework for interpreting 'discrepant events' moderated their experience of disturbance, the associated symptoms of disruption and subsequent attempts at moral sanction.

In both of the experiments reported so far, there is a kind of 'breaching' going on. But although in the first cases the basic rules constitutive of 'ticktacktoe' were not complied with, while, in the second set, the assumption of the reciprocity of perspectives was breached, what both have in common is that the 'perceived normality' of events was impugned. In both cases, what is breached is a set of 'more fundamental' presuppositions in terms of which behavioural instances are attended by actors as instances of intended actions that a group member assumes 'anyone can see'. (Garfinkel, 1963: 198)

Given that those actors who could 'find a sense' for the breaching moves showed least anxiety, indignation or demands for explanation, then the possibility arises, as Garfinkel puts the point, that

> with respect to the problematic relationship between the normative regulation of action and the stability of concerted action, the critical phenomenon is not the 'intensity of affect' with which the 'rule' is 'invested', or the respected or sacred or moral status of the rule, but the perceived normality of environmental events as this normality is a function of the presuppositions that define the possible events.

And it can be conjectured that

> *all* actions as perceived events may have a constitutive structure, and that perhaps it is the threat to the normative order of events as such that is the critical variable in invoking indignation and not the breach of the 'sacredness' of the rules. (ibid.)

With these experiments, the basic relationship between normative rules and socially organized events appears to be a strongly cognitive one in which 'rules' (concertedly applied) are *constitutive* of 'what the events are', or of 'what is going on here'. By comparison, the more conventional *regulative* sense of rule in which rules are said to mark out 'proper' or 'desirable' conduct appears a more secondary matter. By the same token, the 'force' of the rules appears not to derive from a 'moral consensus' on the 'sacredness' of the rules, but rather from the fact that, if conduct cannot be interpreted in accordance with the rules, the social organization of a set of 'real circumstances' simply disintegrates.

These experiments, taking their cue from Schutzian assumptions, imply an order of normative organization at the level of action and interaction which contrasts with the Parsonian 'top-down' version of normative constraint in which consensually defined values determine the character of a stable system of action 'from above'. This order of organization is implemented 'from the bottom up' and, within it,

> structural phenomena . . . are emergent products of a vast amount of communicative, perceptual, judgemental and other 'accomodative' work whereby persons, in concert, and encountering 'from within the society' the environments that the society confronts them with, establish, maintain, restore and alter the social structures that are the assembled products of the temporally extended courses of action directed to these environments as persons 'know' them (Garfinkel, 1963: 187–8)

Yet, even though these demonstrations show that interactants hold themselves and one another morally accountable for the 'accomodative work' through which they make sense of their circumstances, they do not show what the tasks of 'making sense' consist of or what their limits are, and it is to Garfinkel's explorations of these latter topics that we now turn.

THE CONSTITUENT TASKS OF MAKING SENSE

One of the most commonly cited terms in Garfinkel's conceptual armoury is 'the documentary method of interpretation'. Garfinkel derived the term from Mannheim who proposed that the documentary method involves the search for 'an identical homologous pattern underlying a vast variety of totally different realizations of meaning' (Mannheim, cited in Garfinkel, 1967c: 78). As Garfinkel elaborated it, 'the method consists of treating an actual appearance as "the document of", as "pointing to", as "standing on behalf of" a presupposed underlying pattern' (ibid.).

Although Garfinkel took the term itself from Mannheim, the basic idea had previously received very considerable theoretical explication at the hands of phenomenologists from Husserl onwards. The phenomenologists had, indeed, developed an analysis of perceptual and cognitive activity which treated all acts of consciousness as involving a 'documentary' process. For example, the brief discussion of the phenomenological treatment of the perception of a chair in the previous chapter — in which it was indicated that as we walk towards 'a chair', successive presented appearances are referred to the intended object 'this chair' — was in effect a reference to the workings of the 'documentary method'. Although Garfinkel's discussion of the latter has sometimes been interpreted as a recommendation of it as a special sociological technique, it is clear that this interpretation is incorrect. As the above example implies and as we shall subsequently see, Garfinkel endorses the phenomenological treatment of acts of cognition and proposes the documentary method as an invariant and unavoidable feature of all acts of mundane perception and cognition.

Our chair example forms a convenient starting point for discussion of the documentary method because it illustrates two important aspects of its use. The first aspect is easily disclosed by stressing that it is *successive* presentations of 'the chair' which are referred to the intended object 'this chair'. Any intended object, the phenomenologist argues, is constituted as a unity from a succession of appearances which wax and wane in the course of 'inner time' or '*durée*'. Time is thus a constitutive feature of objects. Although the point is most obvious when we are considering a succession of appearances of an object as we move in relation to it, it is just as valid for the perception of an object from a static position. In fact, the similarity of successive presented appearances of an object is one of the means by which we can gauge whether our position is static or not. Thus the existence of an object for an observer is, as it were, permeated with temporal specifications. Time is an integral feature of the organization of a mundane 'world' of objects. The role of time as an integral feature of the constitution of objects and events will become particularly significant in the treatment of action and Garfinkel is generally critical of Parsons's failure to acknowledge its significance in the interpretation of action.

The second aspect of the documentary method in use which must be stressed is that its use is pervasive. To revert to our chair once again, it will be obvious that there is no absolute or privileged 'position-in-general' from which the chair can be viewed or in terms of which perspectival appearances can be abandoned in favour of immediate access to the 'chair itself'. The chair exists as a self-same object *only* insofar as successive perspectival appearances are referred to the intended object 'this chair'. There is, as Garfinkel sometimes puts it, no 'time out' or escape from the documentary process into an all-encompassing viewpoint. Or to put it another way, 'time out' from the documentary process merely results in 'noise' — a state of confusion in which nothing is cognized.

Just as the above points hold for the perception of a physical object such as a chair, so too they hold for social objects. Social objects such as 'a cheerful person' or 'a woman walking to the shops' are the products of complicated judgements in which an 'underlying pattern' is built up from a temporally qualified succession of appearances. It is important to note that the process may operate completely unconsciously as when, after the fashion of Weber's 'observational understanding', we simply 'see' a man running for a train or, alternatively, aspects of the process may be brought to consciousness, for example, when we struggle to 'make out' what somebody is doing or 'form hypotheses' about it.

The documentary process does not, however, end with the assimilation of a set of appearances to an underlying pattern. There is a further, vitally important, dimension of its operation to which Garfinkel alludes when he adds:

> Not only is the underlying pattern derived from its individual documentary evidences, but the individual documentary evidences, in their turn, are interpreted on the basis of 'what is known' about the underlying pattern. Each is used to elaborate the other. (Garfinkel, 1967c: 78)

This second aspect of the documentary method at work, in which the individual evidences 'are interpreted on the basis of "what is known" about the underlying pattern', is comparatively familiar to students of perception. It can be illustrated by taking the well-known figure below and characterizing it with the term 'Duck'.

Under these circumstances, where 'what is known' about the underlying pattern is that figure 2 represents a duck, the protuberances on the left of the figure are interpreted as a beak and the small indentation on the right of the figure is

Figure 2 (Source: Wittgenstein, 1958: 194)

treated as irrelevant. Here the force of Husserl's 'hidden achievements of consciousness' may be such that some time will elapse before a naïve subject can come to see an alternative 'underlying pattern' for the figure. Note, however, that once the figure is viewed as a 'rabbit', not only does the feature previously identified as a 'beak' become the 'ears' but also the small indentation, previously ignored as irrelevant to the interpretation of the figure, becomes relevant as the 'rabbit's' mouth.

Richard Gregory has further demonstrated, with illustrations such as figure 3 below, that the power of 'what is known' about an underlying pattern may be so great as to override all subsequent experience or intellectual knowledge of the object.

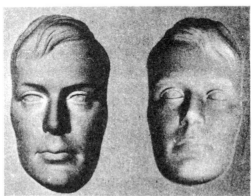

Figure 3 (Source: Professor Richard Gregory)

Naïvely examining Figure 3, we see a pair of faces. But the right-hand face is a hollow mask of the left-hand face. The nose of the right-hand face, which appears to stick outwards, in fact points inwards. Here 'what is known' about faces, i.e. that their features 'stick out' towards us, overrides texture cues (and stereoscopic ones when the mask is seen directly). And Gregory further notes that:

> The actual mask, viewed with both eyes and in a good light, looks, incorrectly, like a normal face, until the observer is close to it when suddenly it looks, correctly, hollow. Drawing back, the 'face' perception will always return. Neither experience nor intellectual knowledge of the hollow mask prevent this dramatically false perception. (Gregory, 1974a: 205)

It may be objected that, after all, these are visual illusions which cannot be brought under conscious, ratiocinative control and that, in any case, they have little connection with the interpretation of action. Let us then try to catch an outline of the process as it manifests itself in the interpretation of action.

Atkinson (1971) has described the following circumstances which were brought before a British coroner's court. The case involved circumstances in which 'a widow aged 83 was found gassed in the kitchen of her cottage, where she had lived alone since the death of her husband. Rugs and towels had been stuffed under the doors and around the window casements' (Atkinson, 1971: 181). At this stage, the reader is likely to have derived a possible 'underlying pattern' from the individual documentary evidences. This pattern will very probably involve the conclusion that the old lady committed suicide. As this pattern emerges, so it 'firms up' the initial impression of the evidence. Loneliness and loss become the underlying psychological dynamic attributed to the act and, rehearsing the widow's last acts, we imagine her putting the rugs and towels in position, switching on the gas taps and sitting in her chair waiting for the end to come. At this stage, we have achieved a 'fit' between the various circumstances and the act — particulars and pattern have elaborated one another to the point of certainty.

Yet, just as we saw earlier with Figure 2 that one interpretation of the figure occluded another alternative interpretation, so a similar process may be going on here: 'At the inquest, the four people who knew her testified that she had always seemed to be a very happy and cheerful person' (ibid.). This evidence introduces a disturbance into our picture. Perhaps the old lady was not so much lonely and depressed as deaf and absent-minded. With this consideration, both the documentary evidences and the underlying pattern seem to shift. It is winter. The rugs and towels were designed to keep the heat in and the draughts out. Our rehearsal of the widow's last hours now depicts her as turning on the gas stove for some purpose and forgetting to light it, or perhaps the gas flame blowing out in a draught. We envisage the old lady sitting down unaware of the gas hissing into the atmosphere and nodding off in the gas-filled room. Every individual documentary appearance is accounted for, but they now combine to form a quite different underlying pattern. Atkinson reports that the coroner in this case recorded an 'open' verdict on the grounds 'that there was no evidence to show how the gas taps had been turned on' (ibid.).

It can be noted here that while the original conclusion 'she committed suicide' was being formed, there was no conscious entertaining of alternative hypotheses. Rather there was a rather rapid and 'intuitive' judgement. In the formation of the original conclusion, 'evidences' and 'underlying pattern' came into alignment in a way which, quite unconsciously, excluded alternative interpretations of the evidences. The evidences simply came together to produce unambiguous and obvious fact. Just as, in viewing Figure 2 as a duck, the indentation on the right of the figure is ignored as irrelevant, so too, in viewing the old lady as a 'suicide', her cheerfulness and the wintry circumstances of her death are discounted. If attention is focused on the previously discounted elements, then the 'underlying pattern' begins to undergo a shift. In both cases too, the development of an alternative pattern involved a total transformation of 'the evidences'. Despite the fact that, in both cases, 'the physical facts' remained the same, their interpretative weighting and significance were utterly transformed. Moreover finally, just as, in the case of Figure 2, the two versions of the figure cannot be entertained simultaneously, so with the widow's death the two versions of 'what the evidences are' or 'amount to' constitute two alternative entities which cannot be juxtaposed except by a 'gestalt switch'.

In his studies of the documentary method at work, Garfinkel developed a demonstration which was designed to exaggerate the process and, as he put it, 'catch the work of "fact production" in flight' (Garfinkel, 1967c: 79). The demonstration consisted of a 'student counselling experiment' in which undergraduates were invited to participate in research exploring 'alternative means to psychotherapy "as a way of giving persons advice about their personal problems" (sic)' (ibid.). In each case, the subject was asked to describe the background of his problem and to ask the 'counsellor' at least ten questions about it. Each question was to be designed so as to permit a 'yes' or 'no' answer. The subject and experimenter-counsellor were situated in adjoining rooms and connected by intercom. The subject was required to tape-record his reflections on each answer after disconnecting the intercom 'so that the counsellor will not hear your remarks'. Unknown to the subject, the experimenter-counsellor predetermined his sequence of 'yes' and 'no' answers with a table of random numbers. At the completion of the questions and answers, the subject was asked to summarize his impressions of the exchange as a whole. Part of one of these exchanges (Case 1) is reproduced below. Further examples can be found in Garfinkel (1967c: 80–88] and in McHugh (1968).

Case 1

Subject: Okay, this is the situation that I am presented with. I happen to be of the Jewish faith and I have been dating a Gentile girl now for about two months. My dad is not directly opposed to the situation, but I feel at the same time that he is not exactly pleased with it. Mother feels that as long as Dad is not directly opposed to this situation that I should go ahead and continue dating until he makes some direct statement to the contrary. My reason for feeling why he is not too pleased with this is that he has never said don't date her, but at the same time he will come up with digs and sayings that make me feel very ill at ease about dating the girl. My question is, do you feel under the present circumstances that I should continue or stop dating this girl? Let me put that in a positive way. Do you feel that I should continue dating this girl?

Experimenter: My answer is no.

Subject: No. Well, that is kind of interesting. I kinda feel that there is really no great animosity between Dad and I but, well, perhaps he feels that greater dislike will grow out of this. I suppose or maybe it is easier for an outsider to see certain things that I am blind to at this moment. I would like to ask my second question now.

Experimenter: Okay.

Subject: Do you feel that I should have a further discussion with Dad about this situation or not? Should I have further discussion with Dad over this subject about dating the Gentile girl?

Experimenter: My answer is yes.

Subject: Well I feel that is reasonable but I really don't know what to say to him. I mean he seems to be not really too understanding. In other words he seems to be afraid really to discuss the situation. I mean at least it appears that way to me so far. But I guess if it is worthwhile to me, if I really want to continue to date her I will go on and have this discussion with Dad. I really don't know what to say because I mean I am dating her. I am not in love with her or anything but I really never know what is going to come out. I guess we should have a discussion based on what the future possibilities might be and how he would feel about that. He may not be too strongly opposed now because we are only dating, but perhaps he sees future complications that he would really like to get off his chest at the moment. I am ready for my third question now. If after having my conversation with Dad and he says to continue dating her, but at the same time he gives me the impression that he is really not, he really does not want me to date her, but he is only doing it because he wants to be a good Dad, should under these conditions, should I still date the girl?

Experimenter: My answer is yes.

Subject: Well I am actually surprised at the answer. I
expected a no answer on that. Perhaps this is because
you are not quite aware of my dad and/his reactions
and he seems to be the type of person that is sensitive
and therefore he is very careful in the way that he
will handle things. (Garfinkel, 1967c: 80–81)

Reflecting on the exchanges from which the above is
excerpted, Garfinkel notes (1967c: 89–94) that the subjects
perceived the experimenter's 'answers' to have been motivated
by their questions and were able to see 'what the adviser had
in mind' in producing his answers. The answers were treated
as 'advice' whose substance was found by interpreting what
the adviser said against the background established by the
question or series of questions. Garfinkel further found that
the subjects' conceptions of 'the underlying problem' which
was being dealt with were extended, elaborated and reshaped
responsively to the 'answers': 'The sense of the problem was
progressively accomodated to each present answer, while the
answer motivated fresh aspects of the underlying problem'
(ibid.). Moreover this elaboration and accomodation of the
problem was done 'so as to maintain the "course of advice" '.
In this process, incomplete or incongruous or unsatisfactory
answers were handled by waiting to see whether they would
be clarified by subsequent answers, by imputing special
reasons or intents to the 'adviser', by deciding that the
'adviser' had 'learned more' about the problem, or changed
his mind or was unfamiliar with its intricacies. Through these
and other means, Garfinkel concludes, the subjects so
managed their interpretations as to view the 'advice' they had
been given as coherent, as compatible with 'given conditions'
as represented by the normatively valued social structures
perceived by the subject, and as the trustworthy product of
properly motivated advisers. This management, moreover,
was not principled in the sense of rule-governed or subject to
well-defined decision procedures. Rather the management was
responsive to whatever exigencies emerged and was accomplished so as to deal with each exigency by whatever means
were available to maintain whatever overall sense could be
be salvaged from the interchange-in-progress.

The findings from the 'student counselling experiment' indicate that the subjects' pursuit of a consistent underlying pattern in the 'advice' they were receiving involved a scarcely conscious recourse to a vast and unpredictable range of considerations which, at best, had the status of partially formulated, recipe-like knowledge. These considerations were consulted in an apparently haphazard manner, being taken up, discounted and dropped 'as the situation demanded'. As in a whirlpool, the documentary 'vortex' retained a degree of focus and clarity while the materials contributing to its maintenance rotated around it with varying degrees of ellipse.

These features might reasonably be regarded as artefacts of the highly unusual experimental situation in which the subjects were placed, which, it will be recalled, was a deliberately contrived one. Although plausible, this interpretation of the results is incorrect, for these same features were demonstrated in a complementary study directed at an apparently much simpler task — the clarification of understandings implicit in ordinary conversation.

In this study, students were asked to report the substance of an actual mundane conversation and then to describe what the conversationalists understood they were talking about. Garfinkel reproduces the following conversation and its explication as an exhibit from the study.

Husband:	Dana succeeded in putting a penny in a parking meter today without being picked up.	This afternoon as I was bringing Dana, our four-year-old son, home from the nursery school, he succeeded in reaching high enough to put a penny in a parking meter when we parked in a meter parking zone, whereas before he has always had to be picked up to reach that high.
Wife:	Did you take him to the record store?	Since he put a penny in a meter that means you stopped while he was with you. I know that that you stopped at the record store either on the way to get him or on the way back. Was it

on the way back. Was it on the way back, so that he was with you or did you stop there on the way to get him and somewhere else on the way back?

Husband: No, to the shoe repair shop.

No, I stopped at the record store on the way to get him and stopped at the shoe repair shop on the way home when he was with me.

Wife: What for?

I know of one reason why you might have stopped at the shoe repair shop. Why did you in fact?

Husband: I got some new shoe laces for my shoes.

As you will remember I broke a shoe lace on one of my brown oxfords the other day so I stopped to get some new laces.

Wife: Your loafers need new heels badly.

Something else you could have gotten that I was thinking of. You could have taken in your black loafers which need heels badly. You'd better get them taken care of pretty soon.

(Garfinkel, 1967b: 38–9)

The exercise revealed that the participants in 'ordinary conversation' engage in the same practices that the subjects in the 'counselling experiment' engaged in. Characteristically, utterances were not treated 'literally' or at 'face value' but were understood by reference to unspoken assumptions and presuppositions that each party attributed to the other. Each utterance was understood by being treated as a member of a developing sequence and, as such, as having 'retrospective' and 'prospective' significances. Each party permitted some present sense of an utterance to be altered by what was subsequently said with the result that 'many expressions had the property of being progressively realized and realizable through the further course of the conversation' (ibid. 41). For example, the sense 'finally' attributed to the wife's utterance 'What for?' may not have been available to the husband until after she subsequently remarked 'Your loafers need new heels badly'. Thus at any given point both the 'sense' of the utterances and 'what was talked about' with the utterances remained 'specifically vague' and open-ended with respect to 'internal relationships, relationships to other events and relationships to retrospective and prospective possibilities' (ibid.). Garfinkel further reports (1967a: 26–30) that the students were unable to arrive at a complete and accurate 'literal' description of 'what was understood' in the talk. No matter how elaborately the students filled in the contents of the right-hand column, they could always be persuaded that its contents were incomplete and required further elaboration to be strictly accurate.

With this much to hand, we can now begin to see some of the force of the demonstration of moral outrage which we encountered at the beginning of this chapter. For, given the local 'occasionality' of the meanings of utterances, their referential vaguenesses, their possibilities of reinterpretation over time, and their lack of scientific specificity, the 'common understandings' achieved by the parties to conversations can only be achieved by the parties doing whatever is necessary at the time to 'fill-in' a background of 'seen but unnoticed' interpretation for whatever is said as it is said. An announced failure to accomplish this task, as in 'What do you mean a flat tire?'|threatens the very possibility of mutual understanding and, with it, the existence of a shared world.

Taken together, the studies described above demonstrate a number of highly significant and previously unknown aspects of the maintenance of social order. First, the studies demonstrate the staggering range of assumptions and contextual features which may be mobilized *ad hoc* to sustain a particular 'documentary version' of a sequence of events. The 'student counselling experiment', in particular, demonstrated the considerable lengths to which participants would go, with only a minimum of apparent discomfort, to sustain the interchange as a 'course of advice' and hence to sustain not only a reciprocity of perspectives but a specific formulation of it established at the outset as involving 'adviser' and 'advice recipient'.

Second, the 'unifying thread', in terms of which some set of *ad hoc* contextual considerations were made relevant to one another, was not some set of rule-governed procedures in terms of which the 'underlying pattern' was assimilated from a set of 'appearances'. On the contrary, the 'underlying pattern' was assumed from the outset to be the basis on which the appearances should be interpreted. At every possible point, the participants seemed to be willing to give the 'underlying pattern' the benefit of the doubt. They assumed it was operative despite appearances which could be held to argue to the contrary and, in all three studies to a greater or lesser degree, they waited for the pattern to reassert itself in new evidences which would enable them to discount any prior discrepancies. In short, in accordance with Schutz's characterization of the 'natural attitude', the participants disattended or suspended any emerging doubts about possible discrepancies between 'appearance' and 'reality' for as long as possible.

Third, the participants treated their use of interpretative resources for the contextual 'filling in' of 'what anyone can see' and their suspension of doubt concerning 'what the appearances amounted to' as a deeply moral matter. Thus the subjects of the 'breaching experiments' assumed an entitlement to explanations from the experimenter concerning the latter's actions and, further, when such explanations were not forthcoming the subjects assumed positions of 'righteous hostility'. Garfinkel summarizes this morally sanctionable demand for the various forms of interpretative co-operation by suggesting that they constitute the conditions under which persons

> are themselves entitled and entitle others to claim that they know what they are talking about and that what they say is understandable and ought to be understood. In short, their seen but unnoticed presence is used to entitle persons to conduct their common conversational affairs without interference. (Garfinkel, 1967b: 41–2)

We thus arrive at the following conclusion. Given the enormous array of possible contextualizations for a statement and hence of possible interpretations for it, and given also that the producers of the statements can never literally say what they mean, then the producers of statements can only make themselves understandable by assuming that the recipients are accomplishing the relevant contextual determinations for what is being said. Moreover the producers must assume that the recipients are accomplishing this task by 'trusting' and relying on the proposed documentary pattern over the course of its emergence. If a socially organized and intersubjective world stands or falls with the maintenance of this interpretative trust, then it is not surprising to find that it is attended to as a deeply moral matter. We should, indeed, be surprised if it were not.

THE MORAL ENFORCEMENT OF 'TRUST'

In concluding this initial discussion of Garfinkel's experiments, it will prove useful to reconsider the question of quite *why* breaches of interpretive 'trust' were sanctioned so powerfully. Just what is it that secures the ordinary actor's motivated compliance with the set of procedures which, together, constitute 'interpretative trust' and provide for an environment of actions and events which 'anyone can see'?

A host of explanatory possibilities immediately suggest themselves. The actor can be viewed as having 'internalized' a commitment to the use of these procedures as a 'need disposition'. Alternatively, the actor could be viewed as concluding that, if the other cannot understand 'plain English', the actor's projects (depending, as they do, upon the co-operation of the other) will be confounded. Hence we are witnessing a 'frustration reaction' pure and simple. Again, the actor could be understood as intuiting the 'inherent fragility' of the symbolically constituted environments of 'real circumstances' which is stressed by, *inter alios*, Berger and Luckmann (1967). Accordingly, the actor's reaction can be treated as that of a 'lay functionalist' who is committed to the maintenance of the existing symbolic order. Or we could be witnessing, in the actor's violent responses ('You know what I mean! Drop dead!'), a form of 'ontological insecurity' (Laing, 1965) which is ultimately based upon the actor's 'psychologically primitive' disposition to adopt the expectancies of the attitude of everyday life.

While each of these interpretations has its attractions, none of them is entirely satisfactory. Indeed each requires us to assume considerably more about the actor's conscious (or semi-conscious) desires or psychological dispositions than we need to. Fortunately, a more economical and extremely productive alternative is directly available from the results of Garfinkel's experimental procedures.

To gain access to this alternative, we need to recall a significant aspect of Garfinkel's experiments which is not often remarked upon. Garfinkel expressly designed some of his experiments (reported in Garfinkel, 1952; 1963; 1967) as a way of discovering the conditions required 'to produce and sustain anomic features of perceived environments and disorganized interactions' (Garfinkel, 1963: 187). It will be apparent from the previous discussion that Garfinkel's use of the term 'anomic' here is designed to catch at more than its conventional sense of 'normatively unregulated'. For norms, as we have seen, do not merely regulate actions in 'pre-existing' circumstances, they are rather constitutive of the 'sense' of the circumstances, of 'what the circumstances are' in the first place. Garfinkel's early experiments were thus aimed at creating situations which were literally unintelligible or, as he puts it, 'specifically senseless'. Now it is striking that, despite the ingenuity of many of the experimental procedures, this goal was rarely achieved. Participants who might have been expected to be unable to comprehend the situations into which they were plunged and who, consequently, should have been reduced to complete confusion and inactivity were, in fact, only rarely at a complete loss. Their actions, in general, failed to exhibit fully complete levels of anomia and disorganization.

If we return to the conversations described earlier in this chapter (cases 1, 3 and 6, 80–2 above) in which breaches of the reciprocity of perspectives occurred, it will be apparent that although the subjects of the experiments may not have fully understood what was going on, their conduct does not reveal that they found the interchanges senseless. Rather it indicates that they analysed the experimenters' behaviours as involving 'active', i.e. 'chosen' or 'motivated', *departures* from the normal which, reasonably enough, they viewed as illegitimate and offensive. Rather than their belief that 'anyone could see what they meant' being shaken by the experimenters' behaviour, the subjects held fast to this belief. And, holding to this belief, the subjects inferred instead that the experimenters were 'up to something'. Further, their expressions of 'righteous hostility' indicate that, while they could not fathom quite what the experimenter was up to, they saw it as uncooperative and somehow directed 'at them'. (Other interpretative possibilities, including the possibility that the experimenter had temporarily taken leave of his senses, also seem to have been entertained. Nonetheless, the conclusion that the experimenters' behaviours were intelligibly motivated seems to have been the most viable across a range of interactional exigencies and, hence, the predominant one.)

These considerations yield two significant conclusions. Firstly, as we have seen, Garfinkel adopts a 'procedural' approach to intersubjective meaning. Within this approach, the actors are conceived as agreeing about their circumstances by virtue of the fact that they share, rely on sharing, and trust one another to implement common methods or procedures in terms of which circumstances and their constituent actions are 'brought to book'. Just as there is no 'external guarantee' which anchors the objective status of the actors' circumstances, so too there is no 'external guarantee' which ensures the shared implementation of the procedures through which the factual character of events is determined. So, to repeat our earlier question: by what means is the implementation of the procedural bases of shared understandings insisted upon?

The solution to this question is to note that, while the procedures for 'making sense' are normally relied upon in a 'seen but unnoticed' fashion, deviations from these procedures were instantly interpreted as 'motivated' departures on the part of the experimenters who were treated as acting from 'special', if presently undisclosed, motives. The experimenters, it will be recalled, were immediately treated as having departed from the use of shared procedures for producing and recognizing 'sensible plain talk'. And, in turn, that visibility gave rise to 'secondary interpretations' by the subjects which, though non-specific, involved the subjects' belief that the experimenters were behaving in a fashion which was 'somehow hostile'. In short, the experimenters were sanctioned, as agents, for conduct which the subjects believed was under the experimenters' voluntary control and was produced for some purpose. We can thus conclude that the subjects' choices in interpreting the experimenters' conduct were not simply between 'normal, sensible' behavior and 'senseless' behaviour. Rather, it seems to have been between 'normal' behaviour and behaviour 'for which a sense has yet to be found and when it is it won't be pleasant'. Deviations from a norm are always analysable as *departures* from it and may be responded to as such.

Earlier in this chapter, it was noted that there is no 'time out' from the documentary method of interpretation. We can now add the rider that, in the interpretation of actions, there is no 'time out' either from the normative accountability of the actions, analysed as 'chosen', which are visible through the application of the method. At the end of the previous chapter, the issue was raised as to whether the maintenance of intersubjective understanding might not depend on the maintenance of co-operation among the interacting parties; whether, in short, the 'chessboard of meaning' might not be wilfully disrupted and overturned under conditions of conflict. This disruption was the very task attempted in Garfinkel's early experiments. The finding is that departures from the norm are visible, through the availability of the norm which should have been followed, as meaningful and 'wilful'. In just this sense, the task could not be accomplished. The 'chessboard of meaning' is revealed to be self-righting. The normative accountability of action is thus a seamless web, an endless metric in terms of which conduct is unavoidably intelligible, describable and assessable.

A second conclusion arises from considering in finer detail some aspects of the motivations of the subjects of the experiments in acting as they did. It is hardly necessary to reject the supposition that, for example, the subjects reacted with hostility to the 'breaching experiments' out of a 'lay functionalist' concern to defend the integrity of a cognitive order which they perceived as threatened. They reacted rather to an unaccountable breach of 'trust' which they perceived as somehow directed 'at themselves'. This characteristic reaction often persisted even after the experimental nature of the encounter had been revealed. Thus Garfinkel reports that, at the end of one of the experiments conducted by student experimenters,

> subjects were only partially accepting of the experimenter's explanation that it has been done 'as an experiment for a course in sociology'. They often complained, 'All right, it was an experiment, but why did you have to choose *me*?' Characteristically, subject and experimenter wanted some further resolution than the explanation furnished but were uncertain about what it could or should consist of. (Garfinkel, 1967b: 72–3)

Such outcomes indicate that breaches of perceivedly normal conduct may be characteristically treated by recipient parties as particularized to them. In this context, the demand for a restoration of normal conduct is not produced as an abstract demand for proper behaviour in general, but as a demand for proper behaviour from this particular individual with respect to this particular recipient. The maintenance of the expectancies of the attitude of daily life (and, as we shall see, any normative framework), instanciated as 'perceivedly normal' courses of conduct, is thus achieved within, and motivated by and with respect to, particular circumstances and particular individuals. These individuals accountably treat their own and one another's actions as the products of 'motivated choices' and, as such, designed with respect to the specifics of settings and their constituent participants.

CONCLUSION

In the present chapter, we have examined Garfinkel's discovery that the constitutive expectancies of the attitude of everyday life are treated by mundane actors as profoundly normative, and morally sanctionable, matters. Associated with this discovery is Garfinkel's view that 'norms' of all kinds are most productively regarded as constitutive features of 'perceivedly normal' environments. These proposals give us an elegant analysis of the basic features of common-sense knowledge and an economical treatment of the 'moral force' with which common-sense knowledge 'that anyone knows' is invested. Together, they represent core propositions in the framework both of Garfinkel's analyses and of those influenced by him.

As yet, however, the analysis remains formidably abstract. The attitude of daily life is hardly the most concrete of 'normative systems'. Moreover, the full implications of these propositions have scarcely been developed in the present chapter. Accordingly, we next attempt the task of teasing out some of the implications of this analysis for the treatment of concrete actions and their circumstances. To the extent that Garfinkel has a 'theory of action' in the traditional sense of the term, we shall surely approach its core propositions in the chapter which follows.

CHAPTER 5

Actions, Rules and Contexts

The difficulty — I might say — is not that of finding a solution but rather of recognizing as the solution something that looks as if it were only a preliminary to it . . . This is connected, I believe, with our wrongly expecting an explanation, whereas the solution of the difficulty is a description, if we give it the right place in our considerations. If we dwell upon it, and do not try to get beyond it.

Wittgenstein, Zettel

Throughout the previous chapter we pursued the insight, established by Schutz and developed by Garfinkel, that in order to provide for the stable organization of some set of social activities, detailed consideration must be given to the participants' understandings of their empirical circumstances. Garfinkel's experiments offer vivid testimony to the vast domain of interpretative and 'accomodative' activity through which 'order' and 'organization' is sought and found in everyday affairs as 'perceivedly normal' courses of conduct. Garfinkel further stresses the ways in which this 'found' order is, in turn, overwhelmingly and unrelievedly used and relied upon by participants as the basis on which further components in courses of action are initiated and developed. In a word, the located organization of a scene of conduct is both 'trusted' and acted upon and, as Garfinkel's 'breaching' experiments demonstrated, treated as a morally sanctionable 'matter of fact'.

Central to the business of locating order and organization in a scene are the reflexive processes of the documentary method of interpretation. Through these processes, intelligible patterns and their constituent particulars are adjusted to one another. At the minimum, these processes can be treated as purely cognitive phenomena in which a hypothetically invisible actor analyses an on-going scene of activity without displaying or otherwise conveying the resulting analysis to others. In the present chapter, we will concentrate on adding a new element to this treatment which, in the interests of orderly exposition, has been understated thus far. This is the element of *action*. It is of central importance because, as we shall see, once the actors are no longer conceived as passive 'fly on the wall' spectators of a scene, but instead as engaged in activity within it, the significance of the reflexive aspects of the 'documentary method' is utterly transformed. For the actors find that, willy-nilly, their actions reflexively contribute to the sense of the scene which is undergoing development as a temporal sequence of actions.

In order to illustrate this aspect of Garfinkel's analysis, some time will now be spent in a treatment of a very simple interactional exchange — a greetings sequence. In part, this example is chosen for its simplicity. In a more complicated case, the theoretical points could easily be lost in the escalating complexity of empirical analysis. Moreover, the greetings exchange is a paradigmatic example of what is usually treated as 'rule-governed' behaviour. It thus provides a useful vehicle through which the rule-governed model of human action can be examined.

In essence, the 'rule-governed' model of human conduct is a very simple one. It begins from the presumption that human actors are generally equipped with an array of rules which they 'follow' (or by which they are 'guided' or 'governed') in situations of action (see Collett, 1975 for a useful discussion). The actual basis on which the actors are proposed to acquire the rules varies from theory to theory. In Parsons's analysis the rules are viewed as internalized as 'need dispositions' and in symbolic interactionist writings too an element of identification is involved in the process of 'self-lodging' through which social rules are acquired (Foote, 1951; Denzin, 1971). Regardless of how the rules are acquired however, the traditional model of 'rule-governed' conduct works in the following fashion. The actors are treated as encountering a situation of action to which one or more of the rules they have learned or internalized 'apply'. Their actions in this context are then analysed as 'guided' or 'caused' by the rules which they have previously acquired. Co-ordinated ~~social action~~ is given a simple explanation by this model. Two or more actors can co-ordinate their actions with one another, provided they have acquired the same rules of action and provided too that *they have identified the situation in the same way in the first place* (Wilson, 1971). As a concession to 'usage', most proponents of the model are prepared to allow that a certain halo of 'vagueness' may surround the use of the rules, but they are united from Parsons (1951) to Searle (1969) in denying that these marginal cases can weaken the general explanatory value of the core model.

The stultifying effect of this model on the development of the theory of action can scarcely be overestimated. Applied to concrete situations of action, the model has persistently drained the resulting analyses of interest and dynamic. Yet so stifling is the grip of the model that, among those concerned with the analysis of 'subjectively meaningful' action and its co-ordination, it is still widely assumed that social organization could not be explained in any other way. Assimilating all unto itself, the model has enveloped all but its most vigorous opponents (e.g. Blumer, 1969). Its power is such that, despite the best efforts of Wittgenstein scholarship (from Cavell (1962) to Baker and Hacker (1980) and Kripke (1981)) and of those influenced by Wittgenstein in such diverse fields as jurisprudence (Hart, 1961) and the history of science (Kuhn, 1970), the conventional wisdom in sociology is − often out of a misinterpretation of Winch (1958) − that Wittgenstein recommends a 'rule-following' model of human action. And so too, according to the same conventional wisdom (e.g. Denzin, 1971), does Garfinkel.

In the following sections, we will try to trace through some of the weaknesses of this model as Garfinkel identified them. Since Parsons developed the model as consistently as anyone (and more consistently than most), we will use his analysis as a stalking horse. But it should be kept in mind that similar criticisms can be applied to any of the model's versions. Along the way, we shall encounter some very positive by-products of abandoning the model. Among them, most surprisingly and paradoxically, is a highly economical analysis of normative constraint.

THE REFLEXIVITIES OF ACTION: GREETINGS

The greetings exchange is an apt vehicle for examining the 'rule-governed' model of action, not only because it is a simple case, but also because unlike many other social activities it falls within the jurisdiction of a pretty straightforward rule. If we further simplify the case by focusing on the situation faced by the recipient of a (first) greeting, most members of our society could describe the rule which 'covers' the situation as being: when greeted, return the greeting. Moreover, most members of our society may have received explicit training (or at least prompting) in this rule, for example by being rebuked for not saying 'hello' back to a family friend or relative. We are here then, prima facie at least, deep in a domain where the activities of the participants can be adequately accounted for by reference to the rule. If the rule model cannot work satisfactorily here, it surely cannot succeed elsewhere. Let us then work through some of the reflexivities of an elementary greeting sequence.

Consider, to begin with, a situation in which a social actor is walking down the corridor of an office building, interactively disengaged from any others on the scene. From the moment this actor is greeted by another, his or her circumstances are radically reconstituted from a situation of mutal disengagement between the parties to one in which some, at least minimal, engagement is proposed by the other. At this initial and elementary level, the first greeter's action has reflexively reconstituted the scene. Moreover, this first greeting transforms the scene for both parties — for the greeter (who moves from a circumstance of disengagement to one of engagement which he or she proposes, via the norm, will be reciprocated) and for the recipient of the greeting (who must now deal with this reconstituted circumstance).

In this context, and with the use of the norm for greetings, our recipient is now faced with a situation of 'choice'. If the recipient returns the greeting, he or she thereby reciprocates the proposal of interactional engagement made by the first greeter and, in so doing, ratifies it. In this case, the sense of the scene has undergone a further transformation from one in which interactional engagement was merely proposed unilaterally to one in which it is a bilaterally acknowledged fact. It is essential here to keep in mind that the scene does not remain unaltered by the second greeting. Rather it is developed and elaborated in a particular direction — the direction of mutual interactional engagement which was proposed by the first speaker.

Alternatively, of course, the recipient may not return the greeting. In this case, such a recipient will 'observably-reportably' develop the substance of the scene in a different direction — counteracting what was proposed by the greeter. Once again, it is essential to note that, although a circumstance of mutual disengagement may well ensue from such an action, it will not be the 'same' circumstance of mutual disengagement as existed prior to the first greeting. Rather, as in the case of the 'breaching' experiments, the re-reconstituted scene may well be accountably attended to by the participants (and reported to others) as an 'intended', 'produced' or 'motivated' outcome and, probably, as a product of good or bad reasons (Turner, 1971).

A number of important points about the nature of conduct and its normative organization can be made from this elementary example. First, it should by now be obvious that regardless of whether the recipient consciously 'chose' to respond in a particular way, he or she was nonetheless placed in a 'situation of choice'. This is so by virtue of the fact that actions reflexively and accountably redetermine the features of the scenes in which they occur. Thus regardless of what our recipient does — of whether the greeting is returned or not — the scene will be reconstituted. The unfolding scene, in other words, cannot 'mark time' or 'stall' for a while; it will unavoidably be transformed.

Second, it can be noticed that the norm 'return a greeting' may be used as an interpretative base for the scene, regardless of which among the alternatives of action the recipient in fact accomplishes. Thus the parties to the scene not only maintain and develop the 'perceivedly normal' course of the scene by perceiving, judging and acting in accordance with the dictates of the norm, they also use this same norm to notice, interpret and sanction departures from its dictates. The norm is thus *doubly constitutive* of the circumstances it organizes. It provides both for the intelligibility and accountability of 'continuing and developing the scene as normal' and for the visibility of other, alternative courses of action. It follows, therefore, that whatever the outcome of the 'choice', the availability of the norm will provide a means by which the conduct and its circumstances can be rendered sensible, describable and accountable.

Finally, it may be noted that, once the norm 'return a greeting' has made an actor's 'choice' visible, there is available a great mass of interpretative devices in terms of which a 'non-standard' choice may itself become elaboratively interpreted. Thus: recipient did not hear or was preoccupied; recipient did not know the greeter, or failed to recognize him, or thought the greeter was initiating a sexual 'pass'; recipient deliberately 'snubbed' the greeter as a social inferior, or sought to renew a quarrel, or to declare a state of enmity by visibly 'refusing' to return the greeting, and so on. And these interpretative resources are themselves accountably implemented by reference to the particulars of the actions, persons, places and circumstances of their occurrence.

Emerging out of this discussion is a point which is absolutely central both to Garfinkel's work and the subsequent traditions of research which he has stimulated. This concerns the role of norms, or maxims of conduct, in the organization of ordinary actions. A characteristic assumption within the theory of action, Parsons's included, is that the role of norms is essentially one of guiding, regulating, determining or causing the conduct which may occur in *circumstances which are treated as if they are already pre-established or pre-defined.* As already noted, within the terms of such assumptions, the theory treats the actors as cognitively equipped to recognize situations in common and, once the situation is commonly recognized, the application of common norms enables the actors to produce joint actions. Moreover the theory, we can now notice, treats the actors' circumstances as essentially unchanged by their courses of action. Hence the role of time as an essential component in the unfolding succession of 'here-and-now' reconstitutions of the actors' circumstances is ignored. Instead time is treated within the theory as, to use Garfinkel's expression, a 'fat moment' (Garfinkel, 1952: 147).

Garfinkel's perspective, emerging as it does out of a preoccupation with the nature of 'common understandings', reverses this tradition of theorizing. Within his viewpoint, the common norms, rather than regulating conduct in pre-defined scenes of action, *are instead reflexively constitutive of the activities and unfolding circumstances to which they are applied.* The argument, described in the previous chapter, concerning the role of the expectancies of the attitude of daily life in the constitution of 'perceivedly normal' courses of conduct is here simply particularized to specific, 'concrete' norms of conduct. Thus what the activities are, with all the subsequent interpretative elaboration of motive and circumstance, is only visible and available in the first place through the reflexive application of norms and maxims of conduct to temporally extended sequences of actions. Norms and maxims of conduct are, then, materials through which, via the documentary method of interpretation, the reflexive determination of the 'whatness' of conduct is possible. In this perspective, once again, the cognitive and the moral are deeply intertwined.

A concern with the reflexive accountability of action is the central pillar of Garfinkel's work. It makes up his central recommendation that

> the activities whereby members produce and manage settings of organized everyday affairs are identical with members' procedures for making those settings 'account-able'. The 'reflexive', or 'incarnate' character of accounting practices and accounts makes up the crux of that recommendation. (Garfinkel, 1967a: 1)

This concern with reflexive phenomena *as applied to actions* marks an entirely new departure from more traditional phenomenological treatments of reflexivity. Phenomenologists had long been preoccupied with the reflexive aspects of the 'hermeneutic circle', but they had characteristically treated these phenomena from the perspective of an observer who stands outside the events which he or she describes. Thus the phenomena of reflexivity have traditionally emerged (as problematic features when treated from a positivistic standpoint) in discussions concerning the interpretation of texts, of historical evidence and, via gestalt psychology, in relation to topics in perception and cognition. Garfinkel's introduction of these same issues into the theory of action utterly transforms both their significance and the theory of action itself.

Introduced into the theory of action, the relevance of reflexive phenomena can no longer be confined to the essentially academic concerns of the armchair theorizer or observer. Instead, as we have seen, they directly enter as 'seen but unnoticed', but nevertheless constitutive, features of what the actions consist of and hence into the concerns and calculations of ordinary actors pursuing their daily affairs. For it is precisely through the reflexive accountability of action that ordinary actors find themselves in a world of practical actions having the property that *whatever* they do will be intelligible and accountable as a sustaining of, or a development or violation, etc. of, some order of activity. This order of activity is, as Garfinkel puts it, 'incarnate' in the specific, concrete, contexted and sequential details of actors' actions. It is via the reflexive properties of actions that the participants — regardless of their degree of 'insight' into the matter — find themselves in a world whose characteristics they are visibly and describably engaged in producing and reproducing. It is through these same properties that the actors' actions, to adapt Merleau-Ponty's phrase, are condemned to be meaningful.

These considerations further transform the theory of action as it has been traditionally treated within sociology by transforming the sense in which norms, rules, or maxims of conduct can be conceived as applying to actions. As we have seen, this transformation is essentially from a regulative to a constitutive sense of norm or rule, yet, paradoxically, this transformation can enable us to gain a renewed access to the question of normative constraint.

THE 'JUDGEMENTAL DOPE' AND HIS WORLD

In sharing a common preoccupation with the institutionalized and routinely ordered nature of much of social conduct, both

Parsons and Garfinkel are concerned to provide for the ways in which routine institutionalized expectations concerning everyday conduct are routinely fulfilled.

It will be recalled that Parsons addresses this issue with his proposal that norms of conduct are internalized as need dispositions of personality. In this account, norms come to represent enduring directives to act in particular ways under given circumstances which are acquired as a result of the prior administration of rewards and punishments. In this analysis, a psychological theorem about dispositions to act and their sources in conditioning is invoked as a fundamental explanatory principle. Moreover, it will be recalled that Parsons's actors are treated as broadly unreflexive with respect to the norms they have internalized. The result is that his actors can neither adopt a manipulative or game-like stance towards the norms, nor are they capable of the reflection necessary to make a moral choice.

Garfinkel's rejection of this position is well known. It involves, he argues, a procedure in which models of action become based on entirely *retrospective* considerations. In this process, the theorist uses the *outcome* of a sequence of actions as the privileged starting point from which to work back to the 'necessary causes' which are presented as responsible for the actions turning out as they did. In this kind of analysis, Garfinkel points out, 'hierarchies of need dispositions, and common culture as enforced rules of action, are favoured devices for bringing the problem of necessary inference to terms, although at the cost of making out the person-in-society to be a judgemental dope' (Garfinkel, 1967b: 68).

What is being eliminated or suppressed in this form of theorizing is the range of contingencies, as interpreted by the actor, which may influence the actual outcome of a chain or sequence of actions. In Schutzian terminology, 'in order to' motives, having to do with the way in which the actor devises plans and projects to deal with the contingencies in his or her circumstances, are suppressed or eliminated in favour of 'because of' motives, having to do with the generalized backdrop of the actor's actions. The natural tendency of this kind of theorizing is a specious determinism in which, in the interests of accounting for the routine fulfillment of expectations, the theorist builds a model in terms of which the expectations could not but have been fulfilled and the sequence of actions could not have come out differently.

It is noticeable that this theoretical suppression of possible alternative courses of conduct leads to a loss of explanatory scope and flexibility. Thus, notoriously, the Parsonian analysis of 'deviant behaviour', in dealing with it as the product of incomplete or inadequate socialization, fails to grasp such conduct as a possible product of practical choice or 'reasoned' decision-making and thus loses access to the various 'logics' of deviance as organized domains of conduct. More significantly still, the theoretical suppression of alternative possibilities of conduct results in a situation in which the theorist loses the very basis for explaining why — in the face of these alternatives — the sequence of conduct nonetheless regularly assumes a particular form eventuating in a 'standard outcome'. The substance of the suppression involved, Garfinkel suggests, consists of the fact that

> courses of common-sense rationalities of judgement which involve the person's use of common-sense knowledge of social structures over the temporal 'succession' of here-and-now situations are treated as epiphenomenal. (Garfinkel, 1967b: 68)

Yet it is these same common-sense rationalities which provide for the person's ordinary awareness of alternative possible courses of conduct while, simultaneously, they militate against the acting out of these alternatives.

Since the theory is already becoming dense again, let us return to our simplified 'greetings' example and work outwards from it. Before proceeding, by way of contrast, we recall that Parsons's actor has enduring dispositions to act in particular ways under specific circumstances. We can also note with Wilson (1971) that the cogency of this formulation as a theory of co-ordinated interaction depends on our acceptance of the idea that the actors are trained in such a way that not only do they share substantive norms of conduct but also that, from the outset, they share common identifications of the situations for which the norms are appropriate. Thus a consensus on both 'the circumstances' and 'the appropriate course of action given the circumstances' must exist from the outset if Parsonian actors are to be able to co-ordinate their actions.

Returning to our 'greetings' situation, it is reasonable to assume that the population has received explicit and standardized training, supported by rewards and punishments, which as previously noted runs to the effect: return a greeting. This situation should be easily handled within the Parsonian framework. Within the terms of Parsons's analysis, the situation is analysed by proposing that each member of the population has internalized the norm 'return greetings' as a need disposition. As a result, it can be hypothesized that all greetings will be returned within the population with, at worst, random deviations from the norm. Deviations from the norm which are systematic in that they are repeatedly produced by the same individuals will, of course, be handled by reference to the 'faulty socialization' rubric. In this context, however, it may be noticed that this explanation as it stands can only cover total failures. Within the terms of the theory, the population is partitioned into the properly socialized who always return greetings and the improperly socialized who never do so. In short, what the theory cannot presently handle is the 'occasional' or 'intermittent' non-returner: to handle such an actor, the model needs complicating.

Drawing on a little folk knowledge, the Parsonian theorist can complicate the normative framework and propose that the population uniformly acquires the norm: 'return greetings unless the greeter is an enemy.' And the theorist can keep on complicating the norm by adding 'unless' clauses: unless the greeting is ambiguous; unless the greeter is unknown to the recipient; is socially inferior, leering, drunk, has offended a friend of a friend, etc. Whilst a normative structure of this kind is imaginable for a simple greetings situation, it requires little insight to see that given the enormous complexity of talk and interaction and the endless variability of the circum-stances in which they occur, the normative theorist is inexorably drawn into equipping the actor with a huge array of instructions — enough, in fact, to deal with every empirically possible contingency in social life. While such a proposal may be unconvincing, still less convincing is the notion that the entire population is uniformly equipped with such instructions such that each member is capable of commonly identifying, without error, every circumstantial nuance requiring a change in conduct. Yet this is precisely what is required within the terms of Parsons's analysis if intersubjective definitions of the actors' circumstances are to be available and acted upon.

In an influential discussion of fully 'rule-governed' or 'mechanical' jurisprudence, H. L. A. Hart comments:

> If the world in which we live were characterized only by a finite number of features, and these together with all the modes in which they could combine were known to us, then provision could be made in advance for every possibility. We could make rules, the application of which to particular cases never called for a further choice. Everything could be known, and for everything, since it could be known, something could be done and specified in advance by rule. This would be a world fit for 'mechanical' jurisprudence. (Hart, 1961: 125)

This would also be a world fit for a 'mechanical', rule-governed theory of action. Looking back at Parsons's programme for sociology, we can now see the full extent to which it was premised on counter-factual assumptions. For Parsons's analysis of concerted actions required that, through common socialization, particular fact situations should await the actors 'already marked off from each other' (ibid. 123) and, moreover, in identical fashion for each actor. And it required too that the rules applying to them should be exhaustive, specific and unambiguous.

In sum, even if we provisionally accept the plausibility of an actor modelled as a 'judgemental dope', we find that the 'world' which must necessarily be co-ordinated with such an actor is an impossible one. For it is a world requiring limitless specification. Rather like the students in the 'conversation clarification experiment', the normative theorist finds that there is no end to what the participants must know, and know identically, if they are to grasp their circumstances adequately and act appropriately. Sooner or later, the theorist must eventually recognize the 'accomodative' work through which the actors treat specifically differentiated situations as 'identical for all practical purposes' and exhibit these treatments in their actions.

'DOUBLE CONSTITUTION' AND THE LOGIC OF NORMATIVE ACCOUNTABILITY

We have already encountered Garfinkel's alternative to analyses in which social actors are portrayed as rule-governed 'judgemental dopes'. He summarizes this alternative when he remarks that

> social science theorists . . . have used the fact of standardization to conceive the character and consequences of actions that comply with standardized expectancies. Generally they have acknowledged but otherwise neglected the fact that by these same actions persons discover, create and sustain this standardization. (Garfinkel, 1967a: 66–7)

Aspects of this alternative have already been encountered in the earlier treatment of the greetings exchange. There, we found, it was the reflexive characteristics of ordinary actions which play a central role in the creation and maintenance of the sense of a sequence of events and the environing context in which they occur. However, if we now pursue Garfinkel's insight just a little further, we will find that the reflexive accountability of ordinary actions can constitute a most economical basis for the explanation of normative constraint in conduct.

To clarify this, let us re-examine our greetings example once more while holding on to the 'double constitution' property of norms. Viewed from the perspective of the one who performed the initial greeting (which he or she expects, via the norm, to be returned), a return greeting not only meets the standard expectation, it also confirms that some standard relationship (e.g. of acquaintance) continues to hold good between the parties as, indeed, the first speaker had expected it would.

On the other hand, returning to the second alternative action (no return greeting), we have already noted that a mass of considerations might be brought to bear in interpreting an 'observable and reportable' deviation. Our initial greeter may conclude that the recipient did not hear and, accordingly, repeat the greeting; or, noticing the anxious expression on the recipient's face, he or she may enquire into the recipient's circumstances. Alternatively, the greeter may silently attribute the unreturned greeting to the recipient's preoccupation, or to an argument the previous day, or to the recipient's rank or rudeness. Whatever the conclusion, there is a sharp contrast between the 'life-as-usual' nature of the greeting-and-its-return which is not given a second thought, and the occasions where the recipient does not return the greeting, which are commonly the objects of 'post-mortem' thought and discussion.

This contrast instructs us that the 'perceived normality' cf ordinary conduct is, in fact, normatively provided for even though this provision is 'seen but unnoticed' and often becomes visible only in the breach. For, to explain the normal action, we merely cite the norm: 'I said "Hello" to return the greeting.' To explain breaches of the norm, we cite accounts which are overwhelmingly treated as excuses or justifications for the breach: 'I didn't hear him,' 'I had a terrible hangover,' 'I don't speak to people who insult me.' And, given this bifurcation in the types of accounts which are given for conformity to and deviation from the norm, we can begin to see some basis for the participants' belief that breaches of norms are commonly more revealing about the attitudes, motives and circumstances of other people than is conformity.

Turning now to view the greeting situation from the perspective of the recipient of the first greeting, we have already suggested that although the recipient may not be fully aware of it at the time, he or she is, in effect, presented with a choice. The choice is between: (1) returning the greeting and sustaining a 'life-as-usual' stance which, among other things, confirms that the relationship between greeter and recipient holds as the greeter proposes it; or (2) not returning the greeting and creating the circumstances in which the initial greeter may accountably infer that 'normal circumstances' do not obtain and that 'something is up' which needs looking into.

Where, for whatever reasons, actors wish to avoid the

second of these consequences, they will engage in the 'perceivedly normal'/normatively provided for conduct. Given these considerations, it will be apparent that three basic conditions are required to get greetings regularly returned: (1) social participants are aware of the norm; (2) they are, on occasion, capable of reflexive anticipation of the interpretative consequences of breaches of the norm and, (3) they attribute (1) and (2) to each other. Where these three conditions hold, a social world will exist in which the participants hold one another accountable as the producers of 'chosen' courses of action which, particularly in the breach, will be held to reflect significant real dispositions, opinions, characters, commitments and beliefs.

Generalizing the theorem, we can suggest that the 'internalization of norms' is (1) not a necessary source of constraint in engendering normatively appropriate conduct, nor (2) an essential bulwark against the unloosed anarchy of interests. With respect to the production of normatively appropriate conduct, all that is required is that the actors have, and attribute to one another, a reflexive awareness of the normative accountability of their actions. For actors who, under these conditions, calculate the consequences of their actions in reflexively transforming the circumstances and relationships in which they find themselves, will routinely find that their interests are well served by normatively appropriate conduct. With respect to the anarchy of interests, the choice is not between normatively organized co-operative conduct and the disorganized pursuit of interests. Rather, normative accountability is the 'grid' by reference to which *whatever* is done will become visible and assessable. And, subject to this condition of visible accountability, conduct undertaken for whatever objectives will tend to become designed and shaped responsively to the constraints imposed by this visibility (cf. Mills, 1940; Skinner, 1978: xii-xiii). In this sense, normative accountability can best be viewed as organizing, channelling and, in a sense, 'domesticating' the ways in which interests may be realized.

Finally, it will be recalled that, insofar as we are looking for normative constraint, we are looking for a form of constraint that *tends* to bind rather than a form which is absolutely binding. We are looking for a form of constraint which may influence persons to return greetings all their lives but who may yet still refuse to return one on this particular occasion. In this context, it can be noted that the constraint which emerges from the reflexive accountability of action is not 'binding' in the ways envisaged by Parsons. The actor who is determined to 'declare' or continue a quarrel can do so by visibly 'refusing' to return a greeting and leaving the other to draw the conclusion. Here not only is the norm not binding, it actually provides the vehicle for the declaration. In providing for the 'observable and reportable' character of departures from 'perceivedly normal' conduct, the reflexive properties of norms do not eliminate such departures a priori. Such departures are for anyone who can stand or forestall the consequences.

At this stage in the discussion, it should be emphasized that although Garfinkel's critical discussions of treatments of the actor as a 'judgemental dope' may imply for some a view of the actor as an almost endlessly reflexive, self-conscious and calculative Machiavel, this is neither a necessary nor an intended interpretative consequence of his position. On the contrary, Garfinkel repeatedly stresses the *routine* nature of the implementation of 'seen but unnoticed' procedures for accomplishing, producing and reproducing 'perceivedly normal' courses of action. Overwhelmingly, participants in such actions are typically interested in getting their ordinary tasks done and, as Garfinkel emphasizes, the reflexive features of their activities are specifically 'uninteresting' (Garfinkel, 1967a: 7–9). Only in cases of breach or anticipated breach may the reflexive features of conduct come to be fleetingly entertained, for on the whole it is in cases of breach that actors may anticipate being held to account for their actions and, as part of this anticipation, contemplate its being held that they could have known and done differently and therefore should have done so. In these cases, a consultation of the reflexive characteristics of actions and their accountings may arouse the anticipatory anxieties and fears which Garfinkel notes were common among his student experimenters. In these cases, actors may feel impelled to conform to the 'standard-ized' institutional option (Garfinkel, 1967b: 69–70).

Thus, for Garfinkel, it is the very reflexivity of the actors, their awareness of the options together with their anticipation of some of the interpretations to which their exercise of the options will give rise, which may ultimately keep them 'on the rails' of perceivedly normal/normatively provided for conduct. It is in this sense that the treatment of the actor as a 'judgemental dope' whose 'common-sense rationalities of judgement' are ignored misses both the analytical foundations and the empirical grounding of normatively organized conduct. As early as 1952, Garfinkel commented:

> The big question is not whether actors understand each other or not. The fact is that they do understand each other, that they *will* understand each other, but the catch is that they will understand each other regardless of how they *would* be understood. (Garfinkel, 1952: 367)

It is this 'catch' — the catch of accountability with all its reflexive features — which constitutes the foundation of socially organized conduct as a self-reproducing environment of 'perceivedly normal' activities. Without this 'catch', 'order' — in both the cognitive and normative senses — as a feature of social activity simply ceases to exist.

In summary, in order to provide' for the existence of normative *constraint* in conduct, Parsons supplemented the actors' habit of routine conformity with norms with a conception of internalization which positively motivates such conformity. Correspondingly, Parsons viewed the actors' capacity to adopt a reflexive or manipulative stance towards their actions as threatening to the normative underpinnings of the social order. Viewed as an analysis of normative constraint, Garfinkel's treatment yields the opposite conclusion. Whatever the level of sheer habit in generating 'perceivedly normal' conduct, a source of underlying constraint which 'breaks through' on occasions of actual or contemplated breach derives from the reflexive orientation to norms of conduct which actors attribute to one another and in terms of which they hold one another accountable. This opposition between the two thinkers can be extrapolated backwards. For, by the same token, the actors' socialization, which for Parsons is the history of rewards and punishments through which they come to unreflexive normative conformity, is for Garfinkel no more than a history of the ways in which the actors are increasingly treated as aware of — and hence accountable in terms of — the normative organization of the empirical circumstances surrounding them.

Finally, it should be noted that Garfinkel's perspective does not entail the denial of the phenomena of normative internalization, introjection or identification *as empirical phenomena.* Many of the 'breaching' experiments indeed can be viewed as revealing the extent to which ordinary actors are prepared to proclaim and act on the basis of such identifications. However his perspective does essentially argue the claim that such internalization is fundamentally both 'cognitive' and 'moral', or better, 'cognitive-moral'. If cognitive shifts occur, the moral order will undergo corresponding alterations. Thus, to invoke Reiss's (1967) well-known example, if the task of fellating adult homosexuals in a public lavatory can be regarded under the auspices of a 'job of work' by a group of teenagers, then the activity can easily be stripped of its more conventional moral connotations. (For a fuller treatment of related issues, see Garfinkel (1956a).) Rather than rejecting the empirical incidence of the phenomena of internalization, Garfinkel's analysis rejects the view that such internalization is a *sine qua non* for the maintenance of social order. Moreover, a specific consequence of his analysis is the denial that 'rules', no matter how deeply internalized as moral imperatives, can dictate the specifics of a course of action. This latter denial will be the focus of the final section of this chapter.

THE ESSENTIAL INSUFFICIENCY OF RULES IN THE DETERMINATION OF CONDUCT

The doctrine of 'finitism' represents perhaps the most complex legacy of Wittgenstein's mature philosophy. Permeating the paragraphs of the *Philosophical Investigations*, its core assertion, in one succinct summary, 'is that proper usage is developed step by step, in processes involving successions of on-the-spot judgements. Every instance of use, or of proper use, of a concept must in the last analysis be accounted for separately, by reference to specific, local, contingent determinants' (Barnes, 1982a: 30). This doctrine, in its many ramifications, infused Wittgenstein's philosophy of mind, language and mathematics. It has been productively developed in discussions of concepts and paradigms in science (Kuhn, 1970, 1977; Hesse, 1974, 1980; Barnes, 1982a). In relation to rule-oriented phenomena (i.e. rule following, rule application, definition by rule, etc.), Wittgenstein's finitist observations (especially those in Wittgenstein, 1958, paras. 143–242) have found able exposition at the hands of, *inter alios*, Cavell (1961, 1962), Baker and Hacker (1980), Baker (1981) and Kripke (1981). One overall conclusion of these discussions has been a very general awareness of the *insufficiency* of rules as either explanations of, or directives to, human action. This conclusion is clearly stated by Hart in relation to legal rules. In particular, he stresses that

> Particular fact situations do not await us already marked off from each other, and labelled as instances of the general rule, the application of which is in question; nor can the rule itself step forward to claim its own instances. (Hart, 1961: 123)

And he adds:

> Canons of 'interpretation' cannot eliminate, though they can diminish, [interpretative] uncertainties; for these canons are themselves general rules for the use of language, and make use of general terms which themselves require interpretation. They cannot, any more than other rules, provide for their own interpretation. (ibid.)

Just as typifications gloss the particulars they typify, so legal rules cover an indefinite range of contingent, concrete possibilities. The rules must, in short, be applied, and to specific configurations of circumstances which may never be identical. Thus it is possible to get a legal judgement on just *when* it is permissible to drive the wrong way down a one-way street (Paul Drew, personal communication) and, the precedent having been established, there must still be a judgement as to whether the next occasion is sufficiently similar to fall within the scope of the prior judgement. In this sense, the rules, as Garfinkel puts it, are always applied 'for another first time'. (Anticipating the subsequent discussion in part, the reader may wish to refer immediately to Garfinkel's remarks on the 'unstated conditions' of the application of rules (1967b: 73–5) and his treatment of jurors' relevances in arriving at legally binding decisions. Further ethnomethodological studies of discretionary, elaborative and *post hoc* applications of formal rules to the specifics of particular contexts include Zimmerman (1971) and Bittner (1965, 1967a, 1967b).)

A preoccupation with finitist issues is not the exclusive prerogative of those who have been influenced by the later Wittgenstein. Husserl had more than a passing interest in what he termed 'occasional expressions' (Garfinkel, 1967a: 4–5). And Schutz placed finitist concerns at the centre of his sociological writings. It is, for example, difficult to discern any in-principle differences (though there are differences of emphasis and substantive argumentation) between Schutz's observations on the essentially abstractive, open-ended and revisable characteristics of type constructs and Wittgenstein's (1969, 1958) observations on the 'family resemblance' characteristics of category names (Heritage, 1978). Nor, for that matter, can a serious in-principle distinction be maintained between Schutz's insistence on the essential contingency of the maintenance of the reciprocity of perspectives and Wittgenstein's arguments concerning the 'contingent publicity' of rule following conduct (Kripke, 1981). Accordingly, we shall view the finitist perspective as essentially co-extensive in its analytic preoccupations with the ethnomethodological focus on indexical phenomena (see chapter 6, 142–50). As Garfinkel and Sacks themselves put the point, Wittgenstein's later work can be viewed as 'a sustained, extensive and penetrating corpus of observations of indexical phenomena' (Garfinkel and Sacks, 1970: 348).

Remaining, for the present, within the finitist vocabulary, it is not difficult to see that Garfinkel's writings constitute a most complete and unwavering expression of finitism. Moreover he develops its implications in relation to Parsons's central topic — the phenomenon of social order. And he conceives it, as Parsons conceived it, in terms of the means and resources through which the actors concertedly recognize and act upon — and in concertedly recognizing and acting, create and recreate, maintain, restore or alter — the phenomena of social organization. Garfinkel proposes that all social phenomena be

> addressed according to the policy that every feature of sense, of fact, of method, for every particular case of inquiry without exception, is the managed accomplishment of organized settings of practical actions, and that particular determinations in members' practices of consistency, planfulness, relevance, or reproducibility of their practices and results — from witchcraft to topology — are acquired and assured only through particular, located organizations of artful practices. (Garfinkel, 1967a: 32)

In doing so, he is proposing a finitist account of the social organization of fact. Similarly, when Garfinkel proposes that

> by his accounting practices the member makes familiar, commonplace activities of everyday life recognizable *as* familiar, commonplace activities
>
> [and] that on each occasion that an account of common activities is used, that they be recognized for 'another first time' (ibid. 9)

he is proposing a finitist account of ordinary descriptions. By the same token, Garfinkel proposes:

> It is not satisfactory to describe how actual investigative procedures, as constituent features of members' ordinary and organized affairs, are accomplished by members as recognizedly rational actions *in actual occasions* of organizational circumstances by saying that members invoke some rule with which to define the coherent, or consistent or planful, i.e. rational, character of their actual activities.

And he adds that

> a leading policy is to refuse serious consideration to the prevailing proposal that efficiency, efficacy, effectiveness,

intelligibility, consistency, planfulness, typicality, uniformity, reproducibility of activities − i.e. that rational properties of practical activities − be assessed, recognized, categorized, described by using a rule or standard obtained outside actual settings within which such properties are recognized, used, produced and talked about by settings' members. (ibid. 32–3)

He is thereby proposing a finitist account of rule application and, combining it with a finitist account of description and fact production, proposing that no account of socially organized activity which denies or fails to acknowledge the contingently produced and reproduced nature of social actors' descriptions, fact production, rule application and social organization, can hope to gain access to the phenomenon: social organization of practical actions.

If no rule can 'itself step forward to claim its own instances', but always awaits contingent application 'for another first time', it necessarily follows that rules *per se* cannot determine the specifics of actual conduct no matter how deeply internalized they are. (Nor, of course, can they therefore ensure co-ordinated or co-operative activity no matter how consensually held they are.) Nonetheless, these observations do not exhaust the essential insufficiencies of rules as determinants of conduct. Here two further points may be made.

First, rules never completely or exhaustively define the character or 'legally possible' range of conduct of an activity. Even where, as in the case of games, the basic rules constitute the character of a game, they do not define what 'playing a game is' (Cavell, 1962). The fact that the rules do not exhaustively describe even a game is not difficult to demonstrate. In a relaxed seminar discussion, Garfinkel described a procedure followed by his undergraduate classes in order to exhibit this phenomenon:

You can start with a command . . . 'Take a game, any game, write down the instructions as to how to play that game. Finished?' Then you pass it to somebody else. That other person is asked: 'Do you have the instructions to the game? Now find monsters in those instructions so that if you needed to be instructed in that way you couldn't possibly make it out.'

Say we are going to propose a game of ticktacktoe. Two persons play ticktacktoe. Any two persons? When, today? Tomorrow? Do we have to be in sight of each other? Can we play by mail? Can one player be dead? . . . My classes can tell you that creating such problems is the easiest thing in the world. It comes off every time without fail. (Garfinkel, 1968: 211–12)

Not only do the rules of a game not cover all possible contingencies, the explicit rules fail to cover the full range of contingencies of their own application:

For example, although chess would seem to be immune to such manipulations, one can at one's move change pieces around on the board — so that, although the overall positions are not changed, different pieces occupy the squares — and then move. On the several occasions on which I did this, my opponents were disconcerted, tried to stop me, demanded an explanation of what I was up to, were uncertain about the legality (but wanted to assert its illegality nevertheless), made it clear to me that I was spoiling the game for them . . . They were not satisfied when I asked that they point out where the rules prohibited what I had done. Nor were they satisfied when I pointed out that I had not altered the material positions and, further, that the maneuver did not affect my chances of winning. If they were not satisfied, neither could they say to *their* satisfaction what was wrong. Prominently in their attempts to come to terms, they would speak of the obscurity of my motives. (Garfinkel, 1963: 199)

Commenting on these outcomes, Garfinkel argued that we are here in the area of the 'game's version of the "unstated terms of contract" ' which is covered by a 'final "finely printed" acknowledgement, "et cetera" ' (ibid.). Elsewhere, Garfinkel (1968: 216) refers to the practices of et cetera as 'inhabiting' the list of rules and indicates that they are 'practices for burying monsters . . . for refusing the existence of exceptions' (ibid. 213). And he adds:

I am trying to ask: When a person seems to be following rules, what is it that that seems to consist of? We need to describe how it gets done. These practices of etc., unless, let it pass, the pretense of agreeing, the use of sanctioned vagueness, the waiting for something later to happen which promises to clarify what has gone before, the avoidance of monsters even when they occur and the borrowing of exceptions are all involved. I am proposing these as practices whereby persons make what they are doing happen as rule-analysable conduct. (ibid. 220)

In sum, no matter what the circumstances, the clarity of their delineation and the transparency with which their particulars fall under a rule, there always remains an open set of unstated conditions of the rule's application. Moreover, in less clear — but sociologically common — cases, the operation of the rule can itself become implicated in the reflexive reformulation of 'the circumstances'.

For example, suppose there is a rule for greetings which runs to the effect: do not initiate greetings except with persons who are acquaintances. And suppose we subsequently witness a man greeting another who we know is not an acquaintance. We can either conclude that he broke the rule or we can infer that, *via the use of the rule*, he was seeking to treat the other *as* an acquaintance. The second interpretation is more likely when, for example, our man is greeting a new colleague at the office. And this reflexive use of a 'rule-governed action' to redefine the context can itself become oriented to by the participants — for example when our man, as portrayed in a thousand Hollywood movies, greets a new employee in the typing pool and she 'knowingly' (for example 'coyly' or 'brusquely') responds. In this case, not only is the reflexive, redeterminative aspect of the rule's application being used but, we might say, knowingly exploited by both participants who can *display* that exploitation as part and parcel of the greeting and its reciprocation. Here then the unstated conditions of the rule's application and interpretation are conjointly and knowingly manipulated.

We can now, second, conclude this discussion of the insufficiency of rules as directives to conduct by noting what is perhaps most obvious of all: for vast areas of social conduct, no rules of action at all are formulated or entertained by the participants — let alone used or drawn upon in devising courses of action. To illustrate this contention, consider the following from Pomerantz (1980).

(NB:II:2:1) ((Transcript conventions appear in the appendix))
    A: Yer line's been busy.
    B: Yeah my fu(hh)! ·hh my father's wife called me . . .
    ((continues))

In this extract from the early part of a telephone conversation, the first speaker (A) asserts 'limited knowledge' of a 'known to B' event. Whereupon the second speaker (B) gives a fairly extended description of the event in question. This kind of sequence is fairly common in conversation (see Pomerantz, 1980), and undergraduate students, when presented with only the first line of the datum, routinely describe it as 'fishing for' or soliciting the information which is subsequently provided. Yet although most speakers (including probably A in the datum above) would, in the event of the looked-for information not being forthcoming, treat that outcome as a kind of 'withholding', we know of no rule which runs to the effect: if someone asserts 'limited knowledge' of a 'known-to-you' event, tell them what you know. Children are not instructed in such a rule, neither is it listed in books of etiquette. Before Pomerantz described the phenomenon it was, in this sense, 'unknown'. Yet, to repeat, it is an extremely regular phenomenon. It is strongly patterned and will support 'accountability' inferences although, since the information is not specifically requested, its 'withholding' is, correspondingly, not the object of overt sanctions.

Many of the phenomena of action described in the large literature of conversation analysis exhibit this kind of 'strong' patterning. Yet none could conceivably be learned, inculcated or sanctioned by reference to publicly available rules. Knowledge of such actions is characteristically tacit, taken for granted and rarely, if ever, raised to consciousness. The sense of these actions, together with the responses appropriate to them and the inferences which may be drawn from alternative responses, are grasped by inductive inference from 'families' of 'similar' actions. (Compare, for example, the datum above with the kind of sequence in which A — holding an unlighted

cigarette — says 'I've forgotten my lighter', followed by B
producing a box of matches.) Correspondingly, understandings of the import of these actions may be supported by
reference to 'intuition' — a term with which we habitually
refer to matters which are not explicitly formulated or codified
within the culture but which are nonetheless taken for granted
as known in common.

Finally, even when actions — such as questions and answers
— are formulated within the culture as activities to which
'rules' apply, the culture inevitably remains silent on matters
concerning the scope and application of those rules. Thus
even though the culture tells us that 'questions should be
answered', there is no determinate set of overt cultural rules
available which can in any sense instruct us how to recognize a
'question' (Levinson, 1979), still less how to 'answer' it.

In sum, any detailed investigation of the organization of
social action will rapidly arrive at the conclusion that, as
Garfinkel proposes, social action cannot be analysed as
'governed' or 'determined' by rules in any | straightforward
sense. This is so for two basic reasons. First, even where
indisputable rules of conduct can be formulated, their
relevance to action will be found to be surrounded by a mass
of unstated conditions which are, in various ways, tacitly
oriented to by social participants. Thus even in the simplest
cases, such as our greetings example, an analysis of social
action simply in terms of the rule will grossly understate the
complexity of the scene of activity as it is available to the
participants' reasoning procedures.

Second, many classes of actions are not analysable by
reference to clear-cut rules which either delimit them as a
class or, still less, could be held to constrain or determine their
empirical occurrence. Rather these actions are produced and
recognized by reference to reasoning procedures which draw
upon complex, tacit and inductively based arrays of 'considerations' and 'awarenesses'. These reasoning procedures address
such matters as what some particular action accomplishes
with respect to the environment of activity to which it is
addressed; what analysis of that environment is exhibited in
the action; what assumptions about the social and personal
characteristics of the participants in the setting are displayed

in the action, and so on. Both the reasoning processes, involved in such judgements and the knowledge bases on which they draw are undoubtedly very intricate. Though a start has been made on their analysis (see especially chapter 8), they are at best weakly and partially understood. References to underlying rule systems may well have some part to play in this understanding, though it is by no means obvious that this part will necessarily be a large one. Moreover, however large this part turns out to be, the final analysis will not involve an appeal to rules as consciously inculcated or consciously oriented to phenomena. Nor will the analytic appeal to rules involve the proposal that the latter are, in any sense, determinate or determinative causes of action.

At the present time, it is clear that the analysis of actions-in-context is best forwarded by the detailed analysis of families of cases rather than through the formulation of prescriptive systems of rules which gloss over more than they reveal and foster the illusion of understanding and explanation where none exists. It is this illusory quality of such rule-based analyses of social action and rule-governed treatments of normative constraint which Garfinkel has laboured so extensively to expose.

CONCLUSION

Reviewing the previous discussion, the intellectual distance between Parsons and Garfinkel is truly vast. The prima facie gap between the two has indeed appeared so great that, for some, Garfinkel's acknowledgement of his intellectual debts to Parsons has seemed perverse or even disingenuous, while his theorizing has appeared incomprehensible and mystifying. If Garfinkel's work is viewed merely as an attempt to tinker with weaknesses in the Parsonian treatment of cognition with the use of a phenomenological vocabulary and a few conceptions derived from Schutz, then such conclusions will perhaps appear inevitable.

There is, however, an alternative view of his writings. The research culminating in ethnomethodology can be perspic-uously viewed as the product of a consistent attempt to recast the analysis of social organization and social conduct by beginning, in accordance with Schutz's recommendation, with 'the foundational structures of what is pre-scientific, the reality which seems self-evident to men remaining within the natural attitude'. In the context of the theory of action, what is self-evident is that the actors treat their own and one another's actions as the intelligible products of knowledgeable subjects whose talk and conduct is more than a conditioned babble. It is self-evident too that these same actors believe themselves to be, and treat one another as, confronted by real choices in conduct for which, unless 'excused', the chooser will be held accountable as the agent of his or her actions. Moreover, these two sets of beliefs are held to be related to one another in complicated and particular ways which can be glossed by suggesting that an actor (for example a child) who is deemed to be ignorant about some aspect of his circumstances is held less accountable as the producer of a 'choice'. Finally, despite the vague and generalized nature of the actors' 'recipe knowledge' as it appears in 'proverbs, partially formulated advice, partial description, elliptical expressions, passing remarks, fables, cautionary tales and the like' (Garfinkel, 1967a: 34), the actors encounter and know their concrete empirical circumstances in fine detail. It is with these self-evident facts that a theory of action must come to terms. Viewed in these terms, the nature and trajectory of Garfinkel's theorizing represents an enormous step forward in advancing an interpretatively based theory of action, and his writings represent the most sustained attempt to think through the consequences of such a theory that has yet been attempted.

As we have seen, Garfinkel's initial decision was to pursue an analysis of social organisation built 'solely from the analysis of expreience structures' and in which the mundane *recognizability* of actions is the primary consideration. Some cumulative consequences of this decision have been traced out in dealing with the reflexive characteristics of the documentary method of interpretation, the 'trusted' use of shared procedures in the constitution of intersubjective fact and the accountable character of social action as a reflexive product of the implementation of these procedures. These considerations, in turn, exert a transforming influence on the conceptualization of the nature, 'mechanics' and organizational properties of normative frameworks. The following table summarizes some of the major differences between Garfinkel's and Parsons's theorizing on the nature of social action and social organization.

TABLE 1: Parsons and Garfinkel on social action and social organization

Parsons	Garfinkel
1 Seeks an analysis of social organization built from a synthesis between the 'facts of social structure' and the 'facts of personality'.	1 Seeks an analysis of social organization built 'solely from an analysis of experience structures'.
2 In this approach, a central role is attributed to the integrative significance of moral norms.	2 In this approach, a central role is attributed to the procedures by which actors come to share, and rely upon sharing, a common view of their empirical circumstances which are treated as 'morally required matters of fact'.
3 Socialization is treated as the 'introjective' acquisition of social norms as 'need dispositions' of the personality. It is the crucial link between 'personality' and 'social structure'.	3 Socialization is viewed as a process in which actors acquire, and/or are treated as having acquired, a body of normatively organized knowledge in terms of which they treat their own and one another's actions as accountable.
4 Motivation for normatively appropriate conduct is established by a past history of rewards and punishments. These create enduring dispositions to act in normatively prescribed ways for the 'given situation'.	4 Motivation for normatively appropriate ('perceivedly normal') conduct is furnished by the actor's reflexive awareness of the differential accountability of alternative courses of conduct.

TABLE 1 cont.

Parsons	Garfinkel
5 The actor's reflexive orientation to norms would introduce an element of 'calculation' into conduct which tends to undermine the stability of institutionalized conduct.	5 The actor's reflexive orientation to norms of conduct, where it emerges, is likely to be a source of stability for perceivedly normal courses of action.
6 The situation of action is a stable object of consensual identification prior to action. Such identification is essential if normatively co-ordinated conduct is to occur. Such situational identification is essentially a transcendent product of shared substantive knowledge of 'matters of fact' known in advance.	6 The situation of action is essentially transformable. It is identified as the reflexive product of the organized activities of participants. As such, it is on-goingly 'discovered', maintained and altered as a project and product of ordinary actions. Situational constitution is essentially a 'local' and immanent product of *methodic procedure* rather than a result of 'pre-existing' agreement on 'matters of fact'.
7 Time is treated as irrelevant to the constitution of circumstances and the actions they 'contain'. Action is treated as occurring within the confines of a 'fat moment'.	7 Time is treated as an integral feature of the unfolding mutual elaboration of circumstances and their constituent actions. Actions inherently possess 'retrospective-prospective' properties.
8 Stable social organization is viewed as the product of a substantive cognitive and moral consensus among actors which, in turn, provides stable directives for co-ordinated actions.	8 Stable social organization is viewed as the product of *whatever* are the empirically discoverable set of locally managed and implemented procedures through which organized courses of co-operative, conflictual, etc. actions are produced and recognized.

A number of research recommendations flow from Garfinkel's theoretical position. Each of them is the outcome of his insistence on the fact that − regardless of their insight into the matter − social actors are, through their own actions, unavoidably engaged in producing and reproducing the intelligible characteristics of their own circumstances. Accordingly, Garfinkel recommends (Garfinkel, 1967a: 32–4) that:

(1) Any setting whatsoever can be analysed so as to uncover the ways in which the actors' actions effect 'choices' which propose what the sense, factual status, objectivity, causal characteristics, etc. of the setting and its constituent actions are. These characteristics can, of course, only be located *within* the setting because they are the products of actions which are produced within it. It is these actions, and these alone, which accomplish the particular, situated organizational work through which 'what the setting is' is, in every way, on-goingly produced.
(2) Since the sensible characteristics of a setting are contingently produced through practical actions and the inferences which are based on them and expressed through them, it is not sufficient, Garfinkel argues, to invoke general rules to describe how the actors make sense of their circumstances while ignoring how the rules are applied, interpreted and used to make sense of the specifics of the setting within which they are invoked and used.
(3) By the same token, it is not satisfactory to describe or interpret a setting by reference to rules or standards which are external to, or independent of, the ways in which the characteristics of the setting are 'recognized, used, produced, and talked about by settings' members' (ibid.). Instead,
(4) 'The policy is recommended that any social setting be viewed as self-organizing with respect to the intelligible character of its own appearances . . . Any setting organizes its activities to make its properties as an organized environment of practical activities . . . *accountable*' (ibid.).
(5) The members of a setting are, at all times, engaged in producing and interpreting, in 'making out', the sense of their circumstances and the constituent actions of these circumstances as a serious practical task with unavoidably

significant conclusions. The recommendation is for studies which analyse these phenomena seriously, carefully and, above all, non-ironically, for it is through these means that the members of a society create and enact the circumstances in which, through their actions, they find themselves.

The results of these recommendations appear as the studies of institutionally organized conduct described in *Studies in Ethnomethodology* (e.g. 1967d, 1967e, 1967f and also 1967i) and in the subsequent 'studies of work' (Garfinkel, forthcoming).

CHAPTER 6

Accounts and Accountings

Not a method of understanding, but immensely various methods of understanding are the professional sociologist's proper and hitherto unstudied and critical phenomena.

Garfinkel, *Studies in Ethnomethodology*

In the present chapter, we turn to what has probably been the most controversial aspect of Garfinkel's theoretical position, his view of language and its relation to social reality. It is in this context that his well-known emphasis on the 'indexicality' of linguistic expressions arises, which has been the subject of widespread debate (Attewell, 1974; Barnes and Law, 1976; Coulter, 1971, 1973; Goldthorpe, 1973; Heritage, 1978; Hindess, 1973; Mennell, 1976; Phillips, 1978). In his stress on the indexical, and hence interpreted, nature of natural language descriptions Garfinkel sought to focus sociological interest on a grievously neglected topic — the nature of language use and of the practical reasoning which informs it.

In considering Garfinkel's contribution to this area, it is worth recalling that he was writing before speech act theory (Searle, 1969; Grice, 1975) had made it commonplace to view speaking as a form of social action and also before the limitations of Chomskian structuralism as an account of language had become generally realized. Within sociology itself, the programmatic observations of the classical writers on the foundational significance of language in social life (e.g. Marx and Engels, 1965; Durkheim, 1982; Durkheim and Mauss, 1963; Mead, 1934) had been developed only in the relatively limited context of interactionist writings on the symbolic nature of the self.

Garfinkel was thus forced to build almost from scratch a

case for the role of language in the constitution of social relations and social reality. He did so by alluding to existing observations on 'indexical expressions' in the philosophical literature (1967a, 4–7), by examining how conversational utterances are interpreted (ibid. 24–31, see above 90–7) and by examining the management of description in a variety of sociological studies (ibid. 11–24, 1967f; 1967g). While the former observations aroused little reaction within sociological circles, the latter — although wholly consistent with and, in many respects, merely elaborative of the former — stimulated considerable controversy. Garfinkel's discussions of the processes of contextual determination and elaborative inference, which are *necessarily* involved in *any* process of description, were understood, especially in the aftermath of Cicourel's (1964, 1968, 1973) and Douglas's (1967) well-known studies, as proposing that many forms of social scientific research are at best essentially flawed and at worst impossible.

Garfinkel himself made no such assertions and they do not form part of any ethnomethodological programme. Instead he used his observations as a basis on which to recommend a research programme directed at examining *how* various types of social activity are brought to adequate description and thus rendered 'account-able'. Although the issues which he emphasizes raise some awkward questions for certain types of research methodology, it would be quite unwarranted to view Garfinkel's observations on descriptive accounting as the product of an extended exercise in methodological 'navelgazing' designed to mount a negative or nihilistic critique of sociological research. On the contrary, they represent a point of entry into a whole range of investigations into domains which had previously been overlooked including, most immediately, the detailed organization of practical reasoning in social interaction and the bases of institutionalized fact production.

Once attention is switched from the rather narrow area of sociological methodology, the full scope of this domain can readily be glimpsed. To do so, we simply need to recall that during a substantial proportion of their daily lives, ordinary members of society are engaged in descriptive accountings of states of affairs to one another. Discussions of the weather, depictions of goods and services, assessments of character and reports of the day's doings are the routine stock in trade of mundane talk. Such talk is *somehow* done seriously, realistically and as a feature of real practical tasks with significant outcomes for the parties concerned. Yet *how* is it done? There is no apparent answer. Moreover, before Garfinkel raised it, a limited version of the question was asked only within the confines of anthropology in the context of a developing preoccupation with 'folk' taxonomies (see, for example, Tylor, 1969).

Lacking the stimulus from 'exotic' languages or cultures, there has been little sociological interest in the workings of ordinary language. Yet the social world, indeed what counts as social reality itself, is managed, maintained and acted upon through the medium of ordinary description. For many occupations and agencies — including medical personnel, police, lawyers, welfare workers, accountants, journalists, insurance agents, loss adjusters, estimators, technicians and scientists — a concern for adequate description is a central preoccupation. But, despite their centrality to the operations of an overwhelming number of social activities and social institutions, the management of ordinary descriptions has rarely been the focus of sustained sociological interest. In sum, the properties of the ordinary transactions through which real world events are described, sorted and classified remained largely uncharted territory prior to Garfinkel's initiatives.

Although this neglect of ordinary descriptive activity has many tributaries, its major source lies in a pervasive and long-standing view which treats language exclusively in terms of its representative function. Within this view, the meaning of a word is what it references, corresponds with, or 'stands for' in the real world. Within this view the function of sentences is to express propositions, preferably true ones, about the world. Eminently commonsensical and yet possessed of a lengthy and comforting philosophical pedigree, this essentially pre-Wittgensteinian view of language has remained a tacit assumption for generations of social scientists. As such, it has permeated sociological activity at all its levels — empirical, theoretical and metatheoretical.

At the empirical level, the bulk of social scientific research ultimately rests on what ordinary actors report about their circumstances, experiences, attitudes and intentions. In this context, subject to controls on the design and manner of questioning and in some cases the maintenance of 'rapport', informants are routinely treated as competent and properly motivated reporters about their everyday affairs. With all the interest quite naturally focused on *what* the actors substantively report, empirical researchers have only intermittently had occasion to reflect on what the actors might be accomplishing in and through their acts of reporting. It is only in cases where doubts arise about the reliability and validity of reports that social scientists stop to enquire into the range of 'considerations' which might have shaped the respondents' utterances.

In just the same ways, organizational data have generally been treated — from Durkheim onwards — as having a simple factual status which is quite independent of the occasions and contingencies of their production. And, beyond this, the *ways* in which such data are realistic and can be measured so as to yield a real world of social events — all of this is treated as 'essentially uninteresting' (Garfinkel, 1967a: 7–9) for the conduct of practical research directed at real world events. Thus the fact that, through linguistic description and organized data production, social worlds can somehow be made available is necessarily treated as a non-investigable fact. It is 'not a matter for competent remarks'. It manifests itself as a simple bonus of studying a 'languaged' species.

Matters are scarcely different at the theoretical level where sociological interest in actors' descriptions has been severely limited by the assumptions of the 'sociology of error' (see above 67–9). Here the fact that actors can know and describe their everyday affairs competently and adequately is similarly regarded as an uninteresting matter. Instead attention is focused on those areas in which the actors' depictions of their worlds can be found to be significantly inaccurate or faulty. It is these latter areas which tend to be the focus of sociological investigation and explanation.

Finally, at the metatheoretical level, we re-encounter the earlier mentioned reliance on a pre-Wittgensteinian notion of description conceived in terms of correspondences between word and object. We have already met with this notion of language in Parsonian theory (see above 28–9). It is a conception in which 'a "sign" and "referent" are respectively properties of something said and something talked about, and which in this fashion proposes sign and referent to be related as corresponding contents' (Garfinkel, 1967a: 28). Within this conception, the essential task of language is to describe. And language can perform this function because the participants already agree in advance about what the words stand for. The net consequence of this position is the curtailment of sociological interest in language. For not only is the function of language constricted to the role of representation, but also its functioning is conceived as transparent in relation to its task. Sociological interest in the nature and functioning of language is thus narrowed to a vanishing point.

It will be obvious that the cumulative effect of this representative view of language is to drive an interest in the properties of actors' accounts of their everyday affairs to the margins of legitimate sociological concern. Garfinkel's attitude ran entirely counter to this stance of systematic neglect. Preoccupied with the question of how social actors encounter and manage a social world-in-common, he found that the properties of their descriptive accounts could not be marginalized in the prevailing fashion. Indeed their centrality to his theoretical problems could scarcely be avoided. Accordingly he embraced the whole topic as crucial to his concerns by making the 'mastery of natural language' − including the capacity to produce and recognize adequate descriptive representations of ordinary everyday affairs − the defining feature of an actor's membership of a society or collectivity (Garfinkel and Sacks, 1970: 342).

Garfinkel approaches the topic by stressing that understanding language is not to be regarded as a matter of 'cracking a code' which contains a set of pre-established descriptive terms combined, by the rules of grammar, to yield sentence meanings which express propositions about the world. Understanding language is not, in the first instance, a matter of understanding sentences but of understanding *actions* − utterances − which are constructively interpreted in relation to their contexts. This involves viewing an utterance against a background of *who* said it, *where* and *when*, *what* was being accomplished by saying it and in the light of what possible *considerations* and in virtue of what *motives* it was said. An utterance is thus the starting point for a complicated process of interpretative inference rather than something which can be treated as self-subsistently intelligible.

It will be apparent that Garfinkel's approach to the phenomena of mundane description is consistent with his overall focus on the accountable nature of social action. As we have seen, he views social action as designed with reference to how it will be recognized and described. Descriptions are no different. They are not to be regarded as disembodied commentaries on states of affairs. Rather, in the ways in which they (1) make reference to states of affairs and (2) occur in particular interactional and situational contexts, they will unavoidably be understood as actions which are chosen and consequential. Like other actions, descriptions are 'indexical' and are to be understood by reference to where and when etc. they occur. Like other actions too, descriptions are 'reflexive' in maintaining or altering the sense of the activities and unfolding circumstances in which they occur.

Before proceeding to explore these aspects of mundane descriptive accounting in detail, it is important to hold firmly in mind that Garfinkel is not concerned in any way with evaluating whether, or to what degree, the actors' depictions of their circumstances are correct or faulty. Neither, conversely, does he accord any analytical privilege to the actors' descriptions of their circumstances, for example by allowing that an actor's description can validate or invalidate what the social scientist says is happening. This stance is the famous policy of 'ethnomethodological indifference' (Garfinkel and Sacks, 1970: 345). As Garfinkel puts it elsewhere:

> Ethnomethodological studies are not directed to formulating or arguing correctives. They are useless when they are done as ironies. . . . They do not formulate a remedy for practical actions, as if it was being found about practical actions that they are better or worse than they are usually cracked up to be. (Garfinkel, 1967: viii)

This stance is effectively a variant of phenomenological 'bracketing' (see above 41–3) transferred to the study of

social process. Just as phenomenologists systematically suspended judgement on the ontological status of the objects
intended in acts of perception, cognition, etc. so as to
investigate how the latter are constituted in consciousness, so
Garfinkel 'brackets' all external judgements of the 'adequacy,
value, importance, necessity, practicality, success or con-
sequentiality' (Garfinkel and Sacks, 1970: 345) of descriptive
accountings. Instead, he treats the latter as purely and simply
'practical actions' and suspends judgement on their adequacy
etc. in order to focus on *how* they are used as facets of the
organization and management of social settings.

An important consequence of this procedure is that it
neutralizes the assumptions of the 'sociology of error' with its
distorting and one-sided emphasis on adequate correspondence as the only significant index of 'descriptive adequacy'.
For Garfinkel, the important thing about descriptions is that
they are *used* — to make available, maintain, transform or
otherwise manage concertedly organized social activities. In
this context, the question of whether and how mundane
descriptions are evaluated, interpreted, accepted or contested
— and in terms of what criteria and considerations — is an
empirical one. As such, it must be subjected to empirical
scrutiny rather than determined a priori. Thus it is only with
the 'brackets' firmly on that the study of ordinary accountings
can become a fully empirical project to be addressed by
naturalistic methods of study.

In sum, Garfinkel's interest is in descriptive accounts and
accountings as data which are to be examined to see how they
organize, and are organized by, the empirical circumstances
in which they occur. Far from being treated as external to
social activity, accounts are to be treated as subject to the
same range of circumstantial and interpretative contingencies
as the actions and circumstances they describe. In this
context, Garfinkel begins his discussion of accounts by noting
(Garfinkel, 1967a: 3) that their 'fit' to the circumstances they
describe is 'loose' and subject to adjustment by *ad hoc* devices;
that accounts, like actions, are understood by reference to a
mass of unstated assumptions and that the sense of an account
is heavily dependent on the context of its production.
Descriptive accounts, in short, are indexical.

INDEXICAL EXPRESSIONS

Notwithstanding its intricate ramifications, the general idea that the sense of descriptions is context bound is a readily accessible one. We take it for granted that when a speaker says 'That's a nice one', the hearer will need to have access to the context of the utterance in order to make sense of it. For, at the minimum, the referent of 'that's' will not be available to the hearer without such access.

The word 'that' in the previous example is a clear case of an *indexical* or *deictic* expression. It is one of a range of terms — others include here, now, this, that, it, I, he, you, there, then, soon, today, tomorrow — whose properties have been the object of extensive analysis in the fields of logic and linguistics (see Levinson, 1983: 45–96 for an overview). These disciplines have encountered indexical expressions as troublesome sources of resistance to the formal analysis of language and of reasoning practices. Garfinkel and Sacks cite the *Dissoi Logoi* (*c*.300 BC) which

> gives attention to the sentence 'I am an initiate' because it presents difficulties. The issue is that of the truth or falsity of the sentence when, if said by A it was true, but if said by B it was false; if said at one time by A it was true, but if said at another time it was false; if said by A from one status it was true, but if said by A from another it was false. (Garfinkel and Sacks, 1970: 347–8)

The central problem which the indexical terms present is that the referents of the terms, and hence the truth values of the statements in which they occur, vary with the circumstances in which they are uttered. Sentences containing these terms are thus highly resistant to techniques of formal analysis. From a sociological point of view, the interest of these terms derives from the fact that they can only be understood by drawing upon contextual knowledge. Thus in the previous example, the referent of 'that' might have been a photograph in family album, a diamond ring in a jeweller's window, or a lettuce in a greengrocer's shop. Whatever the referent of the utterance was, it could only be grasped by seeing who was speaking, or when or where it was said, or by knowing what had been said just previously.

Although it is sometimes assumed that the deictic expressions are exceptional in requiring contextual knowledge to understand them and that other descriptive terms stand in an unproblematic relationship to what they describe, this is not the case. For, if the other descriptive terms were to be unproblematic, they would have to be related to their referents through some determinate set of 'corresponding contents'. As we have seen, Garfinkel rejects this view and, with the help of a few examples, it will not be difficult to see why.

Consider our example, 'That's a nice one', being said by a visitor to a host while both are looking at a photograph album. The referent of 'that's' is established by the visitor pointing to a particular photograph, but what is the meaning of 'nice' here? It is obvious that 'nice' could mean a number of things in such a context. The visitor could be admiring the composition of the shot, or suggesting that the photograph was a good likeness of the host, or indeed that the host looked particularly well in the photograph. Whichever sense of 'nice' was intended is certainly not available from the utterance alone, but remains to be made out by the host in the light of the specifics of the photograph. Here, then, the 'corresponding contents' invoked by the term *remain to be discovered* by an active search of the referent. Quite a differently organized search will be initiated if the utterance is directed by a girl to her boyfriend in front of a jeweller's window. Once again, the referent may be identified by the girl's pointing to a particular ring, but the ring's property of niceness must be looked for in quite a different way. And different properties again will be looked for in a greengrocer's lettuce described as 'nice'.

These last considerations dramatically widen our sense of what is meant by 'indexical expressions'. Garfinkel uses the term not merely to capture the traditional philosophical problem of the *reference* of deictic terms, but also to note that the *sense* of ordinary descriptive terms is powerfully influenced by the context in which they are uttered. This consideration, in turn, leads him to a radical departure from prevailing assumptions about how natural languages work.

Instead of beginning from the assumption that the terms of a language invoke a fixed domain of substantive content and that their intelligibility and meaning rest upon a shared agreement between speakers as to what this content consists of, Garfinkel proposed an alternative *procedural* version of how description works. In this alternative version, he argues that the intelligibility of what is said rests upon the hearer's ability to make out what is meant from what is said according to *methods* which are tacitly relied on by both speaker and hearer. These methods involve the continual invocation of common-sense knowledge and of context as resources with which to make definite sense of indefinite descriptive terms. A major result of their use is that speaking is inevitably understood as action. In what follows, we will briefly trace through these themes.

MAKING DEFINITE SENSE WITH INDEFINITE RESOURCES

Any sustained observation of mundane description will very quickly yield the conclusion that it is impossible to characterize the relationship between descriptors and described in terms of clear-cut correspondences. Consider the following:

> The human visual system can discriminate some 7,500,000 different colours, but the most colour names reported in any language are 4,000 English names of which only 8 are used very commonly. No two plants — no two leaves, in fact — are identical, nor is any plant quite the same on successive days; however all cultures possess plant classification systems by which, at one or another levels of abstraction, billions of discrete, discriminable plants are rendered equivalent. (Rosch, 1975: 177; see also Bruner et al. 1956: 1 *et seq.*)

This immense order of difference between what we are capable of discriminating and what we are able to communicate about with the use of language is strongly supportive of Schutz's proposal that language is inherently *typifying*, a kind of 'treasure house of ready-made pre-constituted types and characteristics all socially derived and carrying along an open horizon of unexplored content' (Schutz, 1962a: 14). Thus, although│every│state of affairs may be unique, this fact is not reflected in our vocabulary. If it were, the result would necessarily be the continual invention of new terms. It is easy to see the uselessness of such a strategy. A lexicon which was continually expanded to accomodate each new circumstance would be unlearnable and unusable since, once the situation for which each term was formulated had passed, the term itself would lapse from use. Descriptors exist as formulations of commonalities across states of affairs, otherwise they would not 'describe.' Through their use, discriminable items — shades of colour, objects and events — are bundled together and treated as equivalent despite their individual differences from one another. Language is the medium through which these common-sense equivalence classes are constituted and communicated. It embodies a continual compromise between generality and specificity. There is thus an inherently approximate relationship between a descriptor and the range of states of affairs it may be used to describe.

In turn, this suggests that the boundaries of the applicability of a term will be indeterminate, negotiable and subject to change. We have already encountered this claim as a feature of finitist approaches to concepts and rule application (see above 120–2). Schutz too, in his discussion of language as a typifying medium, avoids treating the relationship between a type and the word which nominates it as one defined by reference to some fixed or closed 'corresponding contents' which are depicted by the word and contained in the type. Instead he suggests, following Husserl's observations in *Experience and Judgement* (1973), that mundane common-sense type terms are inherently flexible entities which, 'carrying along an open horizon of unexplored content', are subject to elaboration and extension by new experience and circumstances. For example, the child's conception of 'birds' may originate with small, flying species such as robins and sparrows and gradually expand to incorporate aquatic species (e.g. ducks), semi-flightless species (e.g. chickens), larger predatory species (e.g. hawks, eagles), flightless and aquatic penguins and, ultimately perhaps, birds which are known only through history books or paleontological reconstruction (e.g. the dodo or archeopterix) (cf. Rosch and Mervis, 1975; Rosch, 1977).

A similar process is observable even in the humble chimpanzee. The famous Washoe, it is reliably reported, initially acquired the manual Ameslan sign for 'open' in the context of two doors which had to be opened in order for her to get around her living compound. She subsequently learned to use the sign to request the opening of other doors, the refridgerator, cupboards, drawers, briefcases, boxes, bottles and jars and, finally, to request the turning on of taps. Here we witness the steady extension of a sign's application not only to different object domains, but also to reference actions having different mechanical characteristics and different concrete outcomes. And Washoe's achievement is far outstripped by human speakers. Cavell (1961: 220) invites us to consider the use of the term 'feed' in such expressions as 'feed the kitty', 'feed the lion', 'feed the swans', 'feed the meter', 'feed in the film', 'feed the machine', 'feed his pride' and 'feed wire' (cf. Pitkin, 1972: 61). Plainly the commonalities across this range of expressions are not great, yet somehow resemblances are drawn out from expression to expression such that all are intelligible and none appears as a misuse of the term.

In the context of his famous discussion of 'games', Wittgenstein proposed that numerous categories and concepts are not defined by reference to some fixed core of essential common attributes. Instead, he argued, they are defined by reference to 'family resemblances' which form a 'complicated network of similarities overlapping and criss-crossing: sometimes overall similarities, sometimes similarities of detail' (Wittgenstein, 1958: para. 66). Any network of family resemblances is ultimately established by reference to specific instances and cases. Such networks are open and unbounded and are not capable of exact or exhaustive definition, though in practice this does not inferfere with their use (ibid. paras 68–78). Category terms thus embody a range of within-category similarities and between-category differences. Categories are maintained or altered entirely through the accumulation of individual acts of judgement and their acceptance (or rejection) by other members of a language community (ibid.; see also Barnes, 1981, 1982a, 1982b).

Within this view, description and concept application are contingent, negotiable and revisable. Past usage does not necessarily determine future usage. The meaning of a concept or descriptor *is* the range of states of affairs to which it is applied, and the boundaries of that range are continuously reaffirmed or revised in new acts of speaking. Any category name will necessarily bear an inherently approximate relationship to the full range of its instances. There is an approximate relationship between the category name 'bird' and any particular species, just as there is an approximate relationship between the descriptor 'red' and some segment of those 7,500,000 discriminable colours.

Abstractly considered then, human descriptive resources are undoubtedly approximate. Rather than standing in straightforward correspondences with states of affairs, they seem on the contrary to locate fields of possibilities. This suggests that the earlier discussion of the various contextual meanings of the word 'nice' in the sentence 'That's a nice one' and the procedural basis on which these meanings are established may have a very general application. For given the approximate quality of descriptive terms, the uttering of a description, rather than pinpointing a definite property, must instead establish a focus for active 'contextualizing' work by the hearer which is aimed at interpreting what is meant.

The essentials of this work involve the documentary method of interpretation in which the description and its context elaborate each other. Thus the description evokes a context to be searched and, in turn, the results of this search elaborate the specific sense of the description. Such elaborating contexts may be quite diverse. They may, for example, be referents which are in full view of the speaker and hearer. Thus in the utterance 'There's a red sweater over here', the sense of red is qualified by the actual appearance of the sweater. On the other hand, the sentential context may be sufficient to invoke common-sense knowledge which elaborates the sense of a descriptor. Thus although the general sense of 'feed' may be indeterminate, this is not a problem when, for example, someone is asked to 'feed the meter'. In sum, hearers must

perform active contextualizing work in order to see what
descriptions mean, and speakers rely upon hearers performing
such work in order that their utterances will make definite
sense.

These contextualizing interpretative operations which
hearers perform on descriptive expressions transform the
effectiveness of the 'approximate', typified descriptive resources
which human beings have at their disposal. We have given
considerable attention to the lack of any precise, 'one-to-one'
relationship between descriptors and the states of affairs they
depict. The inherent approximation of the relationship
between, for example, the category name 'bird' and the range
of instances it nominates, or the colour term 'red' and the, say,
750,000 discriminable shades it references, may easily be
taken for a defect. Viewed in these terms, as approximate,
vague or indefinite, human descriptive resources may appear
scarcely adequate to the task of depicting specific objects and
events with clarity and discrimination.

However, such a view of descriptors is wholly abstracted.
It is based entirely on a comparison of the perceptual and
cognitive discriminations which are abstractly possible with
the terms in a language which are abstractly available. To use
this comparison to bemoan the paucity of human descriptive
resources is to tacitly identify the tasks and purposes of
mundane descriptions with the commitments of, for example,
a taxonomist or lexicographer. It is to implicate a standard of
linguistic description which is outside linguistic usage.

Ordinary descriptions are rarely produced with such
interests and are never produced in terms of such standards.
Moreover, ordinary descriptions are never produced in the
abstract. They occur in contexts which elaborate and particu-
larize their sense. For example, the descriptor 'red', predicated
of a London bus coming down the street, has its sense
reflexively elaborated and refined by the particular colour of
the referent object present to the vision of speaker and hearer.
The sense for 'red' that is proposed by the speaker and
achieved by the hearer will therefore be particular and locally
situated. The term, elaborated by its circumstance of use, will
be *sufficient* — to pick out the bus, or identify an aspect of it, or
indicate the colour the speaker plans to paint his front door.

And because this is the case, and the 'redness of red' is not the issue, there is no anxiety about the 'abstract indeterminacy' of the term. Neither the speaker nor the hearer notices or cares that, after all, the hearer's sweater could also be called 'red' and it is not the same colour. The term, understood in relation to its referent context, is adequate-for-all-practical-purposes.

It is, then, the practical and situated use of descriptions which permits their clarification and refinement to the point that they can be supplied with a sense that is adequate to their inferred task. In the same way, a description of a man as 'jealous' may be elaborated with a story of what he did when he thought he saw his wife with another man. Or again if, in a pencil and paper test situation, I am asked to 'name some typical birds', I may very likely mention robins and sparrows (Rosch, 1978). But neither is at all likely to come to mind when I am greeted at the door with: 'I've just put the bird in the oven.' In each case, although the descriptors 'red', 'jealous' and 'bird' — considered in the abstract — seem to locate fields of possibilities rather than nominating objects or their properties with precision, some aspect of the contexts in which they occur will, as Garfinkel puts it, 'unavoidably elaborate' their sense. It will be obvious that this process of contextualization in which descriptor and context mutually elaborate one another contributes immense refinement and definition to an apparently crude and undifferentiated descriptive system.

Many discussions of language use which have been stimulated by Garfinkel's observations take over the logico-linguistic assumption that the indexical features of natural languages are an inherent defect (see Schegloff, 1984 for further discussion). Viewed from the standpoint of the present discussion, such a view is deeply mistaken. For it is by virtue of our contextualizing activities as hearers that, as speakers, we can make good sense with a reasonably small vocabulary whose terms embody a network of criss-crossing resemblances. Our disposition to contextualize, put bluntly, enables us to 'economize' on words and makes the linguistic compromise between generality and specificity easier to establish and cope with. The indexical character of natural language use is thus a positive resource which we exploit, rather than a defect which, ideally, should be eliminated. It is also by virtue of this same contextualizing activity that we engage in a further interpretative process which has been set aside until now. This interpretative process involves the treatment of descriptions as *actions* and it is to this treatment that we now turn.

DESCRIPTION AS ACTION

A leading motif of Garfinkel's various discussions of descriptive accountings in his focus on the variety and complexity of the ways in which descriptions make contact both with the world of objects and the world of social relations. In the discussion of the previous section, this aspect of his thinking was totally ignored and we focused exclusively on a single interpretative task: the task of bringing words and objects into correspondence with one another. And we treated this task as the only one which a speaker imposes on a hearer. In the following discussion, we will widen this focus by examining some ways in which descriptions are unavoidably treated as actions. These matters are obviously immensely complex. When Garfinkel speaks of them as 'awesome', he does so without exaggeration. In what follows, therefore, an attempt will be made only to *illustrate* some features of the processes involved and thus to establish an outline of the issues at stake.

A useful starting point is to notice that no description is strictly *compelled* by the state of affairs it describes. Any description is thus inherently *selective* in relation to the state of affairs it depicts. This is so in several respects. First, no description, however detailed or extensive, can exhaust the state of affairs it describes. At the end of any description, it will always be found that there are further ways in which the referenced state of affairs could have been described. Thus any description 'lifts out' certain aspects of a referenced state of affairs into prominence, while disattending or discarding other aspects. Second, the description will be found to reference those aspects in a particular way. For example, the expression 'the red bus on the right' will be heard (1) to pick out a particular feature of the visual field of speaker and hearer — the bus — and (2) to characterize it in a particular way — in terms of its colour and location, rather than in terms of its passengers or how it is being driven. Third, a description is offered when the speaker might not have spoken. And part of the process of understanding it will involve grasping the purpose or motive for its being produced at a particular moment.

These three choices which underly any description — to describe or not, what to describe and how to describe it — are all sources of clues concerning how the description is to be interpreted. In effect, a hearer may interpret a description by asking: (1) why is the speaker referencing that object, (2) in that way, (3) right now? Moreover, the raising of such questions about an utterance inevitably involves the hearer's wider common-sense knowledge of the context in which it occurs and, more generally still, of social relations and human purposes. Thus, understanding a description involves a procedure in which the bringing of words and referents into correspondence with one another is integrated with a larger interpretation in terms of the wider social context and its relevant purposes.

To illustrate: returning to our host and visitor with the photograph album, if the host interprets the visitor's remark 'That's a nice one' as suggesting that the host looks attractive in the photograph, he or she may treat that remark as a 'compliment' or, if the host does not fully agree with the assessment, perhaps as 'flattery'. The description is not interpreted as simply a 'disembodied commentary' on the photograph, rather it is viewed as 'motivated' by reference to 'why that, in that way, right now?' And the motivational puzzle is resolved by invoking a social relationship which is integrated with the host's view of how the description matches its referent. Moving to the jeweller's window, our utterance may — through the raising and answering of the same questions — be heard as the girlfriend's 'hint' that a proposal of marriage would not be unwelcome. Moving the utterance to the greengrocer's shop and as produced by a customer about a lettuce, it may be interpreted by a salesperson as indicating a desire to purchase the lettuce in question (Levinson, 1979). In each of these latter cases, common-sense understandings of the environing social context are brought to bear on the description. In each case, the sense of the utterance as an action has been made out by seeing it as chosen in a specific context which is invoked and made relevant by the description, and for a particular purpose.

Our original utterance, it may finally be noted, is now triply indexical. Its *referent* could not be determined without a physical (or verbal) context. The *sense of particular expressions* (in this case 'nice') could not be made out without the use of context. Finally the *sense of the utterance* — now, unavoidably, construed as an action — could not be made out without invoking a social context which was co-ordinated with the sense of the particular descriptive terms.

In each of these simple cases, a wider context of interpretation is brought to bear on a description which is simultaneously being brought into rough correspondence with a referent state of affairs. Here are some more complex cases, in which an intendedly 'literal' correspondence between the description and the state of affairs cannot be straightforwardly achieved. All are presented in shorthand form.

(1) Staring out of the window at the pouring rain, a speaker observes: 'What a wonderful summer we're having!' The hearer does not assume that the speaker has lost control of the English language. Rather, viewing the utterance against the referent state of affairs and failing to establish a 'literal' correspondence, the hearer establishes a consistent fit between the two by concluding that the remark was intended to be ironical.

(2) Watching a TV report of an orderly political demonstration, a viewer remarks: 'Just look at that mob.' Rather than referring the speaker to an optician, the hearer interprets the reference to a 'mob' as designed to exaggerate the disorderly aspects of the protest and hence, in all probability, as designed to express political disagreement with the purpose of the demonstration.

(3) A speaker's reference to 'having a little trouble in the bathroom' is heard as a reference to constipation. Its vagueness is heard as euphemistic and is referred to constipation since the latter complaint is of a kind likely to surface in a 'bathroom' and is just the type of complaint

for which a euphemistic reference may be appropriate.
(4) At tea, a speaker observes: 'I could eat the whole of that cake' (Levinson, 1981a: 481). The hearer must make out whether this is a boast, a complaint (about the size of the piece the speaker has just been given), a request (for a large piece, or another piece), a compliment to the maker of the cake or some combination of all of these.

In each of these cases, a descriptive expression is addressed by reference to a range of interpretative procedures. As in the previous examples, this involves seeing how the expression could be referring (or, as in (4), otherwise 'attached') to some invoked state of affairs. It further involves, by a process in which the expression and the invoked state of affairs are permitted to stand in an elaborative relationship to one another, seeing what the sense of the expression — construed in terms of the speaker's purposes or attitude in uttering it — could possibly amount to. All of these procedural matters are directly addressed when Garfinkel writes:

> For the conduct of their everyday affairs, persons take for granted that what is said will be made out according to methods . . . *'Shared agreement' refers to various social methods for accomplishing the member's recognition that something was said-according-to-a-rule and not the demonstrable matching of substantive matters. The appropriate image of a common understanding is therefore an operation rather than a common intersection of overlapping sets* . . . In short, a common understanding, entailing as it does an 'inner' temporal course of interpretative work, necessarily has an operational structure. (Garfinkel, 1967a: 30–1; original italics)

These observations may be underlined by recalling that, just as the hearer makes out the sense of an utterance by methodic contextualizing operations, so the speaker relies upon the hearer's ability and willingness to perform them (see the discussion of 'trust' in chapter 4). In the following well-known example from Labov (1972: 123), there is a failure in this process:

Linus: Do you want to play with me Violet?
Violet: You're younger than me. (Shuts the door)
Linus: (puzzled) She didn't answer my question.

Here Violet relies upon a descriptive statement to accomplish her rejection of Linus's request. Linus's failure is one of failing to see that this statement sets out the grounds for the rejection of his request and that, therefore, it stands as the rejection itself.

In sum, speakers produce descriptive expressions with a view to having hearers make whatever range of contextual determinations as are required in order to find the sense of the description. This may involve invoking, *inter alia*, various aspects of the physical context − both referenced and unreferenced − in which the utterance occurs, conventions about the use of descriptive resources, the conversational or wider social context in which the utterance occurs, its institutional background, together with a range of assumptions about competent speaking, the goals of speaking and the nature of speakers. Here, then, we re-encounter the network of 'background assumptions' (discussed in chapter 4) which speakers trust one another to implement and in terms of which they hold one another accountable as competent users of natural language.

The sense of a descriptive utterance then is always contextually determined. Just as the range of contextual features which may be invoked to make sense of an utterance is wide, so too the range of possible contextual determinations is similarly extensive. A hearer may invoke one or another of these aspects of context so as to find that a description is intended to stand in a relationship of correspondence with what is described and that, in being so intended, the description is clear and definite or, alternatively, vague and ambiguous; that the description is truthful, objective or disinterested or, alternatively, false, biased or self-serving; that the speaker is claiming something or, alternatively, proposing it is an assured fact; that the description, in being incorrect, is the product, alternatively, of a mistake or a lie. The hearer may invoke context in order to hear that a description is being produced as a complaint, an accusation, a slur, slander, rationalization, excuse or justification; or to hear that the speaker was talking euphemistically, tactfully, cryptically, metaphorically or ironically (Garfinkel, 1967: 29). All of these senses of a description and innumerably more are contextually determined. They are some of the 'endless ways' in which a descriptor elaborates its circumstances and is elaborated by them (Garfinkel and Sacks, 1970: 338).

Garfinkel summarizes these proposals by the (much misunderstood) remark that, if we drop the theory of signs that links sign and referent in terms of 'corresponding contents',

> then what the parties talked about could not be distinguished from *how* the parties were speaking. . . . the recognized sense of what a person said consists only and entirely in recognizing the method of his speaking, of *seeking how he spoke*. (Garfinkel, 1967a: 28–9)

The point is exemplified in a later paper:

> For example, the natural language formula, 'The objective reality of social facts is sociology's fundamental principle,' is heard by professionals according to occasion as a definition of association members' activities, as their slogan, their task, aim, achievement, brag, sales pitch, justification, discovery, social phenomenon or research constraint. Like any other indexical expression, the transient circumstances of its use assure it a definiteness of sense as definition, or task or whatever, to someone who knows how to hear it. (Garfinkel and Sacks, 1970: 339)

It is these capacities — the capacity to 'understand' a description, to 'make out' from the description-in-its-context what the speaker is undertaking with the description and, with these resources, to determine what the description presently 'amounts to' — which constitute the defining characterisitics of 'mastery of natural language' or 'membership' (ibid. 342). As Garfinkel and Sacks summarize it:

> We understand mastery of natural language to consist in this. In the particulars of his speech a speaker, in concert with others, is able to gloss those particulars and is thereby meaning something different than he can say in so `many words; he is doing so over unknown contingencies in the actual occasions of interaction; and in so doing, the recognition that he is speaking and how he is speaking are specifically not matters for competent remarks . . . The idea of 'meaning

differently than he can say in so many words' requires comment. It is not so much 'differently than what he says' as that *whatever* he says provides the very materials to be used in *making out* what he says. However extensive or explicit what a speaker says may be, it does not by its extensiveness or explicitness pose a task of deciding the correspondence between what he says and what he means that is resolved by citing his talk verbatim. Instead his talk itself, in that it becomes a part of the self-same occasion of interaction, becomes another contingency of that interaction. It extends and elaborates indefinitely the circumstances it glosses and in this way contributes to its own accountably sensible character. (Garfinkel and Sacks, 1970: 344–5)

'Mastery of natural language' thus involves the speaker-hearer's capacity to use common-sense knowledge so as to make a for all practical purposes determination of the sense of a description as a phase in a contexted social activity. It similarly involves the speaker's capacity to design descriptions with a view to the kinds of determinations which a hearer will accountably make (see Sacks, 1972a; Schegloff, 1972; Drew, 1978; Atkinson and Drew, 1979; Pomerantz and Atkinson, 1984; Drew, 1984a, 1984b, Watson 1978 for some representative analyses of the range of considerations involved in the production and interpretation of descriptions). Within this framework, an actor's treatment of a description will unavoidably address it as *contexted*, as unavoidably an *action* which maintains, transforms or, more generally, *elaborates* its context of occurrence and, hence, as unavoidably a *temporally situated phase of a socially organised activity*. There is, once again, no 'time out' from these indexical and reflexive features of descriptive work.

In an early article, Sacks (1963) noted the incompleteness of a science which goes about its descriptive task by trading off the fact that its subject domain is endlessly generating self-descriptions, yet which fails to investigate what the properties of such descriptive activities might be. In focusing on the indexical and reflexive features of accounts and accountings, Garfinkel proposes that they are inevitably treated as actions. The partiality, incompleteness, to-be-contextually-elaborated vagueness, and contextually-interpreted-as-motivated qualities of descriptions all contribute to the actors' treatment of description in this way. Through these properties, the actor knows that no description is ever non-consequentially, non-methodically or non-alternatively produced (Garfinkel and Sacks, 1970: 359 *et seq.*) and that descriptions, like other actions, reconstitute the circumstances in which they occur.

A RESIDUE OF TROUBLES WITH INDEXICAL EXPRESSIONS

If we consider these characteristics as central to the natural history of descriptions and observe their workings in ordinary scenes of action and interaction, then we find that, for the most part, their presence as characterisitics of descriptions is utterly unproblematic. These properties of descriptions are, as Garfinkel puts it, 'seen but unnoticed', 'essentially uninterest-ing' and 'not matters for competent remarks'. Ordinary people are apparently no more interested in the indexical properties of descriptions than they are in the reflexive properties of action. Thus what we find are speakers who competently and comfortably get on with the business of producing and interpreting talk by reference to sets of contextual considerations; who 'adequately grasp' what descriptions accomplish with reference to their contexts; who determine the purposes of describers by reference to that accomplishment; and who determine what could, or should, be accountably done in response to such descriptions — all without strain or difficulty.

However, Garfinkel insists on one major domain of excep-tions to this prevailing tone of ease and comfort with the indexical features of descriptions. This exceptional domain arises as soon as actors are called upon to make evident, or defend, the clarity, precision, exhaustiveness, consistency, reproducibility, objectivity, disinterestedness — i.e. the ration-ality — of their descriptions, explanations and accounts. In such contexts, the central features of descriptions — the unavoidable reliance by their users on procedures of con-textual determination and their context-elaborative properties — obtrude as problems for which remedies are sought in the 'neutralization', discounting or elimination of contextual attachments. Garfinkel is adamant that, under these circumstances, the contextual attachments of descriptions emerge as difficulties – and emerge in the same ways as difficulties – for natural-language users regardless of whether the latter are ordinary society members or professional social scientists. The problems emerge with obstinate persistence regardless of whether the matter concerns ordinary conversationalists trying to justify a character assessment, or a trans–sexual trying to assert who he/she 'really' is (Garfinkel, 1967e), or persons trying to determine equivalent treatment in plea bargaining (Sudnow, 1965), in social security claims (Zimmerman, 1969a, 1969b), in the administration of reading tests (Cicourel *et al.* 1974) and so on. In each case, the problematic contextual attachments of a description or assessment are met by some attempt at erasure. The description, it is usually proposed, is transcendent of its practical circumstantial features and hence is to be treated as 'literal'. Yet this literalness can never involve a full disengagement from contextual features, but only the claim that the contextual features do not bear significantly on the provenance of the description in such a way as to contaminate or discredit it. Strictly speaking then, a literal description cannot be demonstrably achieved, and, as a result, 'in every actual case without exception, conditions will be cited that a competent investigator will be required to recognize, such that in *that* particular case the terms of the demonstration can be relaxed and nevertheless the demonstration be counted an adequate one' (Garfinkel, 1967a: 6). 'Literalness', then, is always and only achieved 'for all practical purposes'.

Social scientists, of course, are not exempted from the tasks of interpretation through which the sense of descriptions, the propriety of assigning an event to a category, the adequacy of a rule formulation, etc. are achieved and justified. As Garfinkel puts it,

Drawing on their experience in the uses of sample surveys, and the design and application of measurements of practical actions, statistical analyses, mathematical models and computer simulations of social processes, professional sociologists are able to document endlessly the ways in which the programmatic distinction and substitutability [of objective for indexical expressions] is satisfied in, and depends upon, professional practices of socially managed demonstration. (Garfinkel, 1967a: 6–7)

Yet the sociologist's task is further complicated by the fact that the data upon which analysis is based are themselves the products of similar tasks of interpretation and demonstration which have already been accomplished by the members of society. This phenomenon greatly complicates the tasks of sociological analysis. Moreover, it renders the goal of establishing social science investigations on a firm and principled methodological footing extremely difficult to achieve. These difficulties may underly the 'pre-paradigmatic' status of many contemporary social science activities.

In the following few pages, some of these problems will be briefly illustrated by reference to routine aspects of social science research technique involving such matters as the interpretation of questionnaire responses and official data. We begin with Garfinkel's classic observations on coding.

ASPECTS OF INTERPRETATIVE PROCESSES IN SOCIOLOGICAL WORK

Coding Organizationally Produced Data

In the early sixties, Garfinkel participated in a project designed to determine the criteria by which applicants were selected for treatment in a psychiatric clinic. The study attempted to assess the passage of potential patients towards treatment by means of a 'clinic career form' inserted into the case folder of each patient as an adjunct to the patient's other medical records. In this way, decision points and their criteria could be made available in a form suitable for treatment by cohort analysis and related techniques. The researchers were interested in discovering what features of patients, of clinical workers, and of their interactions, etc. were associated with particular treatment 'careers'. Published papers which have resulted from this study include a penetrating discussion of the methodological problems associated with such studies (Garfinkel, 1967g) and an analysis of how the 'clinic career forms' were used by medical personnel (Garfinkel, 1967f).

As part of the project, a coding scheme was devised for the analysis of the 'clinic career forms' and conventional studies were conducted to establish coder reliability. Garfinkel became interested in the coding process itself (Garfinkel, 1967a: 18–24) and found that a strangely circular phenomenon was at work in which 'in order to accomplish the coding, coders were assuming knowledge of the very organized ways of the clinic that their coding procedures were intended to produce descriptions of' (ibid. 20). Investigating the process in detail, Garfinkel found that the coders regularly encountered an interpretative gap between what the coding instructions provided for and what was on the clinic career form. They bridged this gap in the same ways that other kinds of rules are fitted to the specifics of particular circumstances (see above 120–6), i.e. by the *ad hoc* practices of 'et cetera', 'unless', 'let it pass' and so on. The coders did this in order to see the records on the clinic career forms as indices of 'real clinic events' and hence to code them in terms of 'what the coding instructions meant' when applied to the 'records as indices of real events'.

Garfinkel notes that this *ad hocing* occurred despite the fact that strict actuarial coding rules could be formulated and followed. But, for the coders, acting in strict accordance with formal coding procedures was felt to be tantamount to merely 'going through the motions' and as involving an almost hypothetical exercise in which the data were coded without regard to the facts-the-data-documented. Attempts to suppress this use of *ad hoc* considerations, Garfinkel comments (ibid. 21), produced bewilderment in the coders. In sum, the coders used *ad hoc* considerations

in order to recognize the relevance of the coding instructions to the organized activities of the clinic. Only when this relevance was clear were the coders satisfied that the coding instructions analysed actually encountered folder contents so as to permit the coders to treat folder contents as reports of real events (ibid).

Moreover, Garfinkel reports that this presupposed knowledge of clinic activities

> seemed necessary and was most deliberately consulted when-
> ever, for whatever reasons, the coders needed to be satisfied
> that they had coded 'what really happened'. *This was so
> regardless of whether or not they had encountered 'ambiguous' folder
> contents.* (ibid. 20)

Thus even this most mundane and preliminary social scientific task cannot be sensibly accomplished without a measure of 'interpretative realism'. This realism consists of 'seeing the system' in the folder contents, of recognizing the folder contents for 'what they actually are' or 'seeing what a note in the folder "is really talking about" ' (ibid. 22–3). It involves, in short, treating the data as signifying a factual order.

The maintenance of 'interpretative realism' required the mobilization of a range of *ad hoc* practices through which an imputed factual order could be located in the particulars of the data. Thus the coders used *ad hoc* procedures to 'recognize' the clinic's activities in the particulars of the 'clinic career forms'. They used them again to reconcile, or find the 'best fit', between the various categories intended by the coding schedule and the particulars in the forms which they treated as signifying as actual order of clinic events.

In sum, the use of *ad hoc* procedures was an unavoidable feature of coding activities. As Garfinkel puts it:

> To treat instructions as though *ad hoc* features in their use were
> a nuisance, or to treat their presence as grounds for complaint
> about the incompleteness of instructions, is very much like
> complaining that if the walls of a building were only gotten out
> of the way one could see better what was holding the roof up
> . . . It is not the case that 'necessary and sufficient' criteria are
> procedurally defined by coding instructions. Nor is it the case
> that *ad hoc* practices such as 'et cetera' or 'let it pass' are
> controlled or eliminated in their presence, use, number or
> occasions of use by making coding instructions as definite as
> possible. Instead *ad hoc* considerations are consulted by coders

and *ad hocing* practices are *used in order to recognize what the
instructions are definitely talking about.* *Ad hoc* considerations are
consulted by coders in order to recognize coding instructions
as 'operational definitions' of coding categories. They operate
as the grounds for and as methods to advance and secure
researchers' claims to have coded in accordance with 'necessary
and sufficient' criteria. (Garfinkel, 1967a: 22)

If *ad hoc* procedures are unavoidable, and through their use an
order of clinic events is 'pre-delineated' in the data-as-coded,
then it follows that, to the extent that they are reliably
employed by coders, a determinate order of clinic events will
be visible to the user of the data-as-coded which is the
unavoidable product of the coders' own interpretative activities.
Thus

it can always be argued – and so far I do not see a defensible
reply – that the coded results consist of a persuasive version of
the socially organized character of the clinic's operations,
regardless of what the actual order is, perhaps independently
of what the actual order is, and even without the investigator
having detected the actual order. (Garfinkel, 1967a: 23)

To propose this is not, of course, to advocate the abandonment of coding because it 'contaminates' data through an
interpretative process. It is to recognize that the unavoidable
gap between data and its sense is unavoidably and irreversibly
bridged, at least in part, by a coding process having unknown
characteristics.

As we have seen, this interpretative process is an essential
feature even of such a low-level activity as the coding of data.
It is essential because the accomplishment of coding requires
some closure of the interpretative gap between the 'words on a
page' and what they mean. This gap is a familiar one. It is the
one we have already encountered between 'saying' and
'meaning' in the previous discussion of mundane speaking
and hearing. The gap is encountered still more pointedly at
higher levels of social scientific analysis of data. It can be
illustrated by reference to the interpretation of questionnaire
responses, to which we now turn.

Using Aggregate Responses to Questionnaire Items

Consider the following research circumstance: it is an idealized version of a commonplace finding in studies of white-collar organizations.

Interviewing a sample of employees in a large commercial organization, a social scientist finds that equal proportions (say 75 per cent) of both routine clerical workers and managerial staff state, in response to a fixed-choice questionnaire item, that their job has 'a lot of responsibility'. As it stands, this observation has the status of a mere finding. It is puzzling, however, that both groups of employees should respond so similarly since common-sense, conventional managerial wisdom and social scientific analysis all converge in suggesting that different jobs in the hierarchy of the organization carry different levels of responsibility. The social scientist's task is to make sense of the finding. A number of possibilities suggest themselves:

(1) The responses are intended by the respondents as purely descriptive of the facts of the matter. In reality, however, they reflect common normative orientations concerning 'responsibility'.

(2) The responses are intended by the respondents as purely descriptive of the facts of the matter, but reflect the application of different criteria of 'responsibility' by clerks on the one hand and managers on the other.

(3) The responses are intended to be heard by the researcher as purely descriptive of the facts of the matter, but are in fact artefacts of the self-presentation of personnel: no one likes to admit that his or her job is devoid of responsibility.

(4) The responses are intended to be heard by the researcher as purely descriptive of the facts of the matter, but in fact reflect the belief that the researcher may pass on judgements about the attitudes and motivations of individuals to higher management.

(5) The responses are intended to be heard by the researcher as purely descriptive of the facts of the matter,

but in fact reflect tensions and frustrations about current
levels of pay: they implicate complaints about current levels
and justify the demand for higher levels.

(6) However the responses were intended, they were in fact
generated by the interviewer's comportment during the
administration of the questionnaire or of other aspects of
the 'interview situation'.

(7) The responses were intended by the respondents as
purely descriptive of the facts of the matter. Moreover, they
report on an objective fact of organizational life: mistakes or
theft by clerks can cost millions just as similar derelictions
by managers can.

There are many more alternative interpretations including
various combinations of the above.

Plainly, whichever interpretation is finally arrived at, it will
variously excite or disappoint different research interests and
expectations. A social scientist interested in career aspirations
who arrives at (2) above may find this interpretation
supportive of a hypothesis relating clerical status to low
horizons of career aspiration. Arriving at (3), the same social
scientist might be inclined to discard the data as uninformative.
By contrast, an industrial psychologist interested in the
motivating value of 'self-esteem' might find the 'data under
interpretation (3)' to be significant confirmatory evidence for
this viewpoint. Or again, an organizational theorist or a
critical theorist arriving at (1) might, from their different
perspectives, be interested in the ways and conditions through
which persons can be brought to such counterfactually
equivalent assessment – depicted, perhaps, under such head-
ings as 'organizational morale' and 'ideological hegemony'
respectively. Many other, more complex possibilities are available.

Moving beyond the different interests in the various
interpretations of the data, it is clear that the interpretations
themselves will be arrived at as the product of a large and
heterogeneous complex of considerations. Thus the social
scientist may review the notes made at the time of the
interview; reconsider the 'atmosphere' in the company or
office building researched in; he or she may consider the issues

— perhaps a pay negotiation or an organizational restructuring exercise — which were 'live' at the time of the interview; he or she may consider the consistency of the pattern of responses with others in the questionnaire or compare the findings with the literature on respondent bias. Most significantly — for it is this consideration which motivates a treatment of the results as 'puzzling' in the first place — the researcher will invoke some kind of judgement of what it would be reasonable for the employees to believe given the facts-as-the-researcher-knows-them and the facts-as-they-are-probably-available-to-the-employees.

Whatever the bases of the interpretation and whatever the social scientist decides, it will be apparent that *if the data are to be counted as evidence* some interpretation must be arrived at. The mere fact that 75 per cent of each type of respondent answered in the way they did is, as it stands, a mere occurrence. It has the same status as an instrument read out for a physicist. The data in both cases mean nothing without an interpretation.

In the case of the sociological data, what does this interpretation consist of? The answer can only be that, with the aid of various contextual considerations partially illustrated above, the researcher examines what the respondents said with a view to determining *how they spoke*. In this way the researcher will eventually decide whether the responses were veridical, deluded, cynical, self-serving, artefactual or whatever. And in turn, given one or another of these decisions, a determination will have been made which will decide whether, or in what ways, the data is 'evidence' and, as part of this determination, what it is evidence for.

Once again, there is no 'time out' from this process of interpretation because it is necessitated by the unavoidable contextuality of acts of speaking. The problem will not go away even if the investigator issues detailed instructions to respondents about how they should respond 'in order to guarantee that the investigator will be able to study their usages as instances of the usages the investigator has in mind' (Garfinkel, 1967b: 70). For even in this case, the investigator still has to determine whether the instructions were followed and that the responses were instances of what was being looked for. And this involves exactly the same range of interpretative issues as before.

Here then, just as the coder was compelled to find ways of 'seeing the system' in the folder contents as a means of getting the coding realistically done, so too the questionnaire user has to bootstrap a way beyond the literal 'face value' of the responses in order to see them as evidences of a social arrangement whose existence is called into being, but not in its specifics compelled by, this very process of interpretation. This process too involves a parallel range of *ad hoc* practices. Social scientific interpretations of data are not controlled by algorithms, nor are they subject to formal or 'fully interpreted' decision procedures. Instead, the gap between the data and an-order-which-the-data-signify is filled by an unknown procedure of indeterminate scope which is defended and justified by reference to 'reasonable considerations'.

In sum, whenever the gap between the data and the data-as-evidence is bridged, it is bridged through the operation of the documentary method of interpretation. Garfinkel summarizes the issues and their bearing on social scientific research in the following terms:

> In reading a journal account for the purpose of literal replication, researchers who attempt to reconstruct the relationship between the reported procedures and the results frequently encounter a gap of insufficient information. The gap occurs when the reader asks how the investigator decided the correspondence between what was actually observed and the intended event for which the actual observation is treated as its evidence. The reader's problem consists of having to decide that the reported observation is a literal instance of the intended occurrence, i.e. that the actual observation and the intended occurrence are identical *in sense* . . . It is at this point that the reader must engage in interpretative work and an assumption of 'underlying' matters 'just known in common' about the society in terms of which, what the respondent said, is treated as synonymous with what the observer meant. Correct correspondence is apt to be meant and read on reasonable grounds. (Garfinkel, 1967c: 95–6)

Examples of this phenomenon can be multiplied indefinitely and at every level of the research enterprise. For example,

Hindess (1973) has persuasively argued that a census form can always be devised and administered so as to yield a set of results regardless of how nearly it catches at the social arrangements it is designed to illuminate. Yet, as Hindess's own discussion amply demonstrates, the relationship between the results of a census and some actual order of social arrangements — Hindess's own example concerns the 1951 Census of India and the prevailing system of land tenure in that country — is not prescribed 'in' the results or 'by' the results. Rather, it remains to be determined. The gap between what is 'on the record' and 'what the record actually represents' always remains to be interpretatively closed, and closed by reference to what is known about some actual order of arrangements independently of 'the record'. What the record actually represents is thus grasped in an interpretative process in which the record is compared with 'what is known' and the sense of each is elaborated to accomodate the other. In this context, the problem of grounding reasonable findings in evidence consists of the problem of interpreting data as 'evidence' using a background of well-grounded matters 'just known in common' in such a way that the social scientist can be 'instructed' by materials while avoiding being 'misled' by them (Garfinkel, 1967c: 100–3).

In stressing that there is always a gap between the data and 'what the data signify' which is repeatedly bridged by interpretative procedures in the various stages of social scientific enquiry, Garfinkel is insistent that he is not criticizing, ironicizing, correcting or attempting to supplement standard social scientific methodologies (Garfinkel, 1967: viii). Neither does he claim exemption from these interpretative processes for ethnomethodological studies. Moreover, except with respect to the specific investigations he has conducted (e.g. Garfinkel, 1967g), Garfinkel does not claim to have uncovered anything about social scientific methodology which is not already known to a greater or lesser extent by one or another group of social scientists.

What is distinctive about Garfinkel's treatment of these issues is the attitude he takes towards them. As he points out (ibid. 100–1), the vast majority of social scientists treat the interpretative processes as a contaminant of research findings or as an obstacle in the way of fully scientific results. Correspondingly, the significance of these processes is minimized in the. descriptions of methods textbooks. For Garfinkel, by contrast, the unavoidable and overwhelming presumption of and reliance upon common-sense processes of interpretation in the production, recognition and evaluation of reasonable research findings suggests an alternative posture. If common-sense processes of interpretation are, in various ways, unavoidable, then it is essential to know what their properties are. Investigations of the 'reasonable' bases of knowledge and inference at the common-sense level are clearly implicated. And these studies further suggest an investigation of whether, or to what extent, these reasonable bases are modified in the context of specific institutional domains. These suggestions will be further developed after a consideration of our final case study, which concerns the use of offical statistics.

Analysing Official Statistics

Perhaps the single most controversial ethnomethodological contribution to the sociological debates of the past decade has centred on attitudes towards the use of organizationally generated statistics. Major discussions addressing this domain have included Cicourel's (1968) pioneering studies of police processing and disposal of juvenile crime cases, the same author's analyses of the generation and use of demographic data (1974) and Garfinkel's (1967g) profound discussion of the use of cohort analysis in quantitative studies of careers in outpatient clinics. In the present section, however, we will focus on the debate about the use of official statistics in the study of suicide not only because several researchers have contributed to this discussion (e.g. Atkinson, 1978; Douglas, 1967; Garfinkel, 1967i), but also because the prominent status of this topic within sociology may help most readers to keep track of a necessarily rapid discussion.

The use of official statistics of suicide, pioneered by the moral statisticians of the nineteenth century, has been a fertile source of sociological observations and debates ever since the publication of Durkheim's paradigmatic *Le Suicide* in 1897. The sociological fascination of this work has quite transcended its many conceptual and methodological shortcomings (Pope, 1976) and, although it undoubtedly derives from many sources (Atkinson, 1978: 9–32), at least one component of this fascination stems from Durkheim's use of statistical data to debunk common-sense notions of the causes of suicide and to establish the supremacy of sociological analysis in the field.

Naturally these objectives, pursued in the context of competing theories of suicide, have placed a considerable strain on the official suicide statistics which form the data base for the arguments between the major protagonists. One result of this has been a lengthy search for improvements in the detail and completeness of this data base. Ironically, two of the major critiques of the use of official suicide statistics in fact arose out of sociological work originally designed to improve the statistical data base (Atkinson, 1978: 3–5; Douglas, 1967: vii). Paradoxically, a major conclusion of both these studies lay in the recommendation to return to the common-sense conceptions of suicide rejected by Durkheim — though treating them this time as objects of study, rather than as competitive with sociological analysis. In the following paragraphs we will briefly review some of the major steps in the suicide debate, beginning with anxieties about the nature and uses of official data.

Anxieties about the use of official data in analyses of suicide occur at broadly three levels of intensity. At the first, and relatively unproblematic level, researchers have complained about the insufficiency of official data for their investigative tasks. For example, sociologists have criticized the inaccuracy and incompleteness of the 'face-sheet' data relating to the population of suicides. Similarly, psychiatricly oriented researchers have complained about the absence of 'background' information on suicides — in some cases finding this lack sufficiently compelling to deter them from the use of official data altogether. By and large, these doubts are the most superficial and the most easily stilled. The normal response to anxieties of this sort is to dig more deeply into the official records or, alternatively, to instigate parallel studies involving the relatives and associates of suicides so as to check up or fill in the record in more detail.

At a second level of doubt, anxieties have repeatedly arisen concerning the extent of error and the degree of completeness with which the suicide statistics capture the real incidence of suicide. In the literature on suicide, as in other areas of deviancy, the prevailing view is that the statistics understate the real population of suicides (Atkinson, 1978; Douglas, 1967) largely because a substantial but unknown proportion of suicides are successfully concealed. Knowledge of the existence of this 'dark number problem' is widespread, for example, *The Times* newspaper recently carried an item stating that a substantial number of motorway crashes in West Germany might be attributable to suicidal intent and that the suicide rate in that country was consequently higher than previously thought.

With respect to this dark number problem, it is generally held that investigation of the suicide statistics need not be suspended provided that it can be accepted that the statistics report a representative sample of the population of suicides. In this context, the go-ahead for studies of the official statistics is urged on a variety of grounds. Prominent among these are: that we have no reason yet to doubt their representativeness since, in all probability, they capture a high proportion of the real population of suicides; that since the suicide rates are stable over time and since stability is inconsistent with error or unrepresentativeness, studies may proceed; that despite an unknown level of representativeness, the statistics are accurate as far as they go; etc. These proposals are often supported by reference to collateral studies of 'undiscovered deviants' whose characteristics as a population can be compared with the population of the 'discovered' (cf. Atkinson, 1978: 36 *et seq.* for a detailed discussion of these views), even though the support for official data that might be garnered from such strategies would itself be dependent on the unsupported assumption that the newly discovered sample of 'undiscovered' deviants is itself representative of its population.

In sum, this second order of question concerning the representativeness of official statistics is traditionally met by asserting that there is no alternative to regarding the statistics as representative, or no need to do otherwise, or that comparisons with other populations of unknown representativeness are not sources of disquiet (see Atkinson, 1978: 57 *et seq.* for an account of some recent studies). At this stage of the argument, the problem of representativeness appears controllable.

Nonetheless, the assumption that the suicide rates are representative has been seriously challenged by Douglas (1967) who makes a strong a priori case for differential rates of concealment. The argument may be run at several levels and with respect to most of the variables which Durkheim and subsequent researchers have treated as significant. Thus it can be argued (e.g. McCarthy and Walsh, 1966) that Catholic suicides for example, because of the greater sanctions of the Catholic church on suicide, may tend to elect 'more equivocal' modes of death (e.g. by drowning, jumping or, more recently, alcohol-barbiturate combinations) and avoid the creation of other evidence (e.g. suicide notes) in a bid to avoid detection which contrasts with other religious affiliates. By the same token Catholic families may be more strongly motivated to conceal evidence of suicide. Similarly, it can be proposed that a lone individual (or, indeed, an individual without life insurance) may have less motivation to choose an equivocal, but inconvenient or unpleasant, mode of death than a family member: that the persons making up the lone individual's social network may lack the capacity or the motivation to conceal evidences of suicide, and that these capacities and motivations will, more generally, be varyingly structured by a variety of motivative conventions (Douglas, 1967: 203–29).

Viewed from the standpoint of traditional suicidology, Douglas's case is extremely difficult to meet. If his observations find support — and so far they have not been seriously challenged — then the suicide statistics would have to be treated, at least provisionally, as the unrepresentative artefacts of such processes as the above and hence as bearing an unknown relationship to the real population of suicides. This interpretative consequence of Douglas's arguments is plainly unacceptable to traditional workers in suicidology and this fact may go some considerable way towards explaining the 'magnificent isolation' of his observations which are acknowledged, but otherwise ignored, within the suicide literature (Atkinson, 1978: 64–66).

At the third, final and even more problematic level of

doubt, social scientists have become concerned with the definitions and procedures used for identifying suicides. The issue arose initially in the context of sociological definitions. In Durkheim's study, for example, it was apparent that his ingenious definition of suicide (as 'every case of death which results directly or indirectly from a positive or negative act, accomplished by the victim himself which he knows must produce this result' (Durkheim, 1952: 44)) failed to square with those in official use with the result, as Halbwachs (1978) pointed out, that Durkheim's definition of suicide and certain considerations based on it (e.g. the discussion of altruistic suicide) were simply redundant. (Durkheim's careful exercise in definition appears still more quixotic in the British context where no official definition of suicide exists (Atkinson, 1978: 89–93).)

The problem of definition ceases to be a formal, even 'legalistic', problem however when it is recognized that the practices and procedures of death certification may not be uniform. The attempt to compare suicide rates over time, between countries and within countries, is often nullified by the use of different definitions of suicide and different procedures for implementing the classification of deaths. The incompatibility and non-comparability of the resulting statistics have been repeatedly documented in the suicide literature (see Atkinson, 1978 and Douglas, 1967 for reviews). A discussion of these issues by Stengel and Farberow, two leading suicidologists, culminated in the following plea:

> We should press for the certification of suicide being entirely freed from its association with the criminal law and to be made a medical responsibility with proper safeguards . . . And we should aim at uniformity of certification procedures and the adoption of common operational criteria for case finding. (Stengel and Farberow, 1967: 13)

Here, perhaps, we find the paradoxical outcome of the commitment to the use of official statistics: if only the world were run on lines suggested by the social scientist, then the social scientist would be in a proper position to describe the lines the world is run on. But if Stengel and Farberow's plea amounts, to restate an earlier quote from Garfinkel, to instructing 'the construing member to act in accordance with the investigator's instructions in order to guarantee that the investigator will be able to study their usages as instances of the usages the investigator has in mind' (Garfinkel, 1967b: 70), the outcome will nonetheless be just as problematic as before. For it is still necessary to determine that Stengel and Farberow's 'common operational criteria' were, in fact, implemented and this would necessarily involve the social scientist in checks on the certifying officers as they go about their tasks. At the end of the day, the logical outcome of this suggestion is that social scientists should do the certifying in the interests of consistency. We thus arrive at last at the problem which haunts us, namely how do the certifying officers determine the fact of suicide and could a social scientist accompanying these officers know differently or better?

The social scientist who begins to accompany a certifying officer in his work will find, according to Garfinkel, that the officer's enquiries treat a death

> as a precedent with which various ways of living in society that could have terminated with that death are searched out and read 'in the remains'; in the scraps of this and that like the body and its trappings, medicine bottles, notes, bits and pieces of clothing, and other memorabilia — stuff that can be photographed, collected and packaged. Other 'remains' are collected too: rumours, passing remarks, and stories — materials in the 'repertoires' of whosoever may be consulted via the common work of conversations. These *whatsoever* bits and pieces that a story or rule or proverb might make intelligible are used to formulate a recognizably coherent, standard, typical, cogent, uniform, planful, i.e. a professionally defensible, and thereby, for members, a *recognizably* rational account of how the society worked to produce those remains. (Garfinkel, 1967a: 17)

The social scientist will find too that the character of each death is 'continually postdicted and foretold' (ibid.) by reference to whatever data come to hand; that 'the circumstances of the death' — including certain methods, places and times of death, evidences of 'depression' and grounds for depression in debt, separation, isolation and illness (Atkinson, 1978) are used to foretell and postdict suicide verdicts. The social scientist will find that the officer encounters a 'gap' between the data and 'what the data mean' which is closed by reasonable interpretation given 'what is usually the case' and 'what is a defensible conclusion under the circumstances'; that the officer is chronically aware of the possibilities of conceal-ment and its motivations on the part of the deceased and the relatives and that, in considering the evidence, the officer may 'err on the side of caution' in proposing suicide only on the 'strongest' or 'incontrovertible' evidence. He or she will find that the officer entertains beliefs about 'reasons for living' and 'reasons for dying' and about the types of people who die for good and bad reasons. The social scientist may find that a coroner, in weighing the adequacy of the evidence before him, is managing the evidence and its interpretative implications so as to balance the reputation of the court against the distress of the family, or the coroner's judgement as an individual against the outrage of the community or the censure of his peers.

To refer to the above aspects of a certifying officer's judgements — and the above list does not even begin to gloss what is already known about coroner's fact-finding procedures (Garfinkel, 1967i; Atkinson, 1978) — is not merely to suggest that those who research the suicide statistics are seeking to explain materials which have already been subject to expla-nation. Nor is it merely to assert that, at best, the researchers will tend to recover aspects of the more generally used explanatory accounts which have been built into the suicide verdicts as their constitutive features (Atkinson, 1978). Rather it is to notice, to adapt Garfinkel's formulation (Garfinkel, 1967g: 215), that the existence of suicide and its associated rates 'consists only and entirely of the likelihood that socially organized measures for the detection of suicide can be enforced'. And hence that the methodological difficulties associated with a 'real' or 'representative' suicide rate 'consist of the very features of the socially organized activities whereby the existence of culturally defined real suicide is detected, described and reported' (ibid.). A suicide rate, in short, is the constituted product of some set of socially organized methods for the 'making out' of suicides from a variety of remains. What are these methods? In what ways is their implementation shaped by scientific, professional, judicial, sentimental and other considerations? Once these questions are asked, an immense array of accounting practices and their organizational exigencies, previously occluded from view by the preoccupation with accuracy, are laid open as possible avenues of investigation. It would not be an exaggeration to suggest that the sociology of suicide is scarcely born until these questions and their implications have been squarely faced.

At the beginning of this chapter it was observed that Garfinkel's remarks on methodology are in no way nihilistic, either in intention or in implication. It is perhaps appropriate to conclude these case studies of sociological methodology by returning briefly to this proposal. Let us first consider what has been asserted in these sections. Pared to a minimum, the claim is that interpretative processes of unknown scope and variety (Garfinkel, 1967c: 100–3) are necessarily implemented in 'making sense' of sociological data. These processes are overwhelmingly operative, without remission, in every stage and aspect of sociological research. Through these processes, common-sense knowledge of social organization is repeatedly built into the reasonable findings (Garfinkel, 1967: 100) as a constitutive feature of those findings.

A large amount of the interpretative work of social science is directed, to recall a phrase from the earlier discussion of language use, at 'seeing how the parties spoke'. In the coding task, the coders' efforts were directed at understanding the organizational conditions and exigencies in terms of which the comments on the record sheets came to be made. In the study of the commercial organization, the interpretation of the tables of results involved a similar effort aggregated over numbers and types of speakers. In the case of suicide, the coroners were forced to engage in similar interpretations with respect to the possible actions of dead persons prior to their deaths. And, it was suggested, sociologists may either, by accepting the suicide statistics as face value, assume the validity of the coroners' analyses, or engage in parallel interpretations both of the coroners' interpretations and their public statements. The latter procedure, it was argued, may prove profoundly generative for the sociological study of suicide.

It should be emphasized that this task of 'seeing how the parties spoke' is not always or inevitably a complex or onerous one. For example, opinion polls and voting studies are premised on the notion that stating a voting intention to a researcher and casting a vote in a polling booth are such similar 'methods of speaking' that results from the first can be readily and straightforwardly extrapolated to predictions and postdictions about the second. And this assumption has, of course, received extensive validation over the years by an accumulation of successful predictions − helped perhaps, by the growth of public acceptance of polling within western culture.

In much social scientific research however, matters are normally considerably more complicated. Here the abundance of interpretative processes which enter into even elementary observations raises serious issues about the nature and status of evidence in social science. To put it mildly, we are a good distance from fully formulated evidential procedures. As Garfinkel rather pointedly observes:

> Undoubtedly, scientific sociology is a 'fact', but in Felix Kaufmann's sense of fact, i.e. in terms of a set of procedural rules that *actually* govern the use of sociologists' recommended methods and asserted findings as grounds of further inference and inquiries. The problem of evidence consists of the tasks of making this fact intelligible. (Garfinkel, 1967c: 103)

Nonetheless, at the end of the day, the task is far from hopeless. The 'circle of interpretation' is not wholly closed and the growth of knowledge is not a mirage. And neither too is the notion that important discoveries are there to be made about the operation of interpretative processes in social scientific procedures. Findings about social scientific methods of fact finding, especially when contrasted with everyday, journalistic, natural scientific, medical or judicial methods, can scarcely fail to deepen our understanding of the enterprise in which we are engaged as well, of course, of our understanding of these other domains.

CONCLUSION

No analysis of ordinary actors' descriptive accountings can for long avoid coming to terms with their characteristics as actions. Just as actors, in designing their actions, address the unavoidable accountability of those actions, so too in designing the accounts which formulate their actions, actors address the unavoidable accountability of their own accounting practices. This issue has emerged in innumerable ways in the present chapter.

As we have seen, the inherent 'looseness' of fit between a state of affairs and any natural language account used to formulate it both permits and motivates the circumstantial elaboration of any natural language account. Through these indexical and reflexive circumstantial elaborations, social actors determine every aspect of an account's sense, adequacy and motivation. Through these same procedures, they determine too how to treat it — whether to accept, reject, qualify, ignore, ironicize or laugh at the account and the activity of which it is a constituent part. Aware, in locally particularized ways, of the promise and troubles inherent in the possibilities of circumstantial elaboration, actors may be seen to design their accounts with respect to a range of 'considerations' and 'exigencies'. The latter may be particular to the specific participants, or generic to particular kinds of activities — e.g. complaining or making excuses – or indeed 'institutional' in that actors may refer to common understandings of the possible uses and fates of accounts-within-classrooms, accounts-within-courtrooms, news interviews, bureaucratic agencies and so on.

A major import of these observations is that any attempt to grasp the nature and significance of actors' acounts, or to use them as part of an investigation, which does not take account of the above characteristics, will very rapidly prove unsatisfactory. In fact, of course, social scientists regularly make reference to these characteristics: for example when they determine the objectivity or bias of particular evidences or when they decide whether to use or discard information made available to them. These determinations, however, are regularly accomplished 'intuitively' and remain unformulated except as 'decisions'. Given the ubiquity of these determinations at every stage and in every aspect of the research process, the range of practices implicated in these determinations cries out for investigation. The task of such investigations would not be to 'debunk' the results of social scientific research — as if the social scientist's use of intuition is always faulty. Rather it is to deepen significantly our understanding of social scientific procedures and of what is involved in particular varieties and techniques of social scientific investigation.

If anything, the task is even more pressing when we turn to the treatment of the actors' accounts on which social scientists depend in large part for their information. It will be apparent from the earlier discussions that actors' accounts — whether they take the form of questionnaire responses or of statistical rates produced by bureaucratic agencies — cannot be unproblematically treated either as disembodied descriptions or as the 'relaxed' or 'loose' versions of objective states of affairs which can subsequently be tightened up by the judicious application of social scientific methodology. On the contrary, no matter how firmly such accounts are proposed as reporting independently existing fact and no matter how fully they are supported by firm evidence and reasoned argument, these accounts — with their evidences and arguments — still await an analysis which situates them, with all their exigencies and considerations, within the socially organized worlds in which they participate as constituting and constituted elements.

Thus the social scientist can, indeed must, ask: what counts as 'reasonable fact' in casual conversation, in a courtroom, a scientific laboratory, a news interview, a police interrogation, a medical consultation or a social security office? What is the nature of the social organization within which these facts find support? To what vicissitudes, exigencies and considerations are the formulations of these facts responsive?

A consideration of this order of question draws us into a wider range of studies in which both actions and accounts of actions, words and deeds, are integral features of organized social realities and it is to this wider domain that we now turn.

CHAPTER 7

Maintaining Institutional Realities

For Kant the moral order 'within' was an awesome mystery; for sociologists the moral order 'without' is a technical mystery. A society's members encounter and know the moral order as perceivedly normal courses of action — familiar scenes of everyday affairs, the world of daily life known in common with others and with others taken for granted.

Garfinkel, *Studies in Ethnomethodology*

In the preceding chapters, we began to examine the consequences of viewing social action as fundamentally organized with respect to its reflexivity and accountability. A major finding of that examination was that the intersubjective intelligibility of actions ultimately rests on a symmetry between the production of actions on the one hand and their recognition on the other. This symmetry is one of *method* or *procedure* and Garfinkel forcefully recommends it when he proposes that

> the activities whereby members produce and manage settings of ordinary everyday affairs are identical with members' procedures for making those settings 'account-able'. (Garfinkel, 1967a: 1)

As we have seen, this symmetry of method is both assumed and achieved *by the actors* in settings of ordinary social activity. Its *assumption* permits actors to design their actions in relation to their circumstances so as to permit others, by methodically taking account of the circumstances, to recognize the action for what it is. The symmetry is also *achieved* and hence it is contingent. For the production and recognition of actions is dependent upon the parties supplying, and trusting one another to supply, an array of unstated assumptions so as to establish the recognizable sense of an action. A final conclusion to recall is that the production of an action will always reflexively redetermine (i.e. maintain, elaborate or alter) the circumstances in which it occurs.

We are now in a position to add a further 'layer' to the analysis of action — the layer of social institutions. For although we have deliberately ignored the fact until now, it will be obvious that, in maintaining, elaborating or transforming their circumstances by their actions, the actors are also simultaneously reproducing, developing or modifying the institutional realities which envelop those actions. In the present chapter, we shall be concerned with the phenomenon of institutional reality maintenance under a variety of circumstances ranging from overwhelming normative consensus to chronic structured conflict. The four case studies discussed in this chapter all focus on relatively diffuse institutional phenomena. The more recent 'studies of work' undertaken by Garfinkel and his students (Garfinkel, forthcoming) deal with a range of more concrete cases. We begin with Garfinkel's famous discussion of 'Agnes' (Garfinkel, 1967e).

CASE 1:   AGNES AND THE INSTITUTION OF GENDER

'Agnes' is the pseudonym of a patient who was referred to the Department of Psychiatry at the University of California at Los Angeles (UCLA) in 1958. She was born a boy with normal appearing male genitals, certified and named appropriately and, until the age of 17, was generally recognized to be a boy (ibid. 120). Nonetheless, by the time she presented herself at UCLA at the age of 19,

> Agnes's appearance was convincingly female. She was tall, slim, with a very female shape. Her measurements were 38–25–38. She had long, fine dark-blond hair, a young face with pretty features, a peaches-and-cream complexion, no facial

hair, subtly plucked eyebrows, and no make-up except for lipstick . . . Her usual manner of dress did not distinguish her from a typical girl of her age or class. There was nothing garish or exhibitionistic in her attire, nor was there any hint of poor taste or that she was ill at ease in her clothing . . . Her manner was appropriately feminine with a slight awkwardness that is typical of middle adolescence. (ibid. 119)

Agnes's purpose in presenting herself at UCLA was to obtain a sex-change operation and, prior to this, she was examined by a number of specialists. The latter were interested in a range of her characteristics, including her unique endocrinological configuration (Schwabe et al., 1962), her psychological make-up, her gender identity, the causes of her desire to be made anatomically female and her psychiatric management (Stoller, Garfinkel and Rosen, 1960; 1962; Stoller, 1968; 1975). Garfinkel, however, used her case as an occasion to focus on the ways in which sexual identity is produced and managed as a 'seen but unnoticed', but nonetheless institutionalized, feature of ordinary social interactions and institutional workings. He conducted the investigation with the use of tape-recorded conversations with Agnes in which the latter discussed her biography and prospects, triumphs and disasters and the hopes and fears associated with her self-imposed task of 'passing' for a woman. The result of this investigation was a profound analysis of gender considered as a produced institutional fact.

This last observation requires some additional comment. In studies of gender, it has been traditional to treat the conventional categories 'male' and 'female' as starting points from which to portray the different outlooks, life chances and activities of the sexes in relation to social structure. Despite their various differences, this analytic standpoint unites writings as divergent as Parsons's classic essays on sex roles and the family (Parsons, 1940; 1942; 1943; 1954), Engels's (1968) *The Origin of the Family, Private Property and the State* and more recent feminist writings (e.g. Kuhn and Wolpe, 1978). In these studies, sexual status is treated as a 'social fact' in a fully Durkheimian sense as an 'external and constraining' phenomenon. Garfinkel, by contrast, wanted to treat sexual status as a produced and reproduced fact. It is the constitution and reproduction of the ordinary facts of gender which is the object of inquiry. The reproduced differentiation of culturally specific 'males' and 'females' is thus the terminus of his investigation rather than its starting point. This differentiation is an overwhelming fact of social structure. Its reproduction, he proposes, is the outcome of a mass of indiscernible, yet familiar, socially organized practices. It was these latter which, in 1958, Garfinkel sought to disclose with the assistance of Agnes − a person whose determination to achieve 'femininity' and whose insight into its component features greatly helped Garfinkel to distance himself from the familiar phenomena of gender and to come to view them as 'anthropologically strange'.

In reading Garfinkel's account of Agnes, it is useful to bear in mind that she was, in effect, presented with two separate, but overlapping, problems in managing her claims to be female. First, she had the problem of dealing with those who took her at 'face value' and knew nothing of her potentially discrediting male genitalia and previously masculine biography. With these persons − the majority of her associates − Agnes was preoccupied with generating and living within a female identity which was above suspicion. Second, Agnes was compelled to deal with a range of persons − her parents and relatives, the medical and psychiatric staff at UCLA and, ultimately, her boyfriend Bill − who knew about these incongruous aspects of her anatomy and biography. With this second group of persons, Agnes's task became one of insisting that, despite the incongruities, she was 'essentially' and 'all along and in the first place' a female. This task, as we shall see, was necessitated as part of her long-term campaign to secure the sex-change operation as a moral right.

Agnes: Sexual Status as a Methodic Production

As part of her task of maintaining herself as a bona fide female, Agnes − like other 'intersexed' persons − had become a sensitive ethnographer of gender. Continually anxious about the successful management of her self-presentation as a woman, she had indeed become acutely aware of the ways in which sexual status can have implications for the conduct of ordinary social activities. The range and scope of these implications are so great and so easily overlooked (ibid. 118) that it is worth beginning with an initial list of some of their aspects.

There are, first of all, the self-evident problems of achieving convincingly female dress, make-up, grooming and accoutrements as an initial precondition of being taken for female. To judge from Garfinkel's description, Agnes had largely overcome these problems before she presented herself at UCLA for the first time. Then there are the problems of managing appropriately feminine comportment — the behavioural manifestations of femininity: 'sitting like a woman', 'walking like a woman', 'talking like a woman' and so on. These behaviours are minutely accountable. For example, Agnes recollected that her brother had complained about her carrying her books to school like a girl and had 'demonstrated to her and insisted that she carry them like a boy' (ibid. 152). While, once again, Agnes had clearly mastered fundamental aspects of female behavioural comportment by the time she arrived at UCLA, the tasks of 'talking like a woman' continued to prove troublesome. For, it turned out, to talk like a woman required a reservoir of biographical experiences and 'knowhow' — all of which had to have been experienced and appreciated in detail from the point of view of a girl. This reservoir of detailed experiences was necessary, first, to produce appropriately feminine talk and, secondly and more generally, to serve as an accumulating series of precedents with which to manage current situations (ibid. 130–1). In this context, Agnes repeatedly complained of her lack of an appropriate biography. After the change to living as a female, but before her operation, Agnes began to exchange 'gossip, and analyses of men, parties, and dating post-mortems' with roommates and wider circles of girlfriends (ibid. 147). Here, Garfinkel comments, 'two years of arduous female activities furnished for her a fascinating input of new experiences' which she used as resources to construct and reconstruct her own biography (ibid. 178). In what follows, we will briefly consider some aspects of Agnes's management of her sexual identity with those who did not know her secrets and with those who did.

Managing with Those who were Ignorant

In dealing with those who knew nothing of her 'male' anatomy and biography, Agnes's central preoccupation was to avoid the disclosure of her secrets.

> In instance after instance the situation to be managed can be described in general as one in which the attainment of commonplace goals and attendant satisfactions involved with it a risk of exposure . . . Her characteristic situation in passing was one in which she had to be prepared to choose, and frequently chose, between securing the feminine identity and accomplishing *ordinary* goals . . . Security was to be protected first. The common satisfactions were to be obtained only if the prior conditions of the secured identity could be satisfied. Risks in this direction entailed the sacrifice of the other satisfactions. (ibid. 139–40)

The nature and overriding extent of Agnes's sacrifices of ordinary satisfactions can be glossed by noting that, although she could drive, Agnes did not own a car because she feared the exposure of her secret while unconscious from an accident (ibid. 141).

In order to protect her identity, Agnes engaged in extensive pre-planning and rehearsal of ordinary activities so as to minimize the risk of enforced exposure. In 'open' or 'unplannable' situations she adopted a range of procedures, which Garfinkel refers to as acting as a 'secret apprentice' and 'anticipatory following', through which she remained inconspicuous while acquiring important feminine 'knowhow'. In all situations, Agnes was concerned not only with managing to present herself as an accountable (i.e. 'observable-reportable') female, but also with the accountability of her management strategies themselves.

Thus, in pre-planning a medical examination for a job, Agnes determined in advance that under no circumstances would she permit the examination to proceed lower than her abdomen. At the same time, she formulated the reasonable grounds ('modesty') in terms of which her refusal, if necessary, would be made accountable. These same grounds provided the basis for a 'no nudity' rule which Agnes and a girlfriend adopted in their shared appartment. Or again, in visiting the beach,

> She would go along with the crowd, reciprocating their enthusiasm for bathing, if or until it was clear that a bathroom or the bedroom of a private home would be available in which to change to her bathing suit. Public baths and automobiles were to be avoided. If the necessary facilities were not available excuses were easy to make. As she pointed out, one is permitted not to be 'in the mood' to go bathing, though to like very much to sit on the beach. (ibid)

Here then, as in the other cases, there was a concern to make contingent on-the-spot decisions necessary for securing the female identity together with a concern for the secondary accountability of the management devices themselves.

A similar duality is evident in less structured contexts. In the context of gossip exchanges, post-mortems on social events or commentaries on the behaviour of other women, Agnes tended to play a passive role permitting the talk to instruct her as to proper conduct. Here, as Garfinkel comments, 'not only did she adopt the pose of passive acceptance of instructions, but she learned as well the value of passive acceptance as a desirable feminine character trait' (ibid. 147). Or again,

> Another common set of occasions arose when she engaged in friendly conversation without having biographical or group affiliation data to swap off with her conversational partner. As Agnes said, 'Can you imagine all the blank years I have to fill in? Sixteen or seventeen years of my life that I have to make up for. I have to be careful of the things that I say, just natural things that could slip out . . . I just never say anything at all about my past that in any way would make a person ask what my past life was like. I say general things. I don't say anything that could be misconstrued.' Agnes said that with men she was able to pass as an interesting conversationalist by encouraging her male partners to talk about themselves. Women partners, she said, explained the general and indefinite character of her biographical remarks, which she delivered with a friendly manner, by a combination of her niceness and modesty. 'They probably figure that I just don't like to talk about myself.' (ibid. 148)

In these remarks, once again, we find the 'dual accountability' constraints to which Agnes oriented. They surface too in other aspects of her 'secret apprenticeship'. For example, in permitting her boyfriend's mother to teach her to cook Dutch national dishes, Agnes simultaneously learned how to cook, *tout court*. This learning, secretly accomplished, was done under the accountable auspices of 'learning to cook Dutch-style'.

In reviewing Agnes's practices for passing with the ignorant, Garfinkel emphasizes the exceptional precision and detail of her observation of the particulars of ordinary social arrangements. He points to the fact that she was compelled to protect her identity across ranges of contingencies which could not be known in advance and 'in situations known with the most faltering knowledge, having marked uncertainties about the rules of practice' (ibid. 136). In an eloquent description of Agnes's predicament, Garfinkel summarizes it as follows:

> In the conduct of her everyday affairs she had to choose among alternative courses of action even though the goal that she was trying to achieve was most frequently not clear to her prior to her having to take the actions whereby some goal might in the end have been realized. Nor had she any assurances of what the consequences of the choice might be prior to or apart from her having to deal with them. Nor were there clear rules that she could consult to decide the wisdom of the choice before the choice had to be exercised. For Agnes, stable routines of everyday life were 'disengageable' attainments assured by unremitting, momentary, situated courses of improvisation. Throughout these was the inhabiting presence of talk, so that however the action turned out, poorly or well, she would have been required to 'explain' herself, to have furnished 'good reasons' for having acted as she did. (ibid. 184)

The nature of Agnes's task in managing, constructing and reconstructing her social identity is thus perhaps well caught by the famous Neurath-Quine metaphor of being compelled to build the boat while already being out on the ocean. It was, unavoidably, a bootstrapping operation.

Above all, Garfinkel emphasizes, Agnes encountered scarcely any situations which could be treated as 'time out' from the work of passing. Always 'on parade', Agnes was compelled at all times to secure her female identity 'by the acquisition and use of skills and capacities, the efficacious display of female appearances and performances and the mobilization of appropriate feelings and purposes' (ibid. 134). In this context,

> the work and socially structured occasions of sexual passing were obstinately unyielding to (her) attempts to routinize the grounds of daily activities. This obstinacy points to the omnirelevance of sexual statuses to affairs of daily life as an invariant but unnoticed background in the texture of relevances that comprise the changing actual scenes of everyday life. (ibid. 118)

These problems and relevancies extended to the tasks of passing with those who, in part at least (see ibid. 285–8), knew of her secrets and it is to these latter that we now turn.

Managing with Those who Knew

As we have seen, Agnes's purpose in coming to UCLA was to secure a sex-change operation. This operation was the central preoccupation of her life and, as time progressed, it also became critical for the continuation of the relationship with her boyfriend which she treated as a major emblem of her femininity. In order to obtain this operation, Agnes had to undergo a wide variety of tests — anatomical, physiological, psychological and psychiatric — the results of which would form the basis on which the decision to operate or not would be made. In this context, Agnes's task became one of insisting that she had a right to the operation regardless of the results of the technical tests by doctors and others. She treated this right as a *moral* right and advanced it on the basis of what she urged as the *natural facts* of her femininity. Her task then, in a nutshell, was to insist that she was 'all along and in the first place' a *natural* female despite the incongruous anatomical, physiological, psychological and biological facts which might be amassed against the claim, and, on this basis, to urge the surgeons to remedy her condition in the direction 'intended by nature'.

It is clear, especially with the advantage of hindsight, that the task of presenting herself to those who knew her secrets as a 'natural-female-despite-the-incongruities' presented Agnes with management problems every bit as serious as those she encountered in presenting herself as a normal female to those who did not know them.

In her dealings with the specialists, Agnes systematically emphasized all aspects of her appearance, behaviour, motivation, biography and anatomy which could be held to be bona fide 'female' in character. Simultaneously, she down-graded every aspect which could be treated as evidence of her masculinity. Thus, in addition to her very feminine physical appearance described above, Agnes presented herself as 'ultra-female' both in her descriptions of her conduct and motivation in real world situations and in her actual conversations with the medical and psychiatric specialists who, indeed, 'came to refer to her presentation of the 120 per cent female' (ibid. 129). Throughout

> Agnes was the coy, sexually innocent, fun-loving, passive, receptive, 'young thing'. . . . As a kind of dialectical counterpart to the 120 per cent female Agnes portrayed her boyfriend as a 120 per cent male who, she said, when we first started to talk, and repeated through eight stressful weeks following the operation when post-operative complications had subsided and the recalcitrant vagina was finally turning out to be the thing the physicians had promised, 'wouldn't have been interested in me at all if I was abnormal'. (ibid.)

Closely aligned with this self-presentation was Agnes's account of her biography in which all 'evidences of a male upbringing were rigorously suppressed':

> The child Agnes of Agnes's accounts did not like to play rough games like baseball; her '*biggest*' problem was having to play boys' games; Agnes was more or less considered a sissy; Agnes was always the littlest one; Agnes played with dolls and cooked mud patty cakes for her brother; Agnes helped her mother with the household duties; Agnes doesn't remember what kinds of gifts she received from her father when she was a child. (ibid. 128–9)

Similarly, evidences of male sexual feelings were never avowed:

> The penis of Agnes's accounts had never been erect; she was never curious about it; it was never scrutinized by her or by others; it never entered into games with other children; it never moved 'voluntarily'; it was never a source of pleasurable feelings. (ibid.)

Related to this suppression of Agnes's male biography and her non-acknowledgement of male sexual feelings was her attitude to her present anatomical state. Here Agnes downgraded her incongruous anatomical features within a *moral* idiom while upgrading those anatomical features which supported her claims to be female in a *naturalistic* way. Thus Agnes's penis 'had always been an accidental appendage stuck on by a cruel trick of fate' (ibid.). While,

> with genitals ruled out as essential signs of her femininity, and needing essential and natural signs of female sexuality, she counted instead the life-long desire to be female and her prominent breasts. . . . Before all she counted her breasts as essential insignia. On several occasions in our conversations she expressed the relief and joy she felt when she noticed at the age of twelve that her breasts were staring to develop. (ibid. 131–2)

In this way, Agnes presented both her physical development and her female psychological make-up as corresponding elements of a natural feminine development. This insistence on a naturalistic orientation to her female insignia would cost her dear after the operation was finally performed:

> Thus, after the operation she was a female with a 'man-made' vagina. In her anxious words, 'Nothing that is made by man can ever be as good as something that nature makes.' She and her boyfriend were agreed on this. In fact, her boyfriend who, in her accounts of him, prided himself as a harsh realist, insisted on this and taught it to her to her dismayed agreement. (ibid. 134)

It is significant, in this context, that Agnes made her final disclosures concerning the origins of her condition only after a further five years of successful life as a woman and after a leading urologist had told her 'unequivocally that her genitalia were quite beyond suspicion' (ibid. 286–7).

Agnes's successful 'feminization' of her biography was not without its lacunae. Reviewing the data obtained by all the researchers on her case, it was found that, despite their best efforts, no data were available about

> (1) the possibility of an exogenous source of hormones; (2) the nature and extent of collaboration that occurred between Agnes and her mother and other persons; (3) any usable evidence let alone any detailed findings dealing with her male feelings and her male biography; (4) what her penis had been used for besides urination; (5) how she sexually satisfied herself and others and most particularly her boyfriend both before and after the disclosure; (6) the nature of any homosexual feelings, fears, thoughts and activities; (7) her feelings about herself as a 'phony female'. (ibid. 163)

In presenting herself as a natural female, Agnes was concerned to avoid saying or doing anything which might permit others to include her within a category of persons — homosexuals or transvestites — who could be held to be essentially masculine. She had no interest in meeting 'other trans-sexuals' on the grounds of having nothing in common (ibid. 131). She insisted that she had always 'steered clear of boys that acted like sissies' (ibid.) and 'just as normals frequently will be at a loss to understand "why a person would do that", i.e. engage in homosexual activities or dress as a member of the opposite sex, so did Agnes display the same lack of "understanding" for such behaviour' (ibid.). Here, then, Agnes sought to avoid any contamination of her essential feminity which might arise from an interest in, or understanding of, or having something in common with persons whose essential identities could be held to be other than female. Her concern, once again, was to portray herself as an exclusively normal, natural female who was such 'without residue'. So scrupulous was this concern that she would not even permit verbal formulations of her desires and achievements in such terms as 'living or being treated *as a female*'. In these contexts she would insist 'not as a female, naturally' (ibid. 170).

Finally, it will be recalled that Agnes treated her own desire to live as a female as itself evidence of her natural sexual status. In this context, she portrayed these desires as fundamental, axiomatic and inexplicable and avoided any psychological or other form of explanation of them that would relativize their status. Instead, she appealed to their life-long biographical continuity as evidence for their naturalness. Thus,

> In common with normals, she treated her femininity as independent of the conditions of its occurence and invariant to the vicissitudes of desires, agreements, random or wilful election, accident, considerations of advantage, available resources and opportunities ... It remained the self-same thing in essence under all imaginable transformations of actual appearances, time, and circumstances. It withstood all exigencies. (ibid. 133–4)

This achievement of the objectivity, transcendence and naturalness of her feminity was critical for the advancement of Agnes's moral claim to the body which she felt she should have had all along. The nature of her claim, in turn, was sensitive to the character of sexual status as a 'natural-moral' institution, which we will now discuss.

Sexuality: A 'Natural-Moral' Institution

As indicated in the preceding chapters, one of Garfinkel's theoretical preoccupations is with the 'double-edged' character of the accountable objects, events and activities which are treated as existent within a society or collectivity. When he proposes that 'a society's members encounter and know the moral order as perceivedly normal courses of action' or, reversing the formulation, that the real-world features of a society are treated by its members as 'objective, institutionalized facts, i.e. moral facts', he announces an interest in the fact that the ordinary members of a society treat its undoubted, objective features as both 'normal' and 'moral'. Social facts are treated both as 'factual', 'natural' and 'regular' and as phenomena which the member is morally required to attend to, take into account and respect.

This interpenetration of the 'factual' and 'moral' aspects of social activities, Garfinkel proposes, is a core feature of the ways in which society members orient towards the world of everyday life:

> They refer to this world as the 'natural facts of life' which, for members, are through and through moral facts of life. For members not only are matters so about familiar scenes, but they are so because it is morally right or wrong that they are so. (ibid. 35)

In sum, the everyday world as an institutionalized and institutionally provided-for domain of accountably real objects, events and activities is, from the society member's point of view, a 'natural-moral' world.

Sexual status is not excluded from this characterization. On the contrary, it vividly illustrates Garfinkel's analysis of the mutual interpenetration of the 'natural' with the 'moral'. As Garfinkel pointedly puts it, if one examines sexual status from the point of view of those who can take their own normally sexed status for granted, then 'perceived environments of sexed persons are populated with natural males, natural females, and persons who stand in moral contrast with them, i.e. incompetent, criminal, sick and sinful' (ibid. 122). The evidence from Garfinkel's study of Agnes profoundly illustrates this phenomenon. It indicates that everyone — the 'man on the street', Agnes's relatives, the physicians on the case and Agnes herself — treated sexual status as a matter of 'objective, institutionalized facts, i.e. moral facts' (ibid.). Let us briefly review each of their attitudes in turn.

Garfinkel begins by noting that the ordinary member of society finds it odd to claim that decisions about sexuality can be problematic.

> The normal finds it strange and difficult to lend credence to 'scientific' distributions of *both* male and female characteristics among persons, or a procedure for deciding sexuality which adds up lists of male and female characteristics and takes the excess as the criterion of the member's sex. (ibid. 123–4)

The normal, Garfinkel continues, finds these assertions strange because he (or she) cannot treat normal sexuality as a matter of technical niceties or of purely theoretical interest. Ordinary people are interested in normal sexual status as the legitimate grounds for initiating morally sanctionable and morally appropriate (i.e. accountable) courses of action. In this context, normal sexual status is treated as decided by reference to the 'sexual insignia' witnessed from birth onwards and 'decided by *nature*' (ibid.). These insignia subsequently form the accountable grounds for differentiated courses of treatment to their bearers. Decisions about sexual status cannot, if social life is to proceed smoothly, and need not await authoritative zoological or psychiatric determination.

The fact that this 'natural' distribution of sexual status is, simultaneously, a 'moral' distribution is revealed by ordinary reactions to persons who perceivedly deviate from the distribution. These reactions commonly take the form of moral retribution. The reactions of Agnes's family to her various changes illustrate this phenomenon and its vicissitudes. After her initial assumption of female status, Agnes reported, her cousin's attitude changed from one which was favourable to Agnes to one of strong disapproval. Other family members displayed 'open hostility' and 'consternation and severe disapproval' (ibid. 128). Thus, although philosophers have extensively critized the 'naturalistic fallacy' (that is, reasoning from what is the case to what ought to be the case), Agnes's family members repeatedly employed this device to assert the grounds (Agnes's upbringing as a boy) on which she should mend her ways.

However, if the employment of the 'naturalistic fallacy' worked against Agnes before the operation, it worked in her favour afterwards when family members exhibited 'relieved acceptance and treatment of her as a "real female after all" ' (ibid.). In this context, Garfinkel comments:

> . . . although the vagina was man-made it *was* a case of the real thing since it was what she was now seen to have been entitled to all along. Both the aunt and the mother were strongly impressed by the fact that the operation had been done at all 'in this country'. That the physicians at the UCLA Medical Centre by their actions reconstructed and validated Agnes's claim to her status as a natural female needs, of course, to be stressed. (ibid. 128)

Turning now to the physicians, it is again clear that, in making the decision to operate or not, they also sought a determination of Agnes's sexual status and thus similarly employed an 'is-to-ought' line of reasoning to support their decision. This use of what Agnes 'naturally was' as grounds to support the line of treatment decided upon is vividly displayed in Stoller's account of Agnes's case (1968: 133–9). In that part of his account reproduced by Garfinkel (1967: 286–7), Stoller goes to considerable lengths to show the grounds on which he had determined that Agnes did not desire the operation as a matter of wilful election and, in particular, that her condition was not the product of ingesting female hormones (estrogens). He concludes the discussion by accounting for the decision to operate as follows: 'Not being considered a transsexual, her genitalia were surgically transformed so that she now had the penis and testes removed and an artificial vagina constructed from the skin of the penis' (ibid. 286). The critical phrase in this passage is the first: 'not being considered a transsexual'. It expresses the belief of Stoller and his colleagues that Agnes was 'fundamentally' female and did not simply desire to be female as a matter of deliberate choice. The phrase indicates that, despite the technical expertise of Stoller and his colleagues, the fundamental grounds in terms of which he presented their decision to an audience of medical professionals were the same 'natural-moral' grounds which were invoked as the basis of their treatments of Agnes by all of her 'significant others'.

Thus in her dealings with her entire world of associates — family, friends, boyfriend, medical specialists, psychiatrists and Garfinkel himself — Agnes was presented with one consuming and overriding problem: the presentation of herself as someone who was naturally, all along and in the first place a bona fide female. The task had to be carried forward across every possible exigency, across every possible or actual state of knowledge possessed individually or severally by these others. And it had to be managed as a condition, not only of acquiring the 'sexual insignia' which would place her beyond suspicion with those who would meet her in the future, but also as a condition of convincing those who, fully knowing her past, could nonetheless be persuaded that she was, finally, what she had claimed to be all along. To meet these tasks, Agnes had only one asset: her skills as a 'practical methodologist' acquired as a student of normal sexuality:

> Her studies armed her with knowledge of how the organized features of ordinary settings are used by members as procedures for making appearances-of-sexuality-as-usual decidable as a matter of course. The scrutiny that she paid to appearances; her concerns for adequate motivation, relevance, evidence and demonstration; her sensitivity to devices of talk; her skill in detecting and managing 'tests' were attained as part of her mastery of trivial but necessary social tasks, to secure ordinary rights to live. Agnes was self-consciously equipped to teach normals how normals make sexuality happen in commonplace settings as an obvious, familiar, recognizable, natural, and serious matter of fact. Her specialty consisted of treating the 'natural facts of life' of socially recognized, socially managed sexuality as a managed production so as to be making these facts of life true, relevant, demonstrable, testable, countable, and available to inventory, cursory representation, anecdote, enumeration, or professional psychological assessment; in short, so as unavoidably in concert with others to be making these facts of life visible and reportable — accountable — for all practical purposes. (ibid. 180)

To summarize: Agnes subscribed to the 'natural-moral' order of sexual status within which normal sexual status is treated as a 'natural fact' while aberrations from the norm are treated as morally accountable. She subscribed to the objective reality of normal sexual status, despite her knowledge of its intricate management in daily life, both as a condition of maintaining her own identity and as a condition of achieving her desired objective — the operation. In this regard, as Garfinkel remarks, Agnes was no revolutionary (ibid. 177–8). Rather, in deploying her considerable methodological talents, Agnes sought in every way to conform with (and thus reproduce) the 'natural-moral' institutional order in which she so dearly wished to participate — as a normal, natural female.

The Objective Reality of Sexual Status and Its Maintenance

The variety of Agnes's management strategies and procedures, the resistance of ordinary social occasions to her attempts to routinize her daily life as a female and the fact that almost every occasion could somehow take on the features of a ' "character and fitness" test' (ibid. 136) suggest that, in almost any occasion of social life, institutionalized features of sexual status are being produced and reproduced by 'normally sexed' males and females. Agnes's case further suggests that, while institutionalized sexuality is being produced and reproduced in this way as a supremely natural 'matter of fact,' its reproduction is simultaneously supported by a massive 'repair machinery' of moral accountability which is brought to bear in cases of discrepancy or deviance. To make these − potentially relativizing − observations on the socially organized character of accountable sexuality is not to deny its objectivity or facticity. On the contrary, it is to begin to gain some appreciation of what its objectivity and facticity consist of. As Garfinkel summarizes it:

> Agnes's methodological practices are our sources of authority for the finding, and recommended study policy, that normally sexed persons are cultural events in societies whose character as visible orders of practical activities consist of members' recognition and production practices. We learned from Agnes, who treated sexed persons as cultural events that members make happen, that members' practices alone produce the observable-tellable normal sexuality of persons, and do so only, entirely, exclusively in actual, singular, particular occasions through actual witnessed displays of common talk and conduct. . . . The inordinate stresses in Agnes's life were part and parcel of the concerted practices with normals, whereby the 'normal, natural female' as a moral thing to be and a moral way to feel and act was made to be happening, in demonstrable evidence, for all practical purposes. (ibid. 181)

This reference to the stresses which Agnes experienced, however, raises a core problem in Agnes's management of 'normality'. While normals can routinize their management and detection of displays of 'normally sexed' conduct so that the latter become a 'seen but unnoticed' background to the texture of commonplace events, Agnes's secrets were such that she could not lose sight of what, for normals, is so massively invisible:

For Agnes, in contrast to normals, the commonplace recognition of normal sexuality as a 'case of the real thing' consisted of a serious, situated, and prevailing accomplishment ... Her anguish and triumphs resided in the observability, which was particular to her and uncommunicable, of the steps whereby the society hides from its members its activities of organization and thus leads them to see its features as determinate and independent objects. For Agnes the observably normally sexed person *consisted* of inexorable, organizationally located work that provided the way that such objects arise. (ibid. 182)

In this context, Garfinkel remarks that Agnes found psycho-logical and sociological theories of the 'judgemental dope' variety flattering (ibid. 183–4). For these approaches 'theorized out of recognition' her excruciating perception of the work of managing sexual status. They thus 'naturalized' (in the way that ordinary society members 'naturalize') the sexual status which she longed to treat as just that — *natural*. Within these theories, sexual status is unproblematically treated as ascribed and internalized. Whereas what Agnes knew without doubt was that this 'ascribed' status is through and through *achieved* as the product of unnoticed, yet unremitting, work.

Reflecting for a moment on the Agnes study, it is surprising to realize the extent to which gender differentiation consists of a filigree of small-scale, socially organized behaviours which are unceasingly iterated. Together these — individually insignificant — behaviours interlock to constitute the great public institution of gender as a morally-organized-as-natural fact of life. This institution is comparatively resistant to change. To adapt Wittgenstein's famous analogy, the social construction of gender from a mass of individual social practices resembles the spinning of a thread in which fibre is spun on fibre. And, as Wittgenstein points out, 'the strength of the thread does not reside in the fact that some one fibre runs through its whole length, but in the overlapping of many fibres' (Wittgenstein, 1958: para. 67e). But if gender manifests itself as a density of minutiae, the latter are nonetheless stabilized both individually and collectively by the apparatus of moral accountability which we have repeatedly seen in action. In this context it is perhaps ironic that Freud could not trust the facts of culture sufficiently to base his account of the differentiation between the sexes on cultural mechanisms. For Freud, gender differentiation is ultimately based on a single slender thread: the psychological responses of males and females to the facts of anatomy. For Garfinkel, by contrast, the institution of gender appears as a densely woven fabric of morally accountable cultural practices which are throughout both accountable, and accountably treated, as natural.

CASE 2: MAINTAINING AN INSTITUTIONAL
ORDER BY REFERENCE TO RULE ACCOUNTABILITY:
THE CONVICT CODE

In the previous discussion we traced through some of the ways in which Garfinkel, via Agnes, demonstrated that sexual status is maintained as a 'natural fact' through a variety of institutionalized procedures and practices. Through these same procedures and practices, he proposes, sexual status is made relevant to the mundane activities of daily life as a 'seen but unnoticed' background to their enactment. As we have seen, the relevance of sexual status to contemporary everyday life is not confined to a few specific contexts of action. On the contrary, its relevance is general in that it has a potential bearing on a wide variety of social activities. Moreover, sexual status is not normally managed by overt reference to rule or rule-like formulations, but instead it takes in an unbounded and scarcely formulable range of matters.

In this second case study, by contrast, we consider the maintenance of a comparatively boundaried domain of institutionalized conduct within which overt rule formulation turned out to be a crucial device for rendering action accountable. We thus return to a classical sociological topic: the relationship of rules to the management of conduct and the maintenance of institutionalized patterns of activity. We will examine this relationship by reference to a justly famous study by Wieder (1974) of a half-way house for narcotics offenders. In this study, Wieder clearly demonstrates both the role of rules in providing for the observability and account-ability of actions and the *uses* to which such accountability can be put. His study is particularly valuable in showing that the uses of accountability-via-rule-formulation can persist in contexts of normative dissensus and chronic structured conflict.

Background

The half-way house studied by Wieder was established to reduce the rate at which paroled narcotics offenders 'relapsed' into new narcotics offences on their release from prison. It was intended as a sheltered environment in which parolee residents could, by finding work and living in a narcotics-free environment, gradually assume responsibility and control over their lives prior to transfer into the external community. Provision was made for a 'task-oriented program which focuses on staff-parolee-community involvement and interaction' (Wieder, 1974: 60). Within these terms of reference, parolee residents were expected to look for work, participate in weekly committee sessions on 'areas of need' within the half-way house, pay for residence in cash or through work tasks and show increasing responsibility and self-reliance in dealing with their affairs (ibid. 60–8). Efforts were made to maximize the amount of formal and informal interaction between staff and residents so as to establish relationships of trust and mutual respect and support between them. Parole agents and supervising staff maintained a watching brief on such matters as the sale and use of drugs, alcohol abuse, residents' employment status, etc.

Viewed in terms of these objectives, the half-way house was not a success. The residents displayed a lack of commitment — studied in its detail and intensity — to the formal objectives and activities of the half-way house (ibid. 83–92). Informal contact with staff was minimized and, when unavoidable, was designedly 'wooden' and passive in character. Whenever possible, the residents avoided giving staff any information about their personal lives. Similarly, staff were unable to place any reliance in the residents' mandatory reports concerning employment and the use of drugs unless they were supported by objective evidence. Only 30 per cent of the residents left the half-way house in the approved manner to some form of independent residence. The remainder either jumped parole or were re-arrested (ibid. 97).

The Convict Code

From his earliest contacts at the half-way house, Wieder encountered references to 'the code' — a loose set of maxims which identified a range of activities which residents should, or should not, engage in. The residents also spoke of various types of persons — 'snitches', 'snivellers' and 'kiss asses' — who were defined in terms of typical forms of deviance from the code.

The code's provisions covered both conduct in relation to staff members and conduct in relation to other residents. Piecing it together over the course of his fieldwork, Wieder found that, in relation to staff, the code proscribed informing ('snitching') on other residents or admitting responsibility for illegal activities ('copping out'). Further, the code provided that staff members were untrustworthy and that they should be given as little information as possible. In relation to other residents, the code enjoined the 'sharing' of drugs and alcohol, it forbade theft from other residents but also 'snitching' to staff about such thefts, it required residents to help others to avoid detection and punishment for illegal activities and to avoid doing things which might interfere with the illegal business of others. More generally, the code enjoined the parolees to 'show loyalty' to one another. A resident, Wieder reports, 'should not "kiss ass", do favours for staff, be friendly to staff, take their side in an argument, or accept the legitimacy of their rules. Any of these acts can be understood as a defection to their side, and makes a resident suspect of being the kind of "guy" that would snitch' (ibid. 117). As it was portrayed to Wieder by both residents and staff, violations of the code were strongly sanctionable by measures which could include beatings or death. A reputation for 'snitching', it was claimed, could follow an individual through the narcotics culture and seriously disadvantage him within the prison community in the (likely) event of his reconviction for similar offences.

In a variety of ways, as Wieder points out, the code provides an explanation for the accumulated failures to achieve half-way house objectives. The minimized interaction, dramatic disaffiliation from institutional activities, consistent misinformation and rule violations which were characteristic of life in the half-way house are all attributable to the maxims of the code and could be explained by 'treating the code as maxims of conduct that residents follow and enforce on one another' (ibid. 120). Wieder cites many instances in which the code was simply used as an explanation for actions by both residents and staff. For example, referring to a 'group therapy' session which had had to be abandoned in the face of resident resistance, residents complained to Wieder on several occasions that it was based on 'snitching, snivelling and copping out' (ibid. 137).

With the code so frequently invoked as an explanation both for individual actions and general patterns of conduct within the half-way house and elsewhere, professional social scientists have routinely faced the choice of accepting or rejecting it as a 'proximate' explanation for conduct (ibid. 120–5). In this context, faced with the weight of testimony from both prisoners and prison officials, most sociologists have tended to endorse some version of the convict code as a means of interpreting and explaining prisoner conduct.

And yet, as Wieder demonstrates, this choice is not strictly compelled by the situation of inquiry. Nor is the exercise of such a choice the most instructive way of explicating the conduct in question. A further option in fact presents itself, namely of withholding any judgement about the adequacy of the code-as-an-explanation in favour of an examination of the ways in which the code-as-an-explanation was drawn upon and used in actual contexts of activity in the half-way house. It was this latter option which Wieder took up.

The Code as a Sense-Making Device

Wieder began by focusing on the role of the code as an interpretative device. Like any other accounting framework, he proposes, the code is used to establish and identify 'what is going on' within a set of behavioural events. As he puts it, the various participants in the half-way house setting 'told the code' as a means 'to identify and name individual acts and patterns of repetitive action and to collect diverse actions under the rubric of a single motive and, in turn, to name them as the same kind of act' (ibid. 154). In these ways, the code was used to impose an unequivocal meaning on the particular events of resident conduct. This involved assimilating particular events to 'typical instances' of more general patterns of resident conduct using the code as a motivational schema. In the process, resident conduct was rendered familiar, rational and expressive of enduring, trans-situational characteristics. While the code was not, and could not be, used to predict resident conduct in detail, its flexible application was such as to render 'nearly any equivocal act sensible in such a way that it was experienced as something familiar, even though the act might not be "expected" or "predicted" in any precise meaning of those terms' (ibid. 155).

While the staff members often invoked the code as a means of interpreting the daily events of the half-way house, the residents also invoked it as a means of characterizing both staff actions and their own responses. These characterizations would often be highly 'local' and specific. Thus, Wieder reports (ibid. 168) that 'friendly conversations' with residents could often be abruptly terminated with some reference to the code, such as 'You know I won't snitch.' Such utterances simultaneously (1) characterized the immediately prior action of the staff member concerned (as asking the resident to 'snitch'), while (2) constituting the resident's refusal to respond and (3) accounting for that refusal. In these ways, Wieder suggests, the staff member's action and the resident's response are embedded in a larger context of enduring role relationships which were formulated 'yet again' on this occasion (ibid.).

In sum, Wieder found that in the first instance the convict code operated as a sense-making device. As such, it was used in conversations among staff, among residents and between staff and residents as a means of depicting the nature of actions and of patterns of actions which took place in the half-way house. Such depictions were accomplished by invoking the relevances of the code as the primary framework in terms of which the activity in question was to be viewed and understood. In this way, actions became defined in terms of the code to the exclusion of other possible definitional frameworks. In turn, they came to be recognizable as 'further instances' of a typical pattern of activity which was persisting and trans-situational in character.

Using the Code as a Persuasive Device

Wieder reports that although the code was used as a sense-making device, it was not invoked as a disembodied commentary on events or as a means of providing descriptions 'for description's sake'. On the contrary, he found, descriptions in terms of the code were produced as consequential interventions in the very fields of events they were being used to formulate.

As an initial illustration of this phenomenon, Wieder cites the work of an utterance such as 'You know I won't snitch' when produced in a commonplace interaction between a staff member and a resident. Here, he argues, not only does the utterance formulate the character of the prior talk, but also this formulation constitutes a specific move within the field of action-as-formulated:

> By saying 'You know I won't snitch,' (a) the resident negatively sanctioned the prior conduct of the staff member or myself. Saying that the question called for snitching was morally evaluating it and rebuffing me or the staff. The utterance (b) called for and almost always obtained a cessation of that line of the conversation . . . In terminating that line of talk, it (c) left me or staff ignorant of what we would have learned by the question had it been answered. And it (d) signalled the consequences of rejecting the resident's utterance or the course of action it suggested. (ibid. 169–170)

Plainly then, the invocation of the code to characterize a conversational event was not, in the daily context of the half-way house, an activity which was devoid of consequences.

These characteristic features of invoking the code so as (1) to formulate a texture of events and (2) to intervene in the texture of events-as-formulated was not confined to the residents. Staff members too, in their dealings with one another, portrayed a variety of aspects of resident conduct in its terms. Once again, however, such portrayals were not simply used to bring resident conduct under the jurisdiction of an interpretative scheme which rendered it coherent and sensible, rather they were used in a variety of persuasive activities. For example, unpleasant resident conduct could be portrayed as compelled or motivated by the code rather than, for example, specifically directed at the staff or produced in response to their own inadequacies. Staff members frequently used the code to account for their failures to achieve formal half-way house objectives while avoiding any implication that they were failing to do their jobs properly. More generally, and in a variety of ways, the code was used to

> relieve staff members of some of their responsibilities for motivating residents to participate in the program. It tempered staff's obligation to be knowledgeable about the affairs of residents, since they could explain their ignorance by referring to the residents' unwillingness to cop out or snitch. A staff member could defeat a proposal for the program by 'telling the code' to show that the proposal was 'unrealistic'. 'Telling the code' served to defend staff and staff ideas against the complaints of residents. It was also consequential in justifying staff's control over residents and staff's unwillingness to trust or give responsibilities to residents. (ibid. 171–2)

Staff members, in short, used the code both as a means of describing resident conduct and as a means of explaining, justifying or otherwise persuasively dealing with the fact that their actions demonstrably fell short of what the half-way house programme required of them.

Thus, despite their conflicting attitudes and objectives and their differing perspectives on the conduct which the code formulated, both the staff and the residents used the convict code as a means of making sense of a range of activities which occurred within the half-way house regime. To this extent, both groups used the code as a definitive means of formulating events and, in this context, the code came to function as a prominent accounting device both in structuring the 'front line' interactions between staff and residents and, within the 'back stage' deliberations of each group, as a means of evaluating actual or intended courses of conduct. In this sense, the code became a predominant feature of the institutionalized reality of the half-way house and one to which both staff and residents portrayed themselves as adapting.

Indefinite Maxims and Institutional Realities

One of the most striking features of the convict code as described by Wieder is its indefiniteness. Its maxims, such as 'Do not snitch' or 'Show loyalty to the residents' are scarcely specific and, as Wieder found during the early months of his investigation, they had to receive extensive exemplification before they could be adequately grasped. Viewed from the standpoint of a novice at the half-way house, the code could only be used after the fashion of Garfinkel's documentary method of interpretation (cf. Wieder, 1974: 183–214). In the process, some initial acquaintance with the code could be used to interpret certain elements of observed conduct as 'action in accord with the precepts of the code'. As further components of conduct were assimilated to the operation of the code and could thus be treated as exemplifying it, 'what the code really was' became elaborated and increasingly detailed. And, in turn, the events of the half-way house became 'progressively experienced as more and more complex, elaborate, definite, seeable-in-a-glance' (ibid. 204).

At the same time, Wieder found, this process of cognitive assimilation in which more and more resident conduct became intelligible and 'what the code amounted to' became more and more detailed was not solely a cognitive process. For the extension and 'filling in' of Wieder's knowledge was simultaneously an extension of the domain of accountability in terms of which Wieder could be expected to interpret and conduct his own activities. The more he knew of the code, the more he was expected to 'see' that it was pointless to attempt certain types of conversation, or engage in particular forms of questioning and so on (ibid. 146–9). The result was that the more Wieder grasped of the details of the code, the more he experienced his own conduct as constrained by its maxims. Increasingly, he records, he felt obliged to design his own actions within the half-way house environment so as to exhibit some awareness of the code and compliance with its dictates.

Applying these considerations to the wider pattern of activities in the half-way house, it can be suggested that the indefiniteness of the code, together with the pervasiveness of the occasions of its telling, combined to create an environment in which *any* course of action could, at any moment, be examined to establish its status as compliant with, or departing from, the code's dictates. To the extent that the residents could be seen both to design their conduct by reference to the code and to use the code as a method of accounting for and evaluating their own conduct, they could also enforce it as the staff's method of interpreting, and accomodating to, the unalterable 'facts' of the situation. For all participants therefore, the code 'densely existed' as an external, objective and constraining facticity to the extent that numerous detailed exhibits of its application could be found in the talk and conduct of the half-way house.

But, if the code 'existed' only in its exhibits, its codification as something which could be cited, formulated and talked about only served to extend its reality:

> By offering such accounts of their behaviour and their circumstances to staff, residents effectively dealt with staff demands that they say more about what they and their fellows were really doing. These accounts effectively dealt with staff demands that residents willingly participate in staff-sponsored activities and they they become involved in planning and carrying out the program. In general, the accumulation of incidents in which 'telling the code' defeated staff's plans and staff's tendency to foresee such defeats meant that staff's actual demands for resident participation were reduced well below the level called for in the program plan. This was so to such an extent that the actual round of events at half-way house only vaguely resembled the program plan. (ibid. 174)

Despite its preoccupation with normatively organized conduct, Wieder's study paradoxically undermines the most central tenets of the traditional model of normative order in which institutional structures are portrayed as the products of rule-following conduct. The convict code which so extensively organized the perceptions and actions of residents and staff was 'internalized' by neither. Its maxims did not relate antecedently existing situations to subsequent actions after the fashion required for the rule-following model (Wilson, 1971), nor did they 'cause' those actions. Rather the maxims were employed as interpretative devices with which to provide for a particular texture of relevancies for occasions of action and their constituent activities. The maxims were 'constraining' upon the conduct and interpretations of residents and staff to the extent that the residents could, by their claimings, instancings, etc., convince the staff that the code *was* a fact beyond their individual control. In bargaining terms, the residents' successes rested

> on the paradox that the power to constrain an adversary may depend on the power to bind oneself; that, in bargaining, weakness is often strength, freedom may be freedom to capitulate, and to burn bridges behind one may suffice to undo an opponent. (Schelling, 1960: 22)

Thus, by their creation of a code and by their insistence upon its binding power, the residents created the 'accounting space' which permitted them both to pursue their projects and, in the process, to undermine the half-way house programme.

Finally, it should be recalled that the role of the code in organizing the institutional life of the half-way house did not rest on the definiteness with which its provisions related prescribed actions to sharply defined contexts. On the contrary, its indefinite and 'unbounded' character permitted searches of indefinite scope and detail so as to see and evaluate *whatever* details of conduct that empirically occurred within its rubric. Thus, as a scheme of interpretation and as grounds for action, the code came to exert a 'stranglehold' on the round of activities in the half-way house, while yet permitting the different participants 'workable', if separate and conflicting, spheres of activity.

Conclusion

Wieder's account of the half-way house regime is a minor classic of ethnography. Lucid, analytically powerful and empirically fascinating, it is of outstanding interest and will readily repay detailed study. In drawing this discussion to a close, three general observations from it will be underlined.

The first has to do with Wieder's treatment of accounts. When social scientists are offered some form of account or explanation of action, the prevailing initial response is to determine how much credence can be given to it. This decision is, in effect, the controlling one in determining the use to which the account will be put. For if accounts are treated as credible, efforts are commonly made to correlate them with actions in some way (Heritage, 1983), or to build the matters they report into an analysis of social structure (Gilbert and Abell, 1983). Within this framework, actors' accounts are exclusively treated as *representative* of the motives, actions, circumstances, etc. which they depict. Wieder's study shows both the feasibility and the value of an alternative method of working. This method involves treating *both* the actors' actions *and* their accountings as part of the natural history of the domain under study, i.e. treating both as institutionally organized by reference to some set of accounting frameworks in terms of which the domain's exigencies and considerations are handled. Within this analytic attitude, the critical research question concerns how the accounts work, and are used within the domain. And the question of the truth and falsity of accounts becomes significant only as a problem to be solved by the actors within the domain.

A second point to be drawn from Wieder's study can be more shortly put. His analysis vividly demonstrates that where sociological research encounters institutional domains in which values, rules or maxims of conduct are overtly invoked, the identification of these latter will not provide an explanatory terminus for the investigation. Rather their identification will constitute the first step of a study directed at discovering how they are perceivedly exemplified, used, appealed to and contested. For it is in their flexible application and resourceful use that rules can provide for the accountability of conduct and it is here, necessarily, that their interest and significance lie.

Finally, it is useful to return, if only for a moment, to those indefinite maxims of the convict code and the density of the institutional reality that was projected with them. There is a belief, to which academic writers are perhaps more prone than many, which connects the definiteness of a rule system with the degree to which it is held capable of generating institutional constraint. Indefinite rules, it is sometimes held, are so 'loose' as to admit elements of contingency, indeterminacy and randomness into social arrangements which are hostile to the persistence and stability of social structure, indeed to the very idea of social structure (Alexander, forthcoming). But this is the illusion of theorists who equate conceptual determinacy with determining power. It is not shared by autocrats and dictators who know that open and unbounded sets of rules, backed by force, are just the way to consolidate a set of advantageous social arrangements. At the microcosmic level, Wieder's study demonstrates this fundamental fact in full measure and the conclusion may properly be drawn that the postulation of indefinite maxims of conduct entails no automatic loss of analytic power with respect to the treatment of persistence and change in social structural arrangements.

REPRISE: MAINTAINING SYSTEMS OF
INSTITUTIONAL ACTIVITY: A SIMPLEST CASE

In the previous two sections we have covered a great deal of complicated observation and analysis. Let us therefore pause to review where we have got to and extract some orienting principles which can carry us further.

The empirical studies reviewed thus far demonstrate beyond reasonable doubt that such matters as sexual status and compliance with simple maxims of conduct are managed, as 'observable-reportable' phenomena, through the use of complex and interlocking arrays of accounting practices. These latter find expression both in overt actions and in the socially sanctionable perceptions and judgements which such actions are treated as indexing. Through these accounting practices, actions are constituted as exhibits of particular institutional orders, e.g. of sexual status or of the convict code. In this way, particular institutional orders of events are recognized as *real* orders of events that were 'seen-to-be-manifested', though not necessarily noticed as such. Underlying these orders of events as real orders is the symmetry principle with which we started the chapter. An institutional order of events exists to the extent, and only to the extent, that its local activities can be found to be exhibits of the constitutive accounting practices that comprise it.

The maintenance of an institutional order as a real order of events thus involves two interlocking phenomena:

(1) Actions must be produced in full circumstantial detail so as to be analyzable with the relevant framework of accounts.

(2) The relevant framework of accounts must be available, and in 'good repair', as a means of bringing the activities themselves within a scheme of interpretation.

At an empirical level therefore, it can be suggested that institutional reality maintenance involves two processes: (1) the routine production of actions which can be viewed in terms of the appropriate interpretative framework, and (2) the maintenance of the interpretative framework itself in the face of 'wear and tear' arising from deviant or discrepant courses of action.

In practice, the achievement of these two conditions may be tightly interlocked. This can be demonstrated by returning briefly to our simplified greetings example. We can begin by observing that, plainly, for as long as we encounter events in which the exchange of 'Hello' routinely occurs, and this exchange is understood (with whatever help from *ad hoc* practices) as the activity of 'greeting', the institution of greetings and its associated norm 'return a greeting' will continue to exist as a 'dense' feature of empirical reality. We have already seen in chapter 5 that the special accountability of deviations from the norm 'return a greeting' may motivate speakers to comply with the dictates of the norm. This special accountability thus exerts a pressure towards the routine production of greetings. It thus contributes towards the satisfaction of the first condition for the maintenance of an institutional reality, namely the routine production of actions which can be interpreted with the relevant framework of accounts.

But what of our second condition: that the interpretative framework must itself be kept in good repair? Plainly, the framework will not be threatened by instances of conduct which can be analysed within its terms. But what of the cases when greetings are not returned? Why is our norm for greetings not eroded — as an empirical generalization and as a normative injunction — by such cases? Here the special accountability of non-returns comes into play once more. Greetings, we say, will not be returned under a range of conditions: when the recipient did not hear, or is hostile, or rude. When a greeting is not returned, we suppose that the event is certainly explicable by reference to one or another of these conditions. The non-return of a greeting is, we know, a prima facie indication that one of these conditions presently holds and, indeed, it is a positive signal for us to try and identify which one of these conditions may in fact apply. For greetings, there are no other possibilities. Either the norm is complied with, or one of the special conditions will be found to hold. In short, we treat the norm, together with the range of special conditions, as exhaustive of all the possible contingencies which could arise on the occasion of a greeting. Explanatory closure for every possible greetings occasion has been achieved. The web of accountability is seamless.

The institution of greetings is thus sustained by the secondary accountability of deviations from its primary normative injunction. This secondary accountability accomplishes both of the tasks outlined above. (1) It motivates routine compliance with the norm and (2), by isolating a range of exceptions as 'special cases', it preserves the central relevance of the norm. The special cases are thus 'the exceptions that prove the rule'. For their interpretation — as instances of 'not hearing', 'being angry' or 'rudeness' — rests on the general applicability of the norm as a primary interpretative base. Moreover, from the speaker's point of view, the fact that failures to return greetings are always explicable by reference to some exceptional consideration only goes to show 'how important the normative injunction to return greetings really is'.

In the first two case studies of this chapter, the central focus has been on the routine production of actions which were recognized to be in compliance with some perceived framework of accountability. In the remaining two case studies, we will focus primarily on the second aspect of institutional reality maintenance: the maintenance of frameworks of accounting practices. We begin by considering the maintenance of the most natural and objective phenomenon known to man: the mundane world of perceived objects and events. This maintenance, it will be shown, is also the object of fundamental institutional procedures through which mundane actors find ways to assure one another that they jointly inhabit a 'shared world'. As in the case of sexual status and the convict code, the implementation of these procedures is morally accountable and becomes overtly so under conditions in which the actors persistently disagree in their judgements of reality.

CASE 3: 'WORLD MAINTENANCE' AS AN INSTITUTIONALIZED ACTIVITY

For the starting point of this discussion, we return to the writings of Alfred Schutz who, in his discussion of intersubjectivity, noted that in the natural attitude of everyday life we simply assume that we are jointly seeing an instance of 'the same thing'. And, although this assumption is only contingently maintained 'until counter-evidence', Schutz also proposed that its maintenance is actively worked at. For example, we actively adjust for differences in perspective and, in thus 'making allowances' for them, actively maintain the general assumption that we are confronted by the same state of affairs.

This assumption, of course, receives extensive confirmation in our practical experiences of manipulating and handling objects. One only needs to think, for example, of two furniture-removers calling out warnings and instructions to one another while manoeuvring a large object down the stairs of a house to see how natural and commonplace this co-ordination of action and description with real world states of affairs is. Indeed the naturalness of the experience is such as to occlude the recognition that 'sharing a perception of the same state of affairs' is undergirded by a variety of institutionalized procedures. In order to reveal them, it is necessary to ask some rather counter-intuitive questions and this is exactly what Melvin Pollner has done in a seminal article on 'Mundane reasoning' (Pollner, 1974).

Pollner begins by noting that, despite the ubiquity of

'shared experience' in the social world, cases quite commonly arise in which conflicting testimony is given or observers cannot agree about what it is they are observing. In such contexts, Pollner notes, the conflict of experience is routinely seen as a 'puzzle' which requires an 'explanation'. Yet, he also observes, this is not the only attitude it is possible to take towards these events:

> Specifically, conflicting testimony might be regarded as indicating that the world is how you perceive it and that the 'it' which you perceive exists only in the perception. It is so, to borrow from Pirandello, if you think it is so, and the 'it' which is so is only in the thinking (or saying, or perceiving, etc.). (ibid. 45–6)

And, if this stance were to be adopted, then

> matters adjudicated in the courts, disputations in science, disagreements in everyday affairs, and so on can be conceived of as an ever-growing compendium of instances testifying to the fact that there is no 'same world'. The very conflicts which are mundanely regarded as a 'failure' in the perceptual process through which the world is observed and its features brought to formulation may alternatively be regarded as 'evidence' of the absurd and radical subjectivity of the world. (ibid.)

So then, two possible stances can be adopted to the phenomena of conflicting experience or testimony: (1) given the existence of a single, objective and univocal world, the conflict is a puzzle requiring explanation; (2) there is no puzzle because 'worlds' are subjective and particular to the experiencer and, hence, multiple. Mundane actors, Pollner proposes, always adopt the first of these stances and their adoption of this stance, of course, reasserts their assumption that the world is objective and unitary and not subjective and multiple.

Having got this far, it is not difficult to see that the adoption of stance 1 by mundane actors is profoundly functional. The social world would undoubtedly collapse if the actors simply shrugged their shoulders every time someone came up with a different version of the events going on before their eyes. But to assert the functionality of stance 1 is perhaps the least interesting thing to say about it. The phenomenon begins to become extremely interesting once questions are asked about the 'methodology' of maintaining it *in the face of conflicting experiences or testimony*. This, then, is Pollner's question: just *how* is stance 1 maintained in the face of these conflicts? And his answer turns on the available procedures for reconciling such conflicts. He lists a number of these procedures, and in the following paragraphs we will group them as involving the resolution of discrepancy at the level of perception, the level of cognition and at the level of reportage.

Perceptual resolutions. These take a number of forms. Common among them are proposals that one (or both) of the reporters of a discrepantly characterized state of affairs was prevented by physical circumstances (e.g. physical obstacles, poor visibility, etc.) from observing what the other reported. Relatedly, it may be proposed that, while the two reporters believed themselves to be describing the same state of affairs, in fact they were not: they were looking in different directions, or in the same direction at different times. All of these procedures were routinely employed to resolve discrepant testimony in the traffic courts studied by Pollner. Alternatively again, one reporter may be held to be a deficient perceiver (to have poor eyesight, or hearing), or to have faulty perception (for example colour blindness), or to be deficient in the necessary perceptual aids (he didn't have binoculars) or to have faulty perceptual aids (a gremlin in the 'software' of his radio telescope). Or, in a yet more extreme case, that one reporter 'imagined' or 'hallucinated' what he saw.

Cognitive resolutions. These take the form of drawing a distinction between what is perceived and what is interpreted of what is perceived. Thus it may be granted that 'something' was heard or seen, but asserted that the something is not the thing proposed (e.g. a burglar or a flying saucer). This distinction can take a variety of 'generic' forms. Young children are generically presupposed to perceive the same world as the rest of us, but to be incapable of cognizing fully or adequately what they perceive. Or again, the new biology student who looks down a microscope and sees a 'criss-cross of lines' where he should be seeing cell walls and nuclei is instructed to look again until he becomes a competent processor of what he sees. Thus as Schutz (1962a) intimated, there are many domains of physical and social events which are accountably and properly cognized only by interpreters who have the appropriate social accreditation. Regardless of whether the domain is physics, geology, psychiatry or religion, it is the properly accredited witness whose experience and testimony is normally treated as criterial (Sharrock, 1974). Thus the geology student who fails to recognize a 'glaciated valley' is required to look again; the witness of a UFO is discredited by the testimony of an experienced airline pilot in the region of the 'sighting' (Coulter, 1975a).

Resolution at the level of reportage.   At this level a distinction is drawn between what is perceived and cognized about a state of affairs and the verbal formulation of its features in a report. Thus discrepancies between accounts may be held to result from the fact that one or the other was 'poorly phrased', metaphorical, ironic, a joke or a lie. In some cases, specific interests may be invoked as a basis for the proposedly discrepant account.

Where any of the above grounds (and there are many more) are invoked to reconcile discrepant reports of what is intendedly the 'same' event, *we are encountering a procedure for reinstating or 'repairing' the existence of a 'known-in-common' world.* In each case, discrepant accounts are reconciled by the ascription (and recognition) of error to one or another of the account producers.

To recap: mundane actors operate on the assumption that others will perceive and recognize the same world as they do. This assumption is overwhelmingly confirmed in routine procedures of looking and telling which routinely interlock with the other's looking and confirming. Where there is some breakdown in this procedure and discrepant accounts emerge, the invocation of the repertoire of error accounts partially illustrated above serves as a means by which a 'known-in-common' world can be restored.

In his analysis of these error accounts, Pollner (1974) proposes that the repaired availability of a 'known-in-common' world is incorrigibly assured as, simultaneously, the process, presupposition and product of the reasoning practices involved. To gloss his remarks, a repaired known-in-common world is *processually* maintained in that the repaired intersubjective availability of 'real world' events is assured in no other way than through the practices with which discrepant accounts are reconciled. It is a *presupposition* of these practices in that, from the entire range of possible explanations of discrepancy, only those predicated on the original assumption of a known-in-common world are invoked and used. Each one of this restricted range of explanations respects the availability of a known-in-common world and each 'explains away' discrepancies by reference to conditions which leave that availability intact. Finally, through these means a known-in-common world is accountably *produced and reproduced*. It is, moreover, produced as an incorrigible product, as an objective world which could not have been otherwise. By these means, the transcendent objectivity of the world is produced in such a way as to be invariant to all exigencies. Through these means, the intersubjective availability of real world events is produced and reproduced as the indubitably given, stable feature of real world events which, for producers, it has always been.

This view of an assumption and the socially organized practices through which its secondary elaborations are invoked so as to reproduce it as incorrigible fact can, of course, be applied to more specific assumptions than the one that there exists a world-in-common. For example the analysis can be put to work on the practices through which the incorrigible infallibility of the famous Azande poison oracle is sustained (Evans Pritchard, 1937; Pollner, 1974), or on the maintenance of scientific paradigms or theories (Kuhn, 1970; Barnes, 1982a; Collins, 1975, 1981; Collins and Pinch, 1982), on religious beliefs (Homan, 1981) or on judgements of mental illness (Coulter, 1975a, 1975b). As we have seen, even our lowly interactional norm 'return a greeting' is preserved *as an incorrigible norm* by the interpretative work which is mobilized in cases when it is not fulfilled. In sum, the stability of accountable real world events of every type is sustained by, to use Garfinkel's term, a 'swarm' of secondarily elaborative practices through which some focal event of entity is sustained as, simultaneously, the presupposition, process and reflexive product of those practices.

The Maintenance of a World-in-Common as a 'Moral' Activity

While the reader may, by now, be prepared to acknowledge that the objective reality of real world events is itself sustained through a variety of institutionalized procedures and practices, it may not yet be obvious that the implementation of the latter is in any way normative in character. To see that this is in fact the case, it will be useful to follow Pollner's analysis one step further.

In a subsequent article, Pollner (1975) observes that, while the practices described above may be used to reconcile discrepant accounts, their use by no means *ensures* the success of such attempts at reconciliation. For, as he notes, the very practices used in support of one account may be invoked in support of its alternative. Under the very circumstances in which I assert that you 'need spectacles', you may retort that I am 'seeing things'. For every device through which A can advance a claim for the correctness of some description (and the inadequacy of B's), there is another available to B which can be used to undercut A's claims and advance B's. Thus circumstances can emerge in which

> the choice which culminates . . . is a choice among experiences which by virtue of their intending the same world are capable of discrediting one another's tacit claims to objectivity. That is, which experience of the world is to be treated as having grasped reality and which is to be treated as faulty is assured by neither the experience *per se* nor by any of the reasons offered in support of a particular selection. Neither of the competing experiences can authorize themselves as definitive because any competing experience can be used as grounds for discrediting such an attempt. (Pollner, 1975: 416)

Where this possibility is actualized, a fully fledged *reality disjuncture* occurs in which

> each participant treats his experience of the world as definitive and, hence, as the grounds for ironicizing his opponent's

experience. If consensual resolution is to be achieved, one of the protagonists will have to abandon the use of his experience as the incorrigible grounds of further inference. Of course, the abandonment cannot be secured on empirical or logical grounds alone. Competitive versions equally satisfy (and, with respect to one another, fail to satisfy) the demands for empirical validation and empirically correct conclusions. *Thus, a choice between them cannot be made compelling in empirical or logical terms alone for the choice is between empirically and logically self-validating and self-sustaining systems.* Consequently, relinquishing the faith in the validity of one's own experiences may have the flavour of an existential leap. It is a leap without logical or empirical foundations because it is a leap from and to such foundations. (ibid. 419)

Under these circumstances, a contest over experienced reality may emerge which is 'political' in the sense that a version of reality is adhered to and used as a basis for further activity despite the recognition that it is contested and rendered equivocal by the counter-claims of the other (ibid.). The prosecution of such contests may involve the reassertion of what was experienced together with its factual character; they may involve such activities as

the offering of 'good reasons' for how what the other claims to have experienced as in the world could not be in the world. They would include an appeal to further experiential or reasoned evidence which contradicts the possibility of the disputed experience. They would include instantaneous recognitions of the other's error and the 'subjective' origin of his claims. They would include, as well, activities which are perhaps more readily regarded as political such as mobilizing support for one's version from relevant segments of the community. (Pollner, 1975: 421–2)

In their most complete form, the politics of these disjunctures involve procedures through which the very attempt by each party to uphold his alternative depiction of the state of affairs is treated by the other as grounds for discounting the depiction. Thus, in the case of A's conviction that someone is persistently following him, B's assertion that this is not the case may be sufficient for A to conclude that B is 'in on the plot'. Whilst that conclusion is, in its turn, sufficient to confirm B's conclusion that A is paranoid. Similarly, protagonists of opposed political or religious convictions may find in the other's reassertions the grounds for determining that the other not only cannot, but *will* not, see because of the ideological assumptions and interests which are visible in his very preparedness to contest the matter. Under these circumstances, a potentially endless cycle of assertion and counterassertion is potentiated which permits no means of resolution. Under these conditions, the relationship between community membership and subscription to particular ways of depicting real world events is vividly displayed. For what counts as 'objective fact' is, under these circumstances, increasingly decided on 'tribal' grounds.

When set against this array of possibilities, the general tendency to avoid the production of competing accounts and to concentrate on procedures for securing agreement is striking, though scarcely surprising. One factor which may underly the avoidance of disagreement may be the risks which disagreement engenders. For, in the context of a 'head-to-head' disagreement, one of the parties is very likely to be discredited as, alternatively, a competent perceiver, cognizer or reporter of his or her experiences. Under circumstances in which it may be uncertain as to which of the parties will be discredited, there may be an inherent motivation towards the 'tactful' avoidance of disagreement and a general preference for indirect or mitigated disagreement (see chapter 8, 265–80).

Additionally, since many accounts are produced and understood by reference to the larger interactional undertakings of which they are a part, disagreements and discrepant accounts may be withheld so as to avoid imputations of disaffiliation or a lack of social solidarity. (Alternatively, of course, disagreements of this kind may be vehicles for the expression of such disaffiliation.) Finally, where one of the accounts produced is ultimately discredited, there may be efforts to limit the more 'global' implications concerning the capacities and motives of the discredited witness (Pollner, 1974; Coulter, 1975a). For instance efforts may be made to locate the error in a mistake 'anyone could have made' and thus to restore the credibility of the erroneous witness as a

competent member of the community of experiencers. So it is
normally in cases only of conflict between communities or, as
Pollner notes (1975), great communicative 'distance', that a
discrediting agent assigns 'global' faults (e.g. of ideology) to
discredited witnesses which would render the possibility of
future communal experiences doubtful. The same point can
be made by suggesting that the assignment of global faults is a
means of announcing and perpetuating conflict among experiencers.

With these considerations in mind, account production can
be examined for the ways in which producers provide for the
life-as-usual 'normality' of their descriptions (Sacks, 1984b);
for the ways in which descriptions of unusual or untoward
events are designed so as to propose that the account producer
is not one who is given to bizarre perceptions or experiences,
or to warrant the special competences involved in such
perceptions or experiences (Jefferson, 1979); and for the ways
in which accounts may be designed so as to undercut or
forestall possible grounds for discrepancy (Smith, 1978;
Atkinson and Drew, 1979). By the same token, account
recipients can be observed to avoid outright disagreement
with provided accounts (Pomerantz, 1984) and to seek to limit
the extent of disjunctures and of motives for their perpetuation
by designing disagreements and discrepant accounts which
avoid implicating the more 'global' aspects of account
producers' competences and motivations (Coulter, 1975a).

In this section we have looked at a sub-set of the collection
of practices associated with the activity of maintaining a
known-in-common world. Some of these practices are 'de-
scriber's practices', others have to do with responding to
descriptions and yet others are concerned with the management of discrepancies which may occur in accounts of states of
affairs. We have also noted some of the ways in which the
implementation of these practices may contribute to the
maintenance of a known-in-common world. To cite the
existence and prevalence of these practices is not in any way to
indulge in a general scepticism about the existence of an
objectively available world. Rather it is to point to some of the
ways in which the world is *rendered* objectively available and is
maintained as such. To cite these practices is to find some of the

ways in which the phenomenon which we gloss as a known-in-common world is available as the product of the socially organized work in which parties' subscription to communally held 'facts of life', their affiliation with one another's projects and activities, and their competences as members of the social world are continually, and in specific and located ways, displayed, managed, judged and used as the accountable basis for further inference and conduct. Garfinkel summarizes these points in the observation that: 'The managed production of this phenomenon in every aspect, from every perspective, and in every stage retains the character for members of serious practical tasks, subject to every exigency of organizationally situated conduct' (Garfinkel, 1967a: 34).

CASE 4: MAINTAINING 'OBJECTIVE FACT' IN A RESEARCH DOMAIN

While it may be held that discrepancies of the kind described by Pollner are relatively infrequent in ordinary social life, there are domains — for example the law courts and psychiatric hospitals – in which they are a routine occurrence. They are also common in research science — a domain characterized by a professional preoccupation with the determination of 'objective fact'. In the present section, we will focus on the ways in which scientists account for discrepancies in research findings, drawing on recent research by Mulkay and Gilbert (which is most fully described in Gilbert and Mulkay, 1984). Anticipating the remainder of this section, we will find that research scientists, in addressing research discrepancies, use very similar *forms* of accounting practices to those which we have already encountered in Pollner's study of mundane reasoning. This is significant in indicating that these same basic accounting practices are usable in an intellectually sophisticated domain which is perhaps characterized by more institutionalized conflict over the nature of real worldly events than is mundane interaction.

In a recent series of papers, Mulkay and Gilbert have systematically investigated a variety of accounting practices occurring within a research community in biochemistry. The members of this community are studying a process known as oxidative phosphorylation which is believed to be the major mechanism through which energy is stored in the cells of animals. Three major hypotheses have been advanced to explain this process and each of these has undergone extensive elaboration and revision. The main protagonist of the dominant theory — the 'chemiosmotic hypothesis' — was awarded a Nobel Prize in 1978. Mulkay and Gilbert's research has focused on how the scientists within this community accounted for such matters as their acceptance of particular theories (Mulkay and Gilbert, 1983; Gilbert and Mulkay, 1982a, 1984), their evaluation and use of experimental evidence (Gilbert and Mulkay, 1982b), their construction and deconstruction of scientific consensus and a range of other topics (Gilbert and Mulkay, 1984). The scientists were studied with the use of unstructured interviews which were tape-recorded and tran-scribed. In what follows, we shall not be concerned with the technical details of the biochemists' theories, but only with the general form of their accountings as detailed in Mulkay and Gilbert's (1982a) article 'Accounting for error'.

The authors begin by noting that research scientists are strongly committed to 'producing accurate observations of the natural world; and to formulating, employing and providing support for valid interpretations, hypotheses and theories' (Mulkay and Gilbert, 1982a:165). This interest, they observe, has a strong practical significance:

> For instance, there are often two or more competing clusters of hypotheses or candidate theories available in relation to a given area of experimental investigation; and each 'theory' will usually lead to the design of quite distinctive experiments. Accordingly, if scientists are to do 'good' experimental work, it is of crucial importance that they choose the theory which is most nearly correct. Similarly, in devising experiments, they must decide on the adequacy of others' observational claims, because acceptance of some claims rather than others will have a direct bearing on what experiments should be undertaken next and what results one should expect to achieve. (ibid.)

Similar observations have also been made by Latour and Woolgar (1979: 187–233).

Scientists, like lay actors, are committed to the notion that the natural world exhibits objective and regular properties. This commitment is expressed in the assumption that, if nature is questioned with the right techniques, univocal answers will emerge. This assumption ultimately undergirds the use of experimental methods and the associated commitment to independent validation of experimental results by other investigators in other laboratories. Moreover, scientists hold that, in the long run, 'the truth will out' (Mulkay and Gilbert, 1981) and experimental results will give overwhelming support to one particular theoretical account over others. Yet, in the meantime, divergent results and conflicting theories must somehow be dealt with in active research fields. This is routinely accomplished by identifying 'correct beliefs' and *explaining away* erroneous theories as the product of the 'intrusion into research of non-scientific influences which have distorted scientists' understanding of natural phenomena' (Mulkay and Gilbert, 1982a: 166). Correct belief, by contrast, is treated as unproblematic and as requiring no special explanation (ibid.). Scientists, in short, employ quite different accounts in order to explain correct and incorrect belief.

In Mulkay and Gilbert's interviews with biochemists, these different accounting practices repeatedly emerged. Scientists of conflicting theoretical persuasions presented their own preferred positions as straightforward and unambiguous products of the experimental evidence. They treated correct belief as an exclusively cognitive phenomenon uncontaminated by psychological or social forces. This method of accounting for correct belief, which Mulkay and Gilbert (1983) term 'empiricist', presents correct belief as unproblematically available to be 'read off' from the evidence. In addition to occurring in those passages of the interviews in which the scientists were accounting for their commitment to particular theories, this method of accounting is also dominant in scientific publications (Gilbert and Mulkay, 1980). And this dominant 'empiricist' repertoire of accounts also spills over into textbook (Kuhn, 1970) and other treatments which represent the development of disciplinary areas in terms of a sequence of 'key experiments' and their theoretical consequences (Gilbert and Mulkay, 1982b).

Returning to the interview data, the scientists routinely treated their own views as 'identical with the discernible realities of the natural world' (Mulkay and Gilbert, 1983) and hence as 'an unquestioned context in relation to which other scientists' claims are to be classified, explained and repudiated' (ibid.). In this context however, as Mulkay and Gilbert note, each scientist faces the following paradox: if the natural world is so unproblematically available via experiment, how is it that other experimenters have come to portray it in alternative and, from each scientist's point of view, incorrect ways? It can be noticed that this paradox, and the interpretative problem it establishes, is structurally similar to that faced by Pollner's 'mundane reasoners'. The latter, like the scientists, were confronted with an unproblematically given world which they assumed 'anyone could see' and which, nevertheless, was being viewed in alternative ways by others.

In both cases the resolution of the paradox is achieved in the same way: particular circumstances are cited as giving rise to the discrepancy, which is thus explained away. In the scientists' accounts, the preliminary move towards this kind of explanation often emerged in the claim that other researchers had failed to understand the preferred theory (Mulkay and Gilbert, 1982a: 168). And, by implication or direct statement, it was suggested that those who had not *understood* the preferred theory were not in a position to accept or reject it. Moreover, it was indicated, such persons were scarcely competent to devise experiments which would test the preferred theory or even to interpret the results of their own experiments properly. This proposal that the protagonists of other competing theories did not understand the preferred (or 'correct') one was normally a preliminary step in accounting for the errors of opponents. There still remained the task of accounting for *why* − when, as the speaker's own position 'evidences', it is possible to gain correct understanding − others have failed to do so.

To accomplish this task, the scientists drew upon a repertoire of *contingent* accounts (ibid.). A variety of factors were cited as 'contaminating' the cognitive process of science. These cited factors, which were often depicted as social or psychological in character, were uniformly presented as external to the cognitive domain of science and as matters whose elimination would result in cognitive consensus. Mulkay and Gilbert list some of the factors which were cited as giving rise to opponents' errors as follows:

> prejudice, commitment to one's own theories, reluctance to make the effort, complexity of the theory, dislike of the new theory, extreme naïvety, narrow disciplinary perspective, threat to status, rushing in too quickly, insufficient experimental skill, false intuition, subjective bias, personal rivalry, irrationality and general cussedness . . . not bothering to read the relevant literature and therefore not seeing the force of the argument, being too busy, being trained in terms of a false theory, being friendly with the correct theory's opponents, living in a country where that theory is not popular, stupidity, accepting the views of an authoritative figure, being afraid of a theory, having invested a good deal of effort in a prior theory, having a reputation deriving from work based on an earlier theory, pig-headedness, being out of touch with reality, being American and therefore thinking in a woolly fashion, fear of being discredited with grant-giving bodies, being prevented by disciples from admitting one's mistakes, and believing in one's theory in the same uncritical way that people believe in their religion (ibid. 176)

As can be seen from this list, which was entirely drawn from interview statements, scientists have at their disposal an immense array of 'citeable' factors with which to account for their colleagues' failure to understand, and endorse, the correct theory. Without exception, the list nominates a series of social and psychological factors which, by their intrusion into the cognitive domain of science, obscure the truth or hinder the search for it. In their discussion of these accounts, Mulkay and Gilbert stress that, although the accounts were formulated to deal with a common interpretative task — 'accounting for error' — their variety and flexibility are such as to furnish resources for each individual scientist 'to provide plausible accounts adjusted to the speaker's own perspective and to the variable characteristics of each individual case' (ibid. 173). The accounts, moreover, were finely tuned to specific conversational contexts and were variously and shiftingly employed even within quite short stretches of talk. Thus, as Mulkay and Gilbert put it, 'the main characteristic of these resources is that they can easily be expanded or contracted, withdrawn or supplemented, without creating obvious inconsistencies, to meet the exigencies of each new conversational exchange' (ibid. 177).

Overall, Mulkay and Gilbert stress the universality of these devices for accounting for error within the 'oxidative phosphorylation' research domain. Protagonists of diametrically opposed theories employed them as part of the task of asserting the correctness of their own theories and discounting the theories of their opponents. This observation raises the following question concerning the 'social order' of science: how is 'science', as a collective institution concerned with the establishment of objective fact, maintained in the face of this babble of voices and mutually undercutting accounts of error? In response to this question we will consider two issues: how 'reality disjunctures' are avoided in science and the role of these accounts of error in relation to the phenomenon of objective fact.

As we have seen, in accounting for error the scientists first identified correct beliefs and then proceeded to discount discrepant, 'erroneous' beliefs as having been caused by the intrusion of non-scientific factors. Since incorrect belief itself is treated as prima facie evidence that non-scientific factors must be at work, there is the ever-present possibility that scientists may initiate and perpetuate full-blown 'reality disjunctures' in which rival theoretical positions are attacked with an ever-escalating repertoire of damning, if mutually cancelling, accusations about the social and psychological factors which have intruded into competing research. The net result of such a process world be the 'politicization' of scientific activity.

This kind of escalation is avoided in natural science by restricting the use of these accounting devices to informal settings in which 'shop talk' is exchanged. Thus, while the accounting devices described above are widespread in scientific circles, they are kept out of the formal literature and

> there is seldom, if ever, any published attempt to explain why false theories are accepted by one's colleagues, presumably because this would lead formal debate into the realm of 'non-scientific' considerations. Yet this embargo means that scientific

debates in the formal literature are radically misleading, in that they omit all the social theorizing or social accounting which takes place when members informally read, assess and discuss formal knowledge claims. (ibid. 179)

This embargo, together with the absence within the formal literature of corrections of observational errors, serves to limit the scope of conflicts within science although 'this does mean, however, that the formal literature contains numerous claims which many competent researchers would regard as demonstrably wrong' (ibid. 180). Moreover,| this| restriction| on the formal literature embodies and reinforces the 'empiricist' account of science which treats genuine scientific knowledge as independent of non-cognitive influences (ibid.). And, as we shall see, this same conclusion can emerge from the accounts of errors themselves.

Turning then to the role of these forms of accounting for error in the maintenance of objective truth, it should by now be clear that, as Mulkay and Gilbert put it, 'the conception of scientific error which we see exemplified in these accounts is a necessary implication of scientists' conception of correct belief. It is the reverse side of the same coin' (ibid. 173). In just the way that error accounts in mundane reasoning presuppose the availability of an objectively knowable state of affairs that 'would be known but for distorting factors', so too do scientists' accounts of error. Thus, at the end of the day,

the intellectual disagreements which are endemic in science at the research front and which could be taken as posing a threat to (the) dominant conception of rationality are interpreted in ways which not only take this conception for granted but, in so doing, further strengthen its apparent cogency. Scientists employ asymmetrical accounting to perform interpretative work in such a way that they are able to preserve the underlying assumptions that *genuine* knowledge is immune from non-cognitive influences, and that only one *scientific* theory is possible in a given area. (ibid. 181–2)

In sum, in their situated use of error accounts, research scientists both preserve an underlying commitment to the unitary character of objective scientific knowledge and exploit this commitment to advance their own current theoretical positions. The informal embargo on the use of error accounts in the published literature serves to limit 'error-account escalated' conflict at the frontiers of research and to maintain the publicly accountable character of scientific knowledge as objective knowledge anchored in the observation of nature. To propose, with Mulkay and Gilbert, that this objectivity is presupposed by, and preserved in, scientists' situated use of diverse accounts to 'explain away' discrepancies in experimental results or theoretical interpretations is not, in any way, to suggest that the achieved objectivity of scientific findings is spurious or artefactual. Rather it is to indicate some of the ways in which this objectivity is maintained as an intersubjective, socially organized, accountable and, in all of these senses, as a *real* phenomenon.

Given the permanent possibility that experimental procedures and their interpretations will yield divergent results, some set of socially organized procedures for the accountable discounting of findings will be a necessary facet of the institutionalized achievement of objective fact. Error accounts form a part of the institutionalized resources for the achievement of this task. They are, to recall an earlier phrase from Garfinkel, 'a device for burying monsters' — the 'monsters' being formulated within the dialectic of error-accounting practices as the kinds of mistakes which can always result from incompetent interrogations of nature.

CONCLUSION

In the preface to *Studies in Ethnomethodology*, Garfinkel contrasts the traditional Durkheimian insistence on the objective reality of social facts with the study policy that 'the objective reality of social facts *as* an ongoing accomplishment of the concerted activities of daily life, with the ordinary, artful ways of that accomplishment being by members known, used, and taken for granted is . . . a fundamental phenomenon' (Garfinkel, 1967: vii). Despite his vigorous assertions to the contrary (ibid. viii; Garfinkel and Sacks, 1970: 345), this study policy has persistently been taken as proposing that social structures, and indeed social reality itself, are inherently fragile and that objective reality is a mirage. This understanding of Garfinkel's position is profoundly mistaken. Although the institutional realities discussed in this chapter have been various, none could be appropriately described as inherently fragile nor were their objectivities illusory.

The general misunderstanding of Garfinkel's proposal seems to arise from his refusal to treat social institutions as self-subsistent. But the fact is that no social institution can be treated as a self-subsistent entity which exists independently of the accounting practices of its participants (cf. Giddens, 1979: 47–130). The reproduction of institutional settings and the accounting practices through which they are constituted is an elementary and fundamental fact of institutional life. And to demand that institutions function in independence from these reproductive processes is, to adapt an earlier observation of Garfinkel's, 'very much like complaining that if the walls of a building were only gotten out of the way one could see better what was keeping the roof up' (Garfinkel, 1967a: 22). Each of the institutional realities discussed in this chapter subsisted as the robust product of an interlocking network of reflexively accountable practices. This feature of these realities reminds us that, as Garfinkel puts it, 'in doing sociology ... every reference to the "real world", even where the reference is to physical or biological events, is a reference to the organized activities of everyday life' (Garfinkel, 1967: vii). And it reminds us too that the 'real world' is not any less real for all that. At most, that reality is temporarily placed in brackets during a period in which 'the social scientist treats knowledge, and the procedures that societal members use for its assembly, test, management and transmission, as objects of theoretical sociological interest' (Garfinkel, 1967c: 77).

In each of the case studies discussed in the present chapter, the specific institutionalized reality under investigation has been bracketed so that the practices underlying its maintenance *as* a reality can be more clearly delineated. Drawing upon ideas developed in chapters 5 and 6, this maintenance has been formulated as involving:

(1) The production of actions in full circumstantial detail that are recognizable and accountable within the relevant institutionalized framework of accounts, and

(2) The maintenance of the accounting frameworks themselves in the face of 'entropic' tendencies deriving from 'discrepant' actions.

Naturally, the empirical fulfilment of (1) will, regardless of the habitual or motivated basis of the acts in question, tend to reinstantiate and reproduce the relevant accounting frameworks and will hence maintain or renew their relevance and potency. However, in relation to (2), it has also been suggested that the critical 'repair' mechanism for accounting frameworks derives from the latters' reflexive property of 'double constitution'. This property forms the basis for a range of processes of 'secondary elaboration' which swarm as an ever-present potential around accounting frameworks. These processes supply resources for the maintenance and 'repair' of accounting frameworks which would otherwise be threatened by 'discrepant' actions, and they do so in two ways. First, they can be used to depict 'discrepant' actions as forms of 'motivated deviance' in ways which can legitimate the mobilization of sanctions. In this way, the secondary elaborations of primary accounting frameworks can furnish the regulative resources which, by inhibiting or suppressing the production of actions constituted as deviant, contribute to the maintenance of institutional patterns of action as depicted in (1) above. Second, and still more significant, the secondary elaborations reflexively preserve the presupposed primacy of the core accounting framework as the constitutive ordering principle for the domain of activities analysable within its discursive field. In this double sense, the secondary elaborations of any accounting framework play a critical role in its reproductive maintenance.

In turn, this suggests that a major mechanism of institutional change will involve the constitutive re-embedding of 'discrepant' activities within some new, normalizing, but equally self-replicating accounting framework. The development of new frameworks of accounts is permanently possible through some regrouping of the particulars which instance natural language categories. Under such circumstances, what is constituted from the perspective of an older accounting framework as 'deviant' will be treated under its new alternative as appropriate, normal or natural, and vice versa.

Such a process of change is, perhaps, most evident in the development of 'paradigmatic' revolutions in science in which, as Kuhn (1970) has taught us to see, anomalies become the focus for the development of new accounting frameworks for physical processes. However similar processes are readily discernable in the sphere of social relations. During the past decade relations between the sexes in western societies have arguably begun to undergo the beginnings of a 'paradigmatic shift'. Ways of speaking and acting associated with gender relations which were previously taken for granted, especially within urban middle class groupings, have begun to become subject to the hesitancies and tentativeness which are the hallmarks of an emerging reflexive awareness and uncertainty about gender related conduct. They, in turn, may be indicators of changes in the constitutive expectancies informing relations between the sexes, although the scope and character of such changes are, as yet, profoundly indeterminate.

In this context, it may be observed that all the studies discussed in the present chapter and, still more, Garfinkel's experiments discussed in chapter 4, suggest that it is 'taken for granted' social practices and accounting procedures which constitute the deepest layers of the moral and factual orders. Indeed it may be hazarded that the progressive sedimentation of such practices and procedures 'out of mind' and into the 'taken for granted' is itself the core process of 'internalization'. And in this context processes in which acquisitions of such practices and methods are devoid of conscious awareness should not be left out of account. While the significance and consequences of the substitution of a cognitive-social 'unconscious' for the older, psychodynamic version cannot detain us here, it is surely beyond question that the detachment of social practices and accounting procedures from the domain of the 'taken for granted' which is involved even in the assertion of their legitimacy, may carry with it, in and of itself, a loss in the legitimacy that is sought for. The Parsonian view that the foundations of the moral order lie in norms to which an attitude of expediency cannot be adopted may thus be correct, although the status of such norms may be more appropriately construed, not as the 'need dispositions' of the older motiv-

ational language but rather as part of the 'collective unconscious' of the 'taken for granted'.

We conclude this chapter by noting that the kinds of
theoretical bracketings which have permeated it are, at best,
only transiently possible within the world of everyday life. As a
result, the endogenous reproductive processes through which
institutional realities are maintained remain largely invisible
to those who participate within them. Instead these realities
contine to exist as the natural-moral outcomes of arrays of
detailed accountable activities. These activities are acted out,
and acted on, largely in that 'seen but unnoticed' fashion
which itself undergirds the reproduction of institutions as the
presuppositionally real orders of events which, from the actors'
point of view, they always have been.

CHAPTER 8

Conversation Analysis

A curious fact becomes apparent if you look at the first paragraph — it may occur in the third paragraph — of reportedly revolutionary treatises back to the pre-Socratics and extending up to at least Freud. You find that they all begin by saying something like this: 'About the things I am going to talk about, people think they know but they don't. Furthermore if you tell them it doesn't change anything. They still walk round like they know although they are walking in a dream world.' Darwin begins this way, Freud begins in a similar way. What we are interested in is, what is it that people seem to know and use.

Sacks, *Proceedings of the Purdue Symposium on Ethnomethodology*

Over the past ten years conversation analysis has developed into a prominent form of ethnomethodological work and has come to exert a significant influence — both methodological and substantive — on a range of social science disciplines including linguistics, social psychology, anthropology and cognitive science. During this time its growth and diversification have become very extensive. The mimeographed lectures of Harvey Sacks (Sacks, 1964–72), who founded the field in collaboration with Emanuel Schegloff and Gail Jefferson, run to some two thousand pages and are still a major resource for contemporary researchers. Since the publication of a series of well-known papers on turn-taking and related topics (Sacks, Schegloff and Jefferson, 1974; Schegloff, 1968; Schegloff and Sacks, 1973), a growing number of researchers have published papers on an ever-increasing range of topic areas embracing many different facets of conversational organization, the role of gaze and gesture in interaction, and communication in a variety of institutional domains (see Heritage, 1984c, for an overview).

Conversation analytic studies have proved to be highly

distinctive both in methodology and findings, from a range of linguistic, social psychological and sociological approaches to the data of interaction, and they have proved to be strongly cumulative and interlocking. These studies have tended to be presented in a rather formal style which presumes a competent audience and which understates what is known about a particular domain of action and the implications of that knowledge.

Each of these characteristic features — the extent, diversity, distinctiveness and style — of conversation analytic writings makes access to their methods and findings difficult. Together, they ensure that the field resists easy summary and they impose limits on what can be attempted in the present chapter. In what follows, therefore, only some of the most basic methodological and substantive aspects of the field will be dealt with.

SOME METHODOLOGICAL PRELIMINARIES: INSTANCES VERSUS IDEALIZATIONS

The inception and development of conversation analysis as a distinctive field of research is closely linked with problems surrounding the tendency for ordinary language descriptions to gloss or idealize the specifics of what they depict (see 144–50). This tendency is inherent in the use of type concepts in the social sciences irrespective of whether the types are produced by 'averaging' as recommended by Durkheim (1982) or by explicit idealization as proposed by Weber in his various methodological writings. In an early paper, Sacks (1963) criticized the use of both of these categories of type concepts in sociology on the grounds that they necessarily blur the specific features of the events under investigation. The result, he argued, is that sociological concepts and generalizations can have only a vague and indeterminate relationship with any specific set of events. This, in turn, inhibits the development of sociology as a cumulative body of knowledge because, given this indeterminacy, it can be difficult to decide whether a specific case in fact supports or undermines a given sociological generalization.

Sacks's response to this problem was a deliberate decision to develop a method of analysis which would keep a grip on the primary data of the social world — the raw material of specific, singular events of human conduct:

> When I started to do research in sociology I figured that sociology could not be an actual science unless it was able to handle the details of actual events, handle them formally, and in the first instance be informative about them in the direct ways in which primitive sciences tend to be informative, that is, that anyone else can go and see whether what was said is so. And that is a tremendous control on seeing whether one is learning anything. So the question was, could there be some way that sociology could hope to deal with the details of actual events, formally and informatively? . . . I wanted to locate some set of materials that would permit a test. (Sacks, 1984a: 26)

Sacks's work on tape-recorded conversation was initiated in deliberate pursuit of this methodological aim:

> It was not from any large interest in language or from some theoretical formulation of what should be studied that I started with tape-recorded conversation, but simply because I could get my hands on it and I could study it again and again, and also, consequentially, because others could look at what I had studied and make of it what they could, if, for example, they wanted to be able to disagree with me. (ibid.)

Viewed with the advantage of hindsight, Sacks's decision to study conversation was both courageous and perceptive. It was courageous because few people in the early sixties believed that the concrete details of social interaction were, in fact, strongly organized enough to permit formal description. Indeed the dominant view, reflected for example in Chomsky's (1957, 1965) decision to avoid the analysis of actual speech, was that social interaction is beset by randomizing factors which make any attempt at analysis problematic. The decision was perceptive however because, now that it is known how strongly interaction is organized and to what level of detail that organization extends, it is clear that human conduct could not be so coherent and meaningful, and in such subtle and nuanced ways, in the absence of such an organization.

The contemporary methodology of conversation analysis has maintained Sacks's pioneering focus on the details of actual interactions and his effort to forestall the 'process of idealization. Its insistence on the use of data collected from naturally occurring occasions of everyday interaction is paralleled by a corresponding avoidance of a range of other research methodologies as unsatisfactory sources of data. These include: (1) the use of interviewing techniques in which the verbal formulations of subjects are treated as an appropriate substitute for the observation of actual behavior; (2) the use of observational methods in which data are recorded through field notes or with pre-coded schedules; (3) the use of native intuitions as a means of inventing examples of interactional behaviour; and (4) the use of experimental methodologies involving the direction or manipulation of behaviour. These techniques have been avoided because each of them involves processes in which the specific details of naturally situated interactional conduct are irretrievably lost and are replaced by idealizations about how interaction works.

A range of considerations inform this preference for the use of recorded data over subjects' reports, observers' notes or unaided intuition or recollection. Anyone who has examined conversational materials will be highly conscious of the deficiencies of such resources by comparison with the richness and diversity of empirically occurring interaction. For example, although the following sequence is by no means extraordinary,

```
(1)  (NB:VII:2) ((Transcription conventions appear in the appendix))
    E:  =Oh honey that was a lovely luncheon I shoulda ca:lled you
        s:soo⌐:ner but I:⌐l:⌐lo:ved it. It w's just deli:ghtfu⌐:l.  ⌐
    M:      ⌊.((f)) Oh:::⌋ ⌊( )                            ⌊Well⌋=
    M:  =I w's gla⌐d    you⌝(came).⌝
    E:          ⌊nd yer f:⌋friends ⌋ 're so da:rli:ng,=
    M:  = Oh:::⌐: it w'z:⌝
    E:        ⌊e-that P⌐a:t isn'she a do⌐:ll?⌝
    M:                              ⌊iYe⌐h isn't she pretty,
        (.)
    E:  Oh: she's a beautiful girl.=
    M:  =Yeh I think she's a pretty gir⌐l.
    E:                              ⌊En' that Reinam'n::
        (.)
    E:  She SCA:RES me.=
```

it is difficult to imagine its invention by a social scientist.

Not only is it impossible to imagine the above being invented, it is similarly inconceivable that it could be recollected in such detail either by an ethnographer or by an actual participant. And, even if it could be recollected, it could not be heard again and again. Moreover, as Sacks (1984a) notes, it can be difficult to treat invented or recollected sequences as fully persuasive evidence for analytic claims. And even if they are accepted, such inventions or recollections can tell us nothing about the frequency, range, variety or typicality of the conversational procedures used within the fragment.

The intuitive invention of data is subject to an additional problem which has nothing to do with complexity, but everything to do with the way unaided intuition tends to typify the ways interaction happens. Consider (2) below:

(2) (Sacks 1968, 17 April)
    A: I have a fourteen-year-old-son.
    B: Well that's alright.
    A: I also have a dog.
    B: Oh I'm sorry.

Although (2) is simple enough, it is not the way we imagine interaction happens. If it had been invented, it might have been used to show what is meant by incoherent interaction. But in fact (2) is taken from a conversation in which the would-be tenant of an apartment (A) is describing circumstances to the landlord (B) which might disqualify the rental and, viewed in this context, the datum is perfectly coherent and sensible. The myriad ways in which specific contexts (e.g. particular social identities, purposes and circumstances) are talked into being and oriented to in interaction vastly exceed our comparatively limited, and overwhelmingly typified, powers of imaginative intuition.

A similar range of issues arises in relation to experimentally produced data. The success of social psychological experiments is strongly dependent on the experimenter's ability to identify, control and manipulate the relevant dependent and independent variables. Not only is this extremely difficult to accomplish without some form of experimenter contamination (Rosenthal,

1966; Friedman, 1967), but also it is unlikely that an experimenter will be able to identify the range of relevant variables without previous exposure to naturally occurring interaction. Moreover, without such exposure the experimenter will find it difficult to extrapolate from experimental findings to real situations of conduct, nor will it prove easy to determine which (if any) of the experimental findings are artefacts of the experimental situation, since such a determination can only be achieved by systematic comparison with naturally occurring data. In sum, the most straightforward procedure has been to work with naturally occurring materials from the outset. Naturally occurring interaction presents an immense range of interactional variations in terms of which systematic comparisons may be used both to check and extend particular analyses.

Thus the use of recorded data is an essential corrective to the limitations of intuition and recollection. In enabling repeated and detailed examination of the events of interaction, the use of recordings extends the range and precision of the observations which can be made. It permits other researchers to have direct access to the data about which claims are being made, thus making analysis subject to detailed public scrutiny and helping to minimize the influence of personal preconceptions or analytical biases. Finally, it may be noted that because the data are available in 'raw' form they can be reused in a variety of investigations and can be re-examined in the context of new findings. All of these major advantages derive from the fact that the original data are neither idealized nor constrained by a specific research design or by reference to some particular theory or hypothesis.

THE PRIMACY OF MUNDANE CONVERSATION

The central domain of data with which conversation analysts are concerned is everyday, mundane conversations. Correspondingly, there has been a general tendency to avoid analysing talk which is, for example, highly 'intellectual' in content or specifically 'fateful' for one or another of the participants. Moreover, until recently the various forms of

interaction involving 'institutional' identities — e.g. teacher—
pupil, social worker—client, courtroom, news interview and
other forms of interaction – were avoided. The reasons for this
focusing on apparently 'trivial' interactions are as follows.

Despite the almost fortuitous decision by Sacks to begin
work on conversational interaction, the topic has turned out to
have a central significance for a range of social science issues.
In the first instance, the social world is a pervasively
conversational one in which an overwhelming proportion of
the world's business is conducted through the medium of
spoken interaction. Speech, moreover, is among the most
ancient of human social institutions. The spoken use of
language antedates all other uses and its overwhelming
preponderance among contemporary uses is plainly visible in
syntactic structure itself (Goodwin, 1979a, 1979b, 1981;
Levinson, 1983; Sacks, Schegloff and Jefferson, 1974; Schegloff,
1979b; see also Harris 1980). Second, conversational exchange
is the order of interaction through which, subject to a variety of
simplifications (Bruner, 1975a, 1984; Ervin-Tripp and Mitchell-
Kernan, 1977; Snow and Ferguson, 1977; Ochs and Schieffelin,
1979), the child is first exposed to the social world. It is the
conventions of this communicative framework which the child
must master as a condition of his or her membership of society
and there is considerable evidence that the child is pre-adapted
to achieve this goal (see, *inter alios* Richards, 1971, 1974, for a
particularly vivid discussion of 'conversational' behaviour in
interactions between mothers and very young children). In
short, it is the acquisition of interactional competence and the
common-sense knowledge gained in and through such competence which constitutes the core of childhood socialization.
These considerations are, in themselves, sufficient to warrant a
commitment to the study of mundane conversation.

Additionally, however, there is considerable evidence deriving from the recent application of conversation analytic
techniques to 'institutional' data (Atkinson and Drew, 1979;
McHoul, 1978; Mehan, 1979; Atkinson, 1982; Drew, 1984b;
Heritage, 1984b) that institutional interaction tends to involve
two related phenomena: (1) a selective reduction in the full
range of conversational practices available for use in mundane
interaction; and (2) a degree of concentration on, and

specialization of, particular procedures which have their 'home' or base environment in ordinary talk. These findings support the view that not only is mundane conversation the richest available research domain, but also that comparative analysis with mundane interaction is essential if the 'special features' of interaction in particular institutional contexts are to receive adequate specification and understanding. These latter observations are supported by the consideration that activities which are normally accomplished in 'restricted' or 'specialized' settings may also occur in parallel fashion in ordinary interaction: 'interrogation' or 'cross-examination', for example, may occur over the breakfast table. As a form of interaction it is not restricted to the police station or the court-room.

The same need to establish the characteristic features of ordinary conversation between people of similar status has led to a central focus on casual conversation between peers, neighbours, etc. rather than, for example, looking directly at relationships involving dominance and subordination or focusing exclusively on male—female interactional differences (but see, for example, Zimmerman and West, 1975). Once again, conversation analysts have proceeded on the basis that it is difficult, if not impossible, to explain specific features of such assymetric interaction by reference to social attributes (e.g. status, power, gender, ethnicity, etc.) without a clear knowledge of what is characteristic of ordinary talk between peers.

In one respect, however, the data of conversation analysis have been atypical, namely, in the concentration on telephone calls during the first several years of research. The use of telephone calls as data was designed to eliminate the complexities of non-vocal behaviour from the analysis of interaction, while preserving a naturalistic environment of talk. In this way, the additional tasks of analysing non-vocal behaviour could be legitimately postponed in favour of an exclusive focus on the details of speech. The findings which derived from this procedure have stood up remarkably well in the face of results from an increasing body of studies focusing on face-to-face interaction (see, for example, Goodwin, 1981; Heath, forthcoming).

THE CONVERSATION ANALYTIC APPROACH: SOME BASIC ASSUMPTIONS

Conversation analysis — like the other research streams of ethnomethodology — is concerned with the analysis of the *competences* which underlie ordinary social activities. Specifically it is directed at describing and explicating the competences which ordinary speakers use and rely on when they engage in intelligible, conversational interaction. At its most basic, the objective is to describe the procedures and expectations in terms of which speakers produce their own behaviour and interpret the behaviour of others. As in other aspects of ethnomethodological work, Garfinkel's (1967a: 1) 'symmetry' proposal is employed and it is assumed that both the *production* of conduct and its *interpretation* are the accountable products of a common set of methods or procedures.

The basic outlook of conversation analysis can be briefly summarized in terms of three fundamental assumptions: (1) interaction is structurally organized; (2) contributions to interaction are contextually oriented; and (3) these two properties inhere in the details of interaction so that no order of detail can be dismissed, *a priori*, as disorderly, accidental or irrelevant.

The initial and most fundamental assumption of conversation is that all aspects of social action and interaction can be found to exhibit organized patterns of stable, recurrent structural features. These organizations are to be treated as structures in their own right and as social in character. Like other social institutions and conventions, they stand independently of the psychological or other characteristics of particular speakers. Knowledge of these organizations is a major part of the competence which ordinary speakers bring to their communicative activities and, whether consciously or unconsciously, this knowledge influences their conduct and their interpretation of the conduct of others. Ordinary interaction can thus be analysed so as to exhibit stable organizational patterns of action to which the participants are oriented. These participant orientations, as we shall see, can be demonstrated in a variety of ways.

A second assumption of conversation analysis, which will be familiar from the earlier chapters of this book, is that the contributions to interaction are contextually oriented. Specifically, it is assumed that the significance of any speaker's communicative action is doubly contextual in being both *context-shaped* and *context-renewing*. A speaker's action is *context-shaped* in that its contribution to an on-going sequence of actions cannot adequately be understood except by reference to the context — including, especially, the immediately preceding configuration of actions — in which it participates. This contextualization of utterances is a major, and unavoidable, procedure which hearers use and rely on to interpret conversational contributions and it is also something which speakers pervasively attend to in the design of what they say. The *context-renewing* character of conversational actions is directly related to the fact that they are context-shaped. Since every 'current' action will itself form the immediate context for some 'next' action in a sequence, it will inevitably contribute to the framework in terms of which the next action will be understood. In this sense, the context of a next action is repeatedly renewed with every current action. Moreover, each action will, by the same token, function to renew (i.e. maintain, alter or adjust) any more generally prevailing sense of context which is the object of the participants' orientations and actions. While both aspects of this assumption can be clearly traced to Garfinkel's pioneering remarks on the indexical and reflexive characteristics of talk and action, they have found parallel expression in Goffman's more ethnographically oriented studies (see Goffman, 1955; 1963; 1971; 1981) and a range of other, otherwise unrelated, approaches to interaction which Kendon (1979; 1982) has linked together under the heading of 'context analysis'.

Finally, the assumption that no order of detail in interaction can be dismissed *a priori* as insignificant has had two major consequences for conversation analytic researchers. The first had been a general retreat from premature theory construction in favour of a more strongly empirical approach to the study of social action. Correspondingly, there has been an avoidance of the abstract theoretical constructs characteristic of earlier sociological treatments of action (for example Parsons's (1937) analysis of the 'unit act') in favour of concrete empirical research on 'actual, particular social actions and organized sequences of them' (Schegloff, 1980: 151). Second, a similarly stringent view is adopted towards the analysis of the competences which are employed in the production and recognition of actions. In particular, every effort is made to render empirical analyses answerable to the specific details of research materials and, as we have seen, to avoid their idealization. In their attitudes towards empirical materials, conversation analysts converge with other proponents of 'context analysis' in assuming that the data of interaction will, in all their aspects and unless proved otherwise, exhibit systematic and orderly properties which are meaningful for the participants.

The research objectives of conversation analysis, together with these underlying assumptions, have necessarily shaped the ways in which analysis is done. Specifically, analysis is strongly 'data-driven' — developed from phenomena which are in various ways evidenced in the data of interaction. Correspondingly, there is a strong bias against *a priori* speculation about the orientations and motives of speakers and in favour of detailed examination of conversationalists' actual actions. Thus the empirical conduct of speakers is treated as the central resource out of which analysis may develop. This basic research orientation, with its treatment of the details of talk as an analytic resource, has been summarized by Schegloff and Sacks in the following passage:

We have proceeded under the assumption (an assumption borne out by our research) that in so far as the materials we worked with exhibited orderliness, they did so not only to us, indeed not in the first place for us, but for the co-participants who had produced them. If the materials (records of natural conversation) were orderly, they were so because they had been methodically produced by members of the society for one another, and it was a feature of the conversations we treated as data that they were produced so as to allow the display by the co-participants to each other of their orderliness, and to allow the participants to display to each other their analysis, appreciation and use of that orderliness. Accordingly, our analysis has sought to explicate the ways in which the materials are produced by members in orderly ways that exhibit their orderliness and have their orderliness appreciated and used, and have that appreciation displayed and treated as the basis for subsequent action. (Schegloff and Sacks, 1973: 290)

Conversation analysts have generally pursued their objectives by showing regular forms of organization in a large variety of interactional materials produced by different speakers. However, the delineation of such forms is usually only part of the analytic process. Additionally, steps will normally be taken to show that the regularities are produced and oriented to by the participants as normatively oriented-to grounds for inference and action. Here the analysis of 'deviant cases' — in which some proposed regular conversational procedure or form is *not* implemented — is regularly undertaken. Integral to this is the task of describing the role which particular conversational procedures play in relation to particular interactional activities. Beyond this lie the more general objectives of describing, wherever possible given the current state of knowledge, the roles which particular conversational procedures play in relation to one another and to other orders of conversational and social organization.

In what follows, we will look at some straightforward aspects of conversational organization, at the ways in which evidences for their existence are formulated and at the ways in which quite simple conversational procedures interlock to produce more complicated organizational structures. The reader is warned, however, that in the context of a short expository chapter only coarse presentations of richly detailed observations and findings can be attempted and, in particular, that conversational data are here being used only in an illustrative way. Recourse to the cited articles and texts, therefore, will be necessary to appraise the substantive use of data. Additional introductions to conversation analysis are contained in Atkinson and Drew (1979, chapter 2) and Levinson (1983, chapter 6), while Schegloff and Sacks (1973) and Schegloff (1984) represent clear examples of the working through of a particular problem. Those who wish to gain a sense both of the delicacy and the cumulative complexity of conversation analytic findings are referred to Jefferson (1980a, 1981a, 1981b).

CONVERSATIONAL ORGANIZATION:
PAIRED ACTIONS

In the previous section, it was noted that conversation analysis is centrally occupied with describing the procedures and expectations through which participants produce and understand ordinary conversational conduct. We have already seen that this programme has issued in a strongly empirical research orientation in which attention is concentrated on organizational features of talk which are displayed, appreciated and used in the actual events of interaction. We now turn to consider a second, highly significant, outcome of this programme: namely, the concentration on action sequences. For, anticipating somewhat, the most prominent place at which the character of an action (A) is demonstrably appreciated, used and treated as the basis for some subsequent action (B) is *in that very subsequent action*. Conversation analysis is therefore primarily concerned with the ways in which utterances accomplish particular actions by virtue of their placement and participation within sequences of actions. It is sequences and turns-within-sequences which are thus the primary units of analysis.

At its most basic, conversation analytic research into sequence is based on the notion that in a variety of ways the production of some current conversational action proposes a local, here-and-now 'definition of the situation' to which subsequent talk will be oriented. The most elementary instance of this phenomenon occurs when some current turn's talk projects a relevant next activity, or range of activities, to be accomplished by another speaker in the next turn — a phenomenon generically referred to as the 'sequential implicativeness' of a turn's talk (Schegloff and Sacks, 1973: 296).

In its strongest form, this projection of a relevant next activity may be accomplished through a conventially recognizable pair of actions. Many conversational actions occur within the framework of such a pair linkage, varying from the relatively 'ritualized' exchanges of 'Hello' and 'Goodbye' to more complicatedly paired actions such as question-answer, request-grant/rejection, invitation-acceptance/refusal, and so on. A generic analytic apparatus to handle these paired actions was developed by Sacks in the mid-sixties. He termed the apparatus an 'adjacency pair' and described it in terms of five basic characteristics (Schegloff and Sacks, 1973: 295–6). In this formulation, an adjacency pair is

(1) A sequence of two utterances, which are
(2) adjacent,
(3) produced by different speakers,
(4) ordered as a first part and second part, and
(5) typed, so that a first part requires a particular second part (or range of second parts).

To this list of characteristics, Schegloff and Sacks added a simple rule of adjacency pair operation: 'given the recognisable production of a first pair part, on its first possible completion its speaker should stop and a next speaker should start and produce a second pair part from the pair type the first pair part is recognizably a member of (ibid. 296). Thus baldly stated, it may be difficult for the reader to grasp either the point or the implications of the adjacency pair concept. It may, indeed, simply look like a rather ponderous way of stating the rule that greetings are exchanged, questions answered, etc. In order to gain access to the very important substantive and methodological issues which cluster around the concept and its application, we will first consider what is *not* claimed or implied by the concept and move on from there.

First, when it is proposed that action sequences such as greetings exchanges or question-answer sequences are organized as adjacency pairs, it is emphatically not claimed that these sequences are invariably produced as succeeding actions occurring adjacently. The claim that greetings are always returned immediately, or that questions are always answered in the next utterance would, if it were being made, be palpably incorrect. The adjacency pair notion does not, therefore, command our attention as a statement of empirical invariance.

Neither, second, is the concept properly viewed as describing an empirical generalization. For, while it may be the case that 99 per cent of greetings are promptly returned or 95 per cent of questions are immediately answered, we are here in pursuit of structural organizations which shape the expectations, understandings and actions of interactants. And it may safely be assumed that a speaker, in greeting an acquaintance or asking a question, does not usually initiate the action or assess its outcome on the basis of a statistical calculation of its likely success. Neither does a greeter, for example, whose greeting has not been returned simply conclude that a statistically unlikely event has occurred. Rather, as we have already suggested (see 106–18), he or she may assess whether the greeting was, or could have been, heard or attempt to account in some way for the absence of the return. In all of this our greeter acts on the presumption that a greeting *always* proposes that a return is due next. Altogether it is safe to conclude that interaction is not structured, nor is its structure implemented, on the basis of statistical calculations.

An alternative point of view has already been foreshadowed. This is that the adjacency pair structure is a *normative* framework for actions which is *accountably* implemented. Within these terms, the production of an utterance identifiable as a first pair part (e.g. a question) — the utterance being so identifiable by reference to some combination of its syntactic features, sequential positioning and conventional properties (see, for example, Schegloff, 1980, 1984; Terasaki, 1976) — selects a next speaker who should immediately proceed to produce the appropriate second pair part. In this analysis, the first speaker's production of a first pair part proposes that a second speaker should relevantly produce a second pair part which is accountably 'due' immediately on completion of the first.

What is the evidence for this latter conception? At an intuitive level, there are the inferences about motives, intentions, beliefs, etc. (e.g. the other intended to be insulting, or the other wouldn't answer the question, or couldn't do so without self-incrimination) which we all make when second pair parts are not forthcoming. Although, especially at this stage in the argument, this evidence may seem to be overly subjective, it is strengthened by the fact that other people also report similar absences and inferences to one another and to us — a fact which indicates that, at the minimum, the orientation to these absences and the inferences which they inherit are 'in the culture'.

A second sort of evidence for the normative character of adjacency pairs derives, of course, from the very large numbers of cases in which actions conforming to their prescriptions are implemented and their associated expectations met. However, the status of this evidence is threatened by a range of instances in talk, which are not infrequent, where, for example, greetings are not returned immediately or at all and questions are not answered promptly or at all. Paradoxically, it is consideration of these 'deviant' cases, in which the adjacency pair structure is not implemented fully or unproblematically, which provides the strongest evidence for the normative character of the adjacency pair structure.

In what follows, we will briefly consider evidences from 'deviant' cases, exemplified by reference to the question—answer pair, where firstly intending questioners, then intended answerers, and finally both parties orient to the normative character of the adjacency pair structure.

Questioners.   In the following two cases, an initial question (arrow 1) fails to elicit any response. Whereupon the intending questioner repeats (arrow 2) and, in the further absence of response, re-repeats (arrow 3) the question and finally gets an answer (arrow 4). Notice that in each case the questioner repeats the question in increasingly truncated form, thereby proposing that the recipient in fact heard the original question.

(3) (Atkinson and Drew, 1979:52)
    1→A: Is there something bothering you or not?
            (1.0)
    2→A: Yes or no
            (1.5)
    3→A: Eh?
    4→B: No.

(4) (Atkinson and Drew, 1979: 52)
    1→Ch: Have to cut the:se Mummy.
            (1.3)
    2→Ch: Won't we Mummy
            (1.5)
    3→Ch: Won't we
    4→ M: Yes.

In each of these cases the first speaker, by repeating the question, proposes that the answer to the original question was 'due' and is thus noticeably or 'officially' absent (Schegloff, 1972). In each case, the repeat (and re-repeat) evidences the first speaker's understanding that, while an answer was 'due', it was not provided. The proposed absence is invoked in — and thus simultaneously warrants — the repetition of the question. In each case, the questioned party finally acknowledges the normative requirement to respond by providing an answer (arrow 4). This class of cases, together with related instances in which second speakers' responses are treated as 'not answering the question', demonstrates that questioners attend to the fact that their questions are framed within normative expectations which have *sequential implications* in obliging selected next speakers to perform a restricted form of action in next turn, namely, at least to respond to the question with some form of answer.

The constraint that upon the production of a first action a second is due is usefully described as the *conditional relevance* (Schegloff, 1968) of a second action upon a first. This property permits speakers (and analysts) to find that particular conversational events, e.g. answers to questions, are specifically and noticeably absent. And, in turn, this finding accountably permits speakers to engage in further activities to solicit the looked-for event, to report its absence to third parties and to use its absence as the basis for inferences of various kinds. As we have seen, the producers of first pair parts, e.g. questioners, orient to this property of their actions and we can now proceed to show that their respondents do likewise. This orientation is, once again, particularly visible in those 'deviant' cases where second speakers, e.g. intended answerers, fail to perform the activity proposed by the first speaker.

Answerers. In each of the following cases, second speakers respond to first pair part questions but their utterances are not hearable as answering the question as put.

(5) (Trio:2:II:1)
   M: What happened at (.) wo:rk. At Bullock's this
       evening.=
   P: =·hhhh˙ Well I don'kno:::w::.

(6) (W:PC:1:MJ(1):18)
    J: But the <u>trai</u>:n goes. Does th'train go o:n th'boa:t?
    M: ·h ·h Ooh I've no idea:. She ha:sn't sai:d.

(7) (Rah:A:1:Ex:JM(7):2) ((Concerning a child's welfare))
    M: 'S <u>a</u>lri:ght?,
    J: <u>W</u>ell'e hasn' c'm ba-<u>a</u>ck yet.

In each of these cases, the question is not answered. But rather than failing to reply, the second speaker in each case offers an *account* for the absent answer, the account being produced in the place where the answer is due. Because the point is fundamental and because the forms of accounting differ in the three examples, we will work through them in some detail.

Initially we can notice that a questioner, in addition to proposing that an answer should be provided 'next' by a selected next speaker, also proposes through the production of a question to be 'uninformed' about the substance of the question (e.g. what happened at Bullock's, whether the train goes on the boat, etc.). Moreover the questioner also proposes by the act of questioning that the recipient is likely to be 'informed' about this same matter. Thus a standard way of accounting for the non-production of an answer is for the intended answerer to assert a lack of information and, hence, an inability to answer the question as put. This is exactly what occurs in (5) above.

In (6) and (7), we see an extension of this procedure. Thus in (6) M accounts for her failure to produce an answer by reference to her ignorance ('Ooh I've no idea:.') and then proceeds to account for her 'uninformed' status with 'She ha:sn't sai:d.' In effect, an account (i.e. 'ignorance') is given for the absence of an answer and then a further account is offered for that 'ignorance', which attends to the fact that the questioner had, by the act of questioning, implied that M was likely to have been 'knowledgeable' on the matter.

Finally, in (7), this logic is extended so that only the second kind of account is offered. Here J merely states a possible obstacle (the child has not returned yet) to her knowing whether the child is 'alright'. And this statement, in occurring immediately after the enquiry, is heard as addressing the conditional relevance of the prior question and, hence, as accounting (through implied ignorance) for the absence of an answer to the question as put.

In each of these cases, while the formal requirements of the question—answer adjacency pair are not met, the adjacency pair format is addressed as a normative framework 'and its non-implementation by the second speaker is oriented to and accounted for by that second speaker. Thus although, in each case, the second speakers do not answer the question, their utterances are nonetheless directly responsive to the field of relevances established by the prior act of questioning.

Questioners and Answerers. This discussion can now be concluded by a brief consideration of a further class of cases in which a question is responded to with another question which does not hearably 'answer' the first, but yet the conditionally relevant answer is not treated as officially or noticeably absent. A prototypical instance is (8).

(8) (Schegloff, 1972: 78)
    A: Are you coming tonight?
    B: Can I bring a guest?
    A: Sure.
    B: I'll be there.

Here A does not treat B's first response as inappropriate or as designed to avoid answering (analyses which A could have displayed by, for example, repeating the initial question or challenging B's response). In this context it can be noticed that B's utterance, while not answering the question, does display an analysable relatedness to it and that it is this relatedness which provides its warrant to occur where it does. Furthermore we can see that A, in answering B's question, effectively acknowledges this relatedness. Finally, the completion of A's answer ('Sure.') provides a further opportunity for B to answer A's original question. Thus although strict adjacency is not achieved between A's initial question (line 1) and B's answer (line 4), the entire sequence nonetheless proceeds under the continuously sustained expectation that A's first pair part will ultimately receive its looked-for second.

Insertion sequences (Schegloff, 1972) of this kind, occurring between first and second pair parts of adjacency pairs, are comparatively common. A more complex instance is shown below in which several inserted question—answer sequences are initiated after the first question — 'How many tubes would you like sir'.

(9) (Levinson, 1983: 305 (simplified))
```
 1      A:   How many tubes would you like sir
 2   1→B:   U:hm (.) what's the price now eh with VAT
 3           do you know eh
 4           . . .
 5           . . .
 6           . . .
 7      A:   Three pounds nineteen a tube sir
 8   2→B:   Three nineteen is it=
 9      A:   =Yeah
10      B:   E::h (1.0) yes u:hm ((dental click)) ((in parenthetical
11           tone) e:h jus-justa think, that's what three nineteen
12  3→       That's for the large tube isn't it
13      A:   Well yeah it's the thirty seven c.c.s
14      B:   Er, hh I'll tell you what I'll just eh eh ring you back
15           I have to work out how many I'll need. Sorry I did—
16           wasn't sure of the price you see
17      A:   Okay
```

Here B asks three questions (arrowed 1–3) before dealing with A's original one. In each case, there is a displayed relatedness between B's inserted queries and the original question which permits A to maintain his expectation across the sequence that his question will ultimately be answered. Finally, it may be noted that B eventually (line 14) defers answering the question and, as in examples 5–7, an account is offered for the deferral together with an apology (lines 15–16).

We have now come far enough to see the absurdity of viewing the adjacency pair notion either as an invariantly implemented structure for particular kinds of actions or, alternatively, as merely a statistical generalization about the sequencing of actions. For, although actions are indeed frequently organized in ways that the concept describes, some of the more significant and characteristic aspects of the nature and workings of adjacency pairs come to light when the expected pattern of action is breached. As we have seen, the normative character of the adjacency pair structure and its associated expectations is clearly evidenced in the behaviour of interactants in the context of breaches. In the examples discussed above, both questioners (in (3) and (4)) and answerers (in (5), (6) and (7)) exhibited an orientation to the normative accountability of the question—answer pair structure. Similarly, in (8) and (9) both questioner and answerer collaborated in maintaining the expectation that an original question would ultimately be answered while permitting the projected answerer to defer the moment of its provision.

We have dwelt at considerable length on these elementary features of adjacency pairs, not because they comprise a large proportion of conversational activity, but rather because the *form of analysis* directed to these very straightforward sequences — a form which we previously encountered in chapter 5 — is repeated in the analysis of very much more complex, subtle and nuanced conversational activities. In each case, a 'current' action is analysed as projecting the production of a relevant 'next' (or range of 'nexts') by another speaker. When the relevant 'next' occurs, it is characteristically treated as requiring no special explanation: a relevantly produced next action is specifically non-accountable. (From an analytic point of view, a normatively institutionalized sequence of actions has simply occurred.) When the relevanced or appropriate 'next' does not occur however, the matter is, as we have seen, specially accountable. In such circumstances, accounts may be offered by the party whose conduct has not met the relevant expectation. Or, alternatively, the conduct may become the object of special inferences and thus be explained by invoking aspects of the circumstances of the action, or the role identity, personality, goals, motives, etc. of the breaching party. Throughout, deviations from standard forms can give rise to inferences of these kinds and it is, in part at least, through such deviations that, for example, 'motives' and 'personalities' may become visible in behaviour. The 'mask of politeness' is thus perhaps well named, if only because an interactant's scrupulous adherence to 'normal forms' can leave others strangely ignorant about the person they are dealing with.

AN ARCHITECTURE OF INTERSUBJECTIVITY

Thus far we have concentrated on the adjacency pair notion as a form of action template by looking at some simple ways in which the producers and recipients of first pair parts display their expectation that a particular next action is accountably 'due'. But this 'action template' aspect of adjacency pair organization has a vitally significant *interpretative* corollary, namely that a first speaker can use his or her action as a presumptive basis on which to interpret what a next speaker says. Thus a questioner may assume that his or her question will be met with either an answer or, if not, an account for the lack of an answer. For example, to return to (7):

> (7) (Rah:A:1:Ex:(JM)7:2)
>   M: 'S alri:ght?,
>   J: Well'e hasn' c'm ba-ack yet.

It is plain that J's utterance is to be heard as an account rather than a random observation. But the inference which permits it to be heard as an account arises solely by virtue of its sequential placement. Thus both M (and we) can use this placement as the means to see *that* the utterance is responsive to the question and, hence, *how* it is responsive. It is through these means that J's utterance is analysable as an accounting for ignorance rather than a random remark. Plainly we are back in the area of common understandings and assumptions just known and taken for granted (see the discussion in chapter 4 of Garfinkel's remarks on 'trust' and Grice's (1975) related observations on the 'co-operative principle'). But we can now see that it is precisely because the adjacency pair structure is a reliable and accountable template for *action*, that it is a reliable template for *interpretation* as well.

The idea that particular kinds of actions, in properly coming in ordered pairs, furnish interpretative resources may appear a simple one. Nonetheless, it has far-reaching implications. Consider the following utterance:

> (10)
>   B: Why don't you come and see me sometimes

It is at least conceivable that (10) could be heard as a complaint and responded to as such; for example:

(11) (Invented)
    B: Why don't you come and <u>see</u> me sometimes
    A: I'm sorry. I've been terribly tied up lately

In fact, in the data from which (10) was taken, it was analysed as an invitation and the sequence in fact ran:

(12) (SBL:10:12)
    B: Why don't you come and <u>see</u> me some⌐times
    A: ⌊I would like to

The point here, and it is a crucial one, is that *however* the recipient analyses the first utterance and whatever the conclusion of such an analysis, *some analysis, understanding or appreciation of the prior turn will be displayed in the recipient's next turn at talk*. Thus the production of apologies and excuses would treat (10) as a complaint, the production of an 'acceptance' (as in (12)) would appreciate (10) as an 'invitation', and so on (see Schegloff, 1984 for further discussion).

Again, in the following two sequences, the same individual (J) receives information from two different acquaintances about the recent arrival of furniture, and a more subtle differentiation of response can be observed.

(13) (Rah:B:1:(11):3:(R))
    A: the two <u>b</u>eds'v come this mo:rning, the new
        be:ds. ·hhhh ʌn:d uh b't o⌐nly onc
→J: ⌊↑ <u>Ih</u> <u>b't</u> that w'z
    ↓ quick that w'z °quick them coming.°
    A: Not too ba:d. B't thez only one <u>ma:</u>tress ↓ with it.

(14) (Rah:B:1:(12):1:(R))
    I: the <u>t</u>hings 'ev arrived from Ba:rker:'n Stone'ou⌐:se,
    J: | ⌊<u>Oh</u>:::.
      (.)
→J: O⌐h c'n a⌐h <u>c'm</u> rou:nd, h⌐h
    I: ⌊A n' ⌦   ⌊Yes: please that's w't

These two informings receive quite different treatments from J and these treatments embody quite different assessments of their implications. Thus while the first informing gets a comment about how quickly the order was delivered, J treats the second as implicating that the informant wants her to go round and inspect/admire the new furniture (see Drew, 1984a for further analysis). Here, then, J's assessment of the arrival of the beds in the first sequence treats the informing as 'plain news', her self-invitation in response to the second treats the latter as implicating her informant's desire to have her round.

The important thing is that, once again, the interpretations embedded in these treatments of the prior turn are publicly available as the means by which previous speakers can determine how they were understood. Thus the sequential 'next positioned' linkage between any two actions can be a critical resource by which a first speaker (and, of course, 'overhearing' social scientists) can determine the sense which a second made of his or her utterance. The significance of the pairing, or 'next positioned' linkage, of utterances is summarized by Schegloff and Sacks as follows:

> by an adjacently produced second, a speaker can show that he understood what a prior aimed at, and that he is willing to go along with that. Also, by virtue of the occurrence of an adjacently produced second, the doer of a first can see that what he intended was indeed understood and that it was or was not accepted. Also, of course, a second can assert his failure to understand, or disagreement, and, inspection of a second by a first can allow the first speaker to see that while the second thought he understood, indeed he misunderstood. It is then through the use of adjacent positioning that appreciations, failures, corrections, et cetera can themselves be understandably attempted. (Schegloff and Sacks, 1973: 297–8)

Linked actions, in short, are the basic building-blocks of intersubjectivity.

We are now in a position to complete this analysis by taking it one final step. So far we have seen that a second speaker's utterance displays an analysis of the prior speaker's turn and that this permits the first speaker to determine whether (or how) he or she was understood. How then does the second speaker come to know whether the analysis he or she displayed was, in fact, appropriate?

For those who have followed the argument so far, the answer to this question will already be apparent. The second speaker can determine the adequacy of the analysis displayed in his or her turn by reference to the next action of the first speaker.

This observation can be developed by noticing, firstly, that one 'third turn' option which is open to the first speaker is the explicit correction or repair of any misunderstanding which was displayed in the second speaker's turn. A rather straightforward instance of this kind of 'third position repair' (Schegloff, 1979c) is the following:

(15) (CDHQ:I:52)
    A: Which one::s are closed, an' which ones are open.
    Z: Most of 'em. This, this, ⌈this, this ((pointing))
  →A: ⌊I 'on't mean on the
        shelters, I mean on the roads.

Here Z's analysis of the prior question as referring to the 'shelters' (as displayed in what he says and the direction pointed to) is explicitly corrected by the first speaker in an overlapping next turn. A slightly more subtle exhibit of the same phenomenon is (16):

(16) (Terasaki, 1976:45)
Mom: Do you know who's going to that meeting?
Kid: Who.
Mom: I don't know!
 Kid: Ou::h prob'ly: Mr Murphy an' Dad said prob'ly
        Mrs Timpte an' some o' the teachers.

Here Kid takes Mom's first utterance, not as a question, but as an utterance designed to clear the way for Mom to subsequently announce who will be going to the meeting (see Terasaki, 1976; Levinson, 1983: 349–56). Kid displays this orientation by uttering 'Who.', which constitutes a request for the information he assumes Mom to have. Mom's 'I don't know!' thus constitutes a third turn correction of the misunderstanding which Kid displayed in second turn, whereupon Kid now responds to Mom's lack of information with a reporting of what he knows. Note here that Kid evidently knows a good deal about who will be attending the meeting and he could have responded to Mom's initial turn by providing this information. The fact that he did not do so testifies to the fact that, despite its question form, he did not analyse the first turn as a 'question' (see Schegloff, 1984 for a further consideration of the issues raised).

Each of these two cases illustrates a very general phenomenon, namely that after any 'second action' the producer of the first has a systematically given opportunity to repair any misunderstanding of the first action that may have been displayed in the second. Given the generic availability of this procedure, any second speaker may look to a third action to see whether this opportunity was taken and, if it was not, conclude that the analysis and treatment of the first action that was displayed in his or her second was adequate. Any 'third' action, therefore, which implements some 'normal' onward development or trajectory for a sequence, tacitly confirms the displayed understandings in the sequence so far. By means of this framework, speakers are released from what would otherwise be an endless task of confirming and reconfirming their understandings of each other's actions.

Bearing these considerations in mind, let us return to (12). The three-part sequence partially displayed in (12) runs as follows:

(17) (SBL:10:12)
    B: Why don't you come and <u>see</u> me some⌜times
    A: ⌊I would like to
    B: I would like you to

Here B's third turn ('I would like you to') tacitly confirms A's treatment of the first turn as an invitation.

By contrast, had the sequence in (17) run as follows:

(18) (Invented)
    B: Why don't you come and <u>see</u> me some⌜times
    A: ⌊I would like to
    B: Yes but why *don't* you

then both A (and the 'overhearing' analyst) could see that, given that B did not deal with A's proposed 'acceptance' of the 'invitation' but instead demanded some kind of account, that B's first utterance had 'all along and in the first place' been intended as a complaint, that A's treatment of it as an invitation was being treated as inadequate and that B's third turn was a pursuance or escalation of her first complaint.

To summarize, conversational interaction is structured by an organization of action which is implemented on a turn-by-turn basis. By means of this organization, *a context of publicly displayed and continuously up-dated intersubjective understandings is systematically sustained.* It is through this 'turn-by-turn' character of talk that the participants display their understandings of 'the state of the talk' for one another. It is important to note that, because these displayed understandings arise as a kind of by-product or indirect outcome of the sequentially organized activities of the participants, the issue of 'understanding' *per se* is only rarely topicalized at the conversational 'surface'. Through this procedure the participants are thus released from the task of explicitly confirming and reconfirming their understandings of one another's actions. Mutual understanding is thus displayed, to use Garfinkel's term, 'incarnately' in the sequentially organized details of conversational interaction. Moreover, because these understandings are publicly produced, they are available as a resource for social scientific analysis.

Before leaving this topic, two further fugitive remarks are in order. First, the above observations concerning the way a turn's talk displays an analysis, appreciation or understanding of a prior turn do not simply apply to the responses or 'reactive' second utterances with which we have been primarily concerned in this section. They also apply to 'first' or initiatory actions of various sorts which, in their own various ways, also display analyses of the 'state of the talk'. For example, a speaker who initiates a pre-closing (Schegloff and Sacks, 1973: 303–9) exhibits an analysis that 'there and then' is an appropriate place for that to occur. Moreover, the manner in which the pre-closing is begun will itself display a variety of sensitivities to the conversational context (ibid.). Similar considerations may be suggested for topic inititiations (Button and Casey, 1982, 1984; Jefferson, 1984b) and for a variety of other actions which are initiatory, or even premonitory, of sequences rather than responsive within them (Jefferson, 1980b; Pomerantz, 1980; Schegloff, 1980).

Our second observation takes the form of a warning of certain limitations about the value of sequential analysis in getting at the participants' understandings of prior talk. As we have stressed, participants' analyses of prior talk are not overtly expressed but are indirectly exhibited in their own turns. A speaker shows she understands a prior turn as an 'invitation' by 'accepting' it, rather than some other means. In short, a second speaker's analysis of a prior is presented indirectly and must thus be inferred. As Goodwin and Goodwin have made the point, 'rather than presenting a naked analysis of the prior talk, next utterances characteristically transform that talk in some fashion — deal with it not in its own terms but rather in the way in which it is relevant to the projects of the subsequent speaker' (Goodwin and Goodwin, 1982: 1). It is a commonplace that speakers may respond to earlier talk in ways which may blur, conceal or otherwise avoid displaying their true appreciation of its import. Similarly, speakers may avoid taking up and dealing with what they perfectly well know is accomplished or implicated by prior talk so as to influence the direction of the talk towards some desired objective. These occasions are common in talk and may be varyingly 'transparent' to analytic inspection. Some of their characteristic features can themselves be documented by means of comparative sequential analysis. But their existence serves to emphasize that 'official' treatments of talk occurring at the conversational surface are the *starting point* for interpretative and analytic work and cannot be treated simply as unproblematic representations of what the speakers' understandings or intentions in the talk consisted of.

THE LOCAL STRUCTURING OF CONVERSATION: ADJACENCY AND AGENCY

The alert reader may have begun to notice something of a shift in the way sequences are being described during the past few pages. We started by describing very tightly organized sequences — adjacency pairs — in which the options available to second speakers were relatively constrained. By contrast, we have now lapsed into a looser mode of exposition in which the local positioning of utterances 'next' to one another is crucial.

We need to work in this way because, as was previously stressed, conversation is not an endless series of interlocking adjacency pairs in which sharply constrained options confront the next speaker. Rather conversation is informed by the general assumption — common to both speakers and hearers — that utterances which are placed immediately next to some prior are to be understood as produced in response to or, more loosely, in relation to that prior. This assumption provides a framework in which speakers can rely on the *positioning* of what they say to contribute to the *sense* of what they say as an action.

This assumption that adjacent utterances are, wherever possible, to be heard as related was formulated by Sacks (spring 1972, lecture 4) as a fundamental ordering principle for conversation and he summarized it as the general finding that 'a turn's talk will be heard as directed to a prior turn's talk, unless special techniques are used to locate some other talk to which it is directed' (Sacks, Schegloff and Jefferson, 1974: 728).

As usual, there are a range of different evidences for this finding. There is, first, the fact that the vast majority of utterances — including much of the data shown in this chapter — would be unintelligible if this assumption was not made. Moreover and secondly, there is a good deal of evidence which suggests that if a speaker wishes some contribution to be heard as *unrelated* to an immediately prior utterance, the speaker must do something special to lift the assumption. Thus there are a number of standard prefixes, such as 'by the way . . .', which are designed to show that what follows is to be heard as disjunctive with the immediately prior talk. Intonation may also be employed to the same effect (Sacks, spring 1972, lecture 4). Similarly, misunderstandings in talk may arise from a hearer's assuming a relatedness between utterances which was not intended but where the speaker failed to signal this fact. There are, then, a variety of evidences for the fact that conversationalists assume that adjacently positioned utterances are to be heard in relation to one another and that this is an assumption of 'first resort'. Functioning as such a resource, this assumption is generic. Indeed the very availability of the conventional notion of 'sequence' is dependent on it.

But although this assumption is easy enough to evidence, it is not so easy to explain. One explanation might be that speakers and hearers orient to the juxtapositioning of utterances because they are reflexively aware of the accountability of failing to do so. Just as absent second pair parts are normatively accountable and 'inferentially rich', so too might the failure to orient to the relevance of juxtapositioning. Thus, it may be concluded, the phenomenon of adjacency is its own explanation. As a basic normative expectancy it is accountably implemented and that is that. But this analysis explains only the *maintenance* of the orientation to adjacency as a normative orientation; it does not explain the existence of the normative orientation in the first place. And this is because an explanation in terms of the normative accountability of deviation depends for its force on *the prior institutionalization of adjacent positioning as a generic phenomenon* and it is this that we want to explain.

Another possible explanation for the significance of adjacent positioning in conversation has already been sketched. We have already noted the ways in which adjacency is implicated in the public display of continuously up-dated intersubjective understandings. Surely, it may be argued, it is this essential role of adjacent positioning which accounts for its pervasive use as an assumption in the structuring of talk. Yet the evidence also shows that speakers can in fact produce utterances which can intelligibly be heard, without difficulty, as responsive to, appreciating and displaying an analysis of utterances at some removes away. In short, it is not essential for mutual intelligibility that utterances should always be adjacent to the talk they appreciate and respond to. We are thus returned to our original question which is: why is adjacent positioning so primary and fundamental in the production and interpretation of talk?

A decisive solution to this question can only be arrived at by considering a further order of conversational organization which has not been discussed thus far, namely the turn-taking organization for conversation. Little will be said about the organization of turn-taking in the present chapter (though see Sacks, Schegloff and Jefferson, 1974; Atkinson and Drew, 1979: 34–61 and Levinson, 1983: 296–303 provide further detailed summaries). Suffice it to say that turns are allocated among conversationalists by reference to a set of rules which apply recursively on a local, turn-by-turn basis. As Levinson (1983: 297), following Sacks, Schegloff and Jefferson (1974: 696), has suggested, the rules can be viewed as a sharing device by means of which a scarce resource — the opportunity to speak — is distributed among speakers. This system operates in terms of minimal units or 'shares' in terms of which allocation proceeds. Its operation involves the allocation of one such unit, for example a sentence, a phrase or some other turn constructional unit, to each speaker. After the speaker's production of one such unit, the conversational 'floor' may readily be allocated elsewhere.

The relation between this turn-by-turn allocation system and the pervasive use of adjacency or 'close ordering' in conversation is set out in the following remarks by Schegloff and Sacks:

> Given the utterance by utterance organization of turn taking, unless close ordering is attempted there can be no methodic assurance than an . . . aimed—for . . . utterance type will ever be produced. If a next speaker does not do it, that speaker may provide for a further next that should not do it (or should do something that is not it) . . . Close ordering is, then, the basic generalized means for assuring that some desired event will ever happen. If it cannot be made to happen next, its happening is not merely delayed, but may never come about. (Schegloff and Sacks, 1973: 297)

For example, if A asks B a question and if B, instead of answering, comments on the weather directing his remarks to C who in turn . . . , then A has no means of being assured that his question will ever be answered. Nor, of course, will he have any assured means of knowing whether he was understood. Thus the efficacy and intelligibility of A's question — indeed A's capacities as an agent in the conversation with B and C — are ultimately assured through the pervasive role of adjacent positioning, both as a normative requirement of action and as a constitutive feature of its interpretation.

Generalizing the argument, each speaker in conversation participates in an organization whose contingent outcomes are only partially under his or her control. Individual agency is secured within this framework by the generalized requirement that responses to a current action should properly occur next. In turn, this action requirement is generalized as an interpretative framework for each next utterance and responding adjacently becomes a major resource for each next actor to exert agentive powers *vis-à-vis* a prior. And, once again, the normative character of this framework of action and interpretation — including of course the normative accountability of deviations from the framework — helps to motivate and maintain conformity to its dictates.

METHODOLOGICAL REPRISE

Earlier in the chapter, we noted a number of characteristic aspects of analysis which may be involved in the pursuit of conversation analytic objectives. We have now completed a coarse sketch which illustrates some of the relevant forms of analysis.

We began by noting what appeared to be a regular organizational pattern in conversational activity, namely that many conversational actions are paired. Some examples were greetings, 'goodbyes', question—answer, invitation—acceptance/declination and so on. Selecting the question—answer pair for closer inspection (any other pair would have yielded parallel, though not identical, findings), we determined that the pair structure was not accidental or artefactual, but was produced as the methodical and accountable product of the shared orientations and expectations of the speakers. These orientations, we found, were particularly visible in those 'deviant cases' where the pair format was not straightforwardly implemented.

Having established this, we began to explore the role which the pair structure might play in talk and we focused, in particular, on its role in the maintenance of a framework of continuously up-dated intersubjective understandings. Developing this argument, we were led to extend the arguments derived from the consideration of pairs to a more abstract and generic phenomenon — 'next positioning' — applied over more extended sequences of actions.

Finally, we briefly considered the relation of paired actions (and more abstractly, adjacently positioned actions) to another order of conversational organization — the turn-taking system. This yielded a powerful explanation of the generic role of adjacent positioning in talk: adjacent positioning was found to be the major means by which individual speakers could be assured of exerting some local influence over the conduct of their co-interactants.

We have thus encountered some of the basic methods of reasoning which are employed in conversation analytic research. The discussion above does not, of course, exhaust those methods, nor their applications. Many other analytic procedures are routinely employed in ethnomethodologically oriented studies of conversation. But some indication of the form of reasoning which tends to surface in conversation analytic writings has now been given and we will proceed from here into some more substantive domains.

PREFERENCE, PRE-SEQUENCES AND THE TIMING OF SOCIAL SOLIDARITY

In the present section of this chapter, we will briefly illustrate a variety of ways in which the design of actions can contribute to the maintenance of social solidarity. Anticipating the results of this discussion, it will be suggested that there is a 'bias' intrinsic to many aspects of the organization of talk which is generally favourable to the maintenance of bonds of solidarity between actors and which promotes the avoidance of conflict.

We can begin by recalling that many of the two-part structures discussed earlier in this chapter have alternative second pair parts. For example requests, offers, invitations, proposals and the like may all be either /accepted/ or refused. Characteristically however, these two alternative actions are usually done in different ways. Consider the invitation which we have already discussed earlier.

(12) (SBL:10:12)
      B: Why don't you come and see me some ⌈times
      A: ⌊I would like to

In this example, as Atkinson and Drew (1979: 58) have noted, the invitation is accepted in a simple and unvarnished fashion. Moreover the acceptance occurs 'early' through an utterance which begins in overlap with the completion of the invitation.

By contrast, the following invitation is refused:

(19) (SBL:10:14)
     B: Uh if you'd care to come over and visit a little
            while this morning I'll give you a cup of coffee.
     A: 1→hehh Well that's awfully sweet of you,
        2→I don't think I can make it this morning
        3→·hh uhm I'm running an ad in the paper and-and
            uh I have to stay near the phone.

This refusal is accomplished in a markedly different way from the earlier acceptance. First, in contrast to the 'early' acceptance of (12), the refusal is delayed (arrow 1) by a short outbreath ('hehh'), a turn component associated with refusals ('Well') and an appreciation ('that's awfully sweet of you'). Second, in contrast to the earlier unvarnished acceptance, the rejection (arrow 2) is not asserted as definite (though, of course, it is a 'non-negotiable' refusal), but rather is asserted in a qualified or mitigated form. Third, while the acceptance in (12) is treated as non-accountable, the refusal is treated as requiring an account and in fact is accompanied by a fairly elaborate explanation (arrow 3).

These different ways of accomplishing acceptances and rejections of invitations are not specific to these two examples or to these two speakers. On the contrary, they are characteristic of the general ways in which acceptances and rejections of invitations are accomplished. Thus while most acceptances involve:

(1) Simple acceptance and
(2) no delay.

rejections are routinely designed to incorporate at least some of the following features (Levinson, 1983:334–5):

(1) Delays: (i) by pause before delivery, (ii) by the use of a preface (see (2)), (iii) by displacement over a number of turns via the use of insertion sequences.

(2) Prefaces: (i) the use of markers like 'uh' or 'well', (ii) the use of token agreements, appreciations and apologies, (iii) the use of qualifiers and (iv) hesitation.

(3) Accounts: explanations for why the invitation is not being accepted.

(4) Declination component: which is normally mitigated, qualified or indirect.

And these characteristic differences in the design of acceptances and rejections of invitations are not confined to the latter. They are also found in acceptances and rejections of requests, offers and proposals (Davidson, 1984). They inform the organization of agreements and disagreements (Pomerantz, 1975, 1978, 1984), and, relatedly, corrections (Schegloff, Jefferson and Sacks, 1977; Jefferson, 1983), blamings (Pomerantz, 1978b; Atkinson and Drew, 1979) and a variety of other actions.

The generic term 'preference' is used to reference these basic differences. Actions which are characteristically performed straightforwardly and without delay are termed 'preferred' actions, while those which are delayed, qualified and accounted for are termed 'dispreferred'. To avoid any confusion, it should be asserted immediately that these terms are not intended in any way to refer to the private desires, or psychological proclivities of speakers. On the contrary, we are here dealing with highly generalized and, as we shall see, institutionalized methods of speaking.

As we have suggested, these systematic patternings of the design of particular actions are fundamentally tied to the actions themselves and they vary little in relation to particular speakers or social contexts. Thus, as Wootton (1981) has demonstrated, even when it is a four-year-old child who is making the request and a busy mother who is refusing it, she will nonetheless package her refusal using the 'standard' components for a dispreferred action — delay, mitigation, accounting, etc. These observations stand as substantial preliminary evidence for the fact that the preference organization of the design of actions is strongly institutionalized.

Further evidence that these designs are institutionalized comes from the inferences which are made when the designs are not implemented. For example in invitation sequences, while 'early' acceptance is normal and by no means an

automatic sign of 'enthusiasm', a 'delayed' acceptance is often
heard as 'reluctant'. Similarly an 'early' or unmitigated or
unaccounted-for refusal can easily be heard as 'hostile' or
'rude'. And, once again, our knowledge of these inferential
possibilities may shape our conduct, constraining it in particular
ways. Thus, knowing that refusals of invitations normally have
accounts, we may end up at a party we would rather have
avoided because no account was available and 'we couldn't get
out of it'. And again, as party givers, we may require the pro
forma, dispreferred design for a rejection even though the
rejecting invitee is someone whom we would rather not have
and, indeed, even though we know that he knows it. Plainly
issues of 'face' (Goffman, 1955; Brown and Levinson, 1978) are
closely associated with our maintenance of the relevant forms
and observances. And, once again, it is deviance from these
institutionalized designs which is the inferentially rich, morally
accountable, face-threatening and sanctionable form of action.
And, as in the case of greetings, it may be these latter
considerations which influence the ways in which we design
our talk, constraining us to adopt the institutionalized form
regardless of our private desires and personal inclinations.

Now if it is granted that the two different turn designs —
preferred and dispreferred — are institutionalized methods of
talking which are required and used for accomplishing
particular actions, it may still be asked why these particular
contrasting features are recruited to these contrasting turn
types. Why are such features as accounts and delay built into
dispreferreds such as refusing an invitation and avoided in
preferreds such as accepting one?

Some suggestions for an answer to this question may arise
from a brief examination of just which 'second actions' are
normally done in preferred format and which in dispreferred
format. Some prominent instances are set out in table 2.

It will be obvious enough that the preferred format
responses to requests, offers, invitations and assessments are
uniformly affiliative actions which are supportive of social
solidarity, while dispreferred format responses are largely
destructive of social solidarity. The point is underlined by
consideration of self-deprecations (Pomerantz, 1984). Here,
where agreement would constitute criticism of the other, it is

TABLE 2 PREFERENCE FORMAT OF SOME SELECTED ACTION TYPES

Action	Preferred Format Response	Dispreferred Format Response
Request	Acceptance	Refusal
Offer/invitation	Acceptance	Refusal
Assessment	Agreement	Disagreement
Self-deprecation	Disagreement	Agreement
Accusation/blaming	Denial	Admission

disagreement which is packaged in the preferred response format. The point is further underscored by the fact that denials to accusations and blamings are preferred (Atkinson and Drew, 1979: 122 *et seq.*). Here, where an admission may announce a rift between the accused and others, denial should occur early and be unaccountable. (It may be noted that both these features are preserved in the British legal system where on the one hand suspect silence in the face of a question or accusation may be used in evidence by the prosecution (McBarnet, 1981; chapter 3, Atkinson and Drew, 1979: 112), while on the other the assertion of innocence (and denial of guilt) is specifically unaccountable according to the legal doctrine that the accused is innocent until proven guilty.)

In sum, preferred format actions are normally affiliative in character while dispreferred format actions are disaffiliative. Similarly, while preferred format actions are generally supportive of social solidarity, dispreferred format actions are destructive of it. As we shall see, the uniform recruitment of specific features of turn design to preferred and dispreferred action types is probably related to their affiliative and disaffiliative characters. In what follows, we will concentrate on the role of two of the most distinctive features of the dispreferred format — accounts and delay — to illustrate this notion.

Accounts

The role of accounts in dispreferreds is complex, and to simplify the main lines of the argument it will be necessary to concentrate on offers, invitations and requests. Here it can be suggested that, a priori, none of these projects acceptance and rejection as equivalent actions. On the contrary, each projects acceptance as the action to be accomplished next. This is formally demonstrable. For example, if I do not want Smith to come to my party, I can ensure this outcome by not inviting him. Prima facie therefore, my invitation to him formally projects his acceptance − regardless of my (or his) private feelings on the matter. Thus, just as a question projects the relevant occurrence of an answer next, so an invitation projects the relevant occurrence of an acceptance next. And, just as the failure to answer a question is accountable (see 249–51), so too is the failure to respond affirmatively to invitations (and requests, offers and the like).

This discussion may be extended by noting that, in asking a question or making an invitation, speakers commit themselves to a range of beliefs about themselves, their co-participants and their relationships. A refusal can threaten or undermine any of these beliefs and, hence, the refusal can undermine the 'face' of the first speaker and/or his or her relationship with the second. For example, when a question is not answered, the failure may be a product of the answerer's not knowing the answer, or not being willing to supply it, or not acknowledging the questioner's right to ask it. The accounts which accompany or accomplish refusals commonly address one or another of these possibilities. Thus table 3 is a simplified depiction of the range of grounds which might be used to reject or put off a simple request: 'Would you dust the room?'.

Now although, as we have suggested, any one of these grounds might in principle serve as grounds for the rejection of the request, the striking fact is how few of them are actively invoked. When accounts for refusing requests are examined empirically, they are found to cluster around the issue of *ability* to comply (Levinson, 1983: 350; see also Merritt, 1976). Similarly, invitations are overwhelmingly rejected, as in (19), on the basis of inability (rather than, for example, unwillingness) to accept (Drew, 1984a). As we have seen, questions which are requests for information also get inability accounts of the 'I don't know' or related forms (cf. (5), (6) and (7)). Offers, on the other hand, are commonly rejected by reference

TABLE 3   GROUNDS FOR REJECTING OR PUTTING OFF
A SIMPLE REQUEST
(after Labov and Fanshel, 1977: 86–8)

Ground	Example
Existential status of action	I already dusted it.
Time of performance	It's not time for dusting yet.
Need for the action	It looks clean to me.
Need for the request	Don't worry I'll do it.
Ability	I can't do it today./I can't do it with this wrist.
Obligation	It's not my turn to dust./It's not my job to dust.
Willingness	I hate dusting./I don't feel like it.
Rights	Who are you asking me to dust?

to a 'lack of need' for the offered thing. Thus in (20) below, an offer of help is rejected on the grounds that there are still 'helpers' at home (note the canonical dispreferred rejection format):

(20) (Her:OII:2:4:ST) ((S's wife has just slipped a disc))
   H: And we were <u>w</u>ondering if there's <u>a</u>nything
       we can do to help
   S: ⌜Well 'at's⌝
   H: ⌞I mean⌟ can we do any shopping for her or
       something like tha:t?
       (0.7)
   S:| Well that's <u>most</u> <u>ki</u>:nd Heather<u>ton</u> ·hhh At the moment
  →<u>no</u>:. because we've still got two <u>bo</u>:ys at home.

What is common to all these forms of accounting, of course, is their 'no fault' quality. None of them implicate a lack of willingness to give, or accept, the goods or services on offer. None of them threaten the assumed rights of one party to offer or give, or the other to solicit or receive, such goods and services. None, in short, threaten the 'face' of either party or the relationship between them.

It can further be noted that these accounts are 'no fault'

accounts in a further sense. Second speakers refuse, or account for refusal, by invoking a 'contingency' which might not, could not, or even should not properly be known to the first. First speakers are thereby absolved of a particular sin: that of asking a question, or making an offer or invitation which they 'could' or 'should' have known could not be positively responded to.

Finally, in these accounts, second speakers invoke contingent knowledge of *their own circumstances* to account for the lack of a positive response. In thus invoking knowledge which they have rights and obligations to know as subject-actors (Pomerantz, 1980: 187), second speakers can construct accounts which are properly incontestable by others. At the end of the day, it is the speaker and only the speaker who knows his own 'needs', the state of his own knowledge or the state of his diary. The use of such knowledge as the raw materials of accounts for refusal thus forecloses the development of further argument which, indeed, is only possible through the introduction of other, collateral grounds (though see Drew, 1984a, for many subtle observations on this and related issues). Thus these contingent accounts constructed in terms of observations about the speaker's own local circumstances inherently serve to diminish the opportunities for proliferating disagreement or contest (see also Wootton, 1981, for a further discussion of sequential resources related to these matters for terminating request sequences between parents and very young children).

To sum up, accounts are commonly required as design features of disaffiliative (dispreferred) second actions to invitations, requests and the like because these first actions inherently project affiliative second actions, and invoke a variety of assumptions about the desirability etc. of the relevant second actions which, in turn, implicate the 'face' of, and the relationship between, each participant. The latter are threatened by disaffiliative second actions. Accounts resolve these threats by focusing on 'no fault' considerations. Such accounts, in drawing upon matters properly known primarily to the account giver, tend to short-circuit any potential for further conflict or disagreement (see Pomerantz, 1975, 1984, for further sequential considerations bearing on the resolution of disagreement sequences). Thus accounts designed in the these ways, in functioning as threat- and conflict-avoidance procedures, serve generally to maintain social solidarity.

It needs only to be added that speakers' working knowledge and competences with respect to 'how conversation works' can add a further reflexive twist to these considerations. Thus a rejection or a refusal which is unaccounted for may be held to be suspect because the rejecting party 'would not' or 'could not' explain it in the normal way. Or again, a speaker who asserts unwillingness to attend a party to an intending host may add insult to injury since, it may be held, 'he couldn't even be bothered to invent an excuse'. And it is in virtue of such considerations that speakers may end up attending social functions for the lack of an appropriate excuse. For, lacking such a desirable social asset, they may do the non-accountable thing, and go.

Delay

While the contribution of accounts to the maintenance of social solidarity between speakers is readily available to intuition, the parallel contribution of delay — as a design feature of dispreferreds — is less so. In the following discussion, we will be centrally concerned once again with responses to offers, invitations and the like and will draw extensively from Davidson's (1984) decisive analysis in this domain of actions.

As we have seen, while 'affiliative' acceptances to offers, invitations, etc. commonly occur 'early', i.e. immediately on completion or in slight overlap with their first pair parts, 'disaffiliating' rejecting responses very often occur 'late'. Compare, for example, the overlapping acceptance in (12) with the delayed rejections in (20) and (21).

    (12) (SBL:10:12)
        B: Why don't you come and <u>see</u> me some⌐times
        A: ⌊I would like to

    (20) (Her:OII:2:4:ST:detail)
        H: I mean can we do any shopping for her or
           something like tha:t?
   → (0.7)
      S: Well that's <u>most</u> ki:nd <u>Heatherton</u> ·hhh At the
       ₗmoment <u>no</u>:. because we've still got two bo:ys at home.

(21) (Davidson, 1984: ST)

    A: Oh I was gonna <u>sa</u>:y if you wanted to:, =
        =·hh you could meet me at UCB and I could
        show you some of the <u>o</u>ther things on the compu:ter,
        (.)

    A: Maybe even teach you how to program Ba:sic or
        something. ·hhh

→ (0.6)

    B: Well I don't know if I'd wanna get all <u>that</u>
        invo:lved, hh·hhh

These differences in the timing of preferred acceptances and dispreferred rejections are strongly recurrent and patterned design features of these two classes of actions. As a result, the pauses which occur before the production of dispreferreds can easily be analysed as *prefatory* to rejection. Thus in (22) and (23) such an analysis is displayed by the original enquirer/ suggester after a 'long' pause in (22) and a micro-pause in (23).

(22) (Levinson, 1983: 320)

    C: So I was wondering would you be in your office
        on Monday (.) by any chance?

→   (2.0)

→C: Probably not

(23) (Levinson, 1983: 335)

    R: What about coming here on the way

→   (.)

→R: Or doesn't that give you enough time?

    C: Well no I'm supervising here

In both these cases the first speaker, hearing the pause in progress as foreshadowing some difficulty, steps in to formulate a negative response in (22) and to anticipate a possible problem in (23).

This analysis can be developed by observing that if first speakers can analyse a pause as prefatory to rejection, they can use the time to step in to modify or revise the first utterance to a more 'attractive' or 'acceptable' form, rather than simply using it to formulate an anticipation of rejection. Such a revision is apparent if we re-examine (21).

(21) (Davidson, 1984: ST (detail))
   A: Oh I was gonna sa:y if you wanted to:,=
      =·hh you could meet me at UCB and I could
      show you some of the other things on the compu:ter
→   (.)
→A: Maybe even teach you how to program Ba:sic or
      something. ·hhh

Here A, analysing the micro-pause as foreshadowing a
rejection of his general offer about computing, revises it to the
more concrete one of teaching 'Basic' and does so *before the
rejection is actualized.*

As we have seen, dispreferreds are also routinely prefaced by
objects such as 'well' and 'uh' (Davidson, 1984). These, too,
concretely foreshadow rejection and, again, they take time to
produce. During this time, revisions can be made to prior
offers, etc. and these revisions in response to pauses, can occur
before the anticipated rejection occurs. Thus in (24) a
suggestion is reinforced after an 'uh well', and in (25) a revised
offer is re-revised after 'well'.

(24) (Davidson, 1984: ST)
   A: Listen that could be a job for Sa:mmy::.=
   A: =·hhhh⌜h
→B: ⌞Uh:, we:⌜ll, (   )⌉
→A: ⌞And his station wag⌟on.

(25) (Davidson, 1984: ST)
   P: Oh I mean uh: you wanna go to the store
      or anything over at the Market ⌜Basket or anything?⌉
   A: ⌞ hhhhhhhhhhhhhhh⌟h=
→A: =Well ho⌜ney I⌐⌉
→P: .   ⌞Or Ri ⌟chard's?

Here, in (24), the suggestion of 'Sammy' for the job is
reinforced in advance of rejection by a subsequent reference to
his 'station wagon'. And, in (25), a new store ('Richard's') is
mentioned by P who has heard enough in A's 'Well ho—' to
know that her offer of a trip to the 'Market Basket' is not
attractive enough.

Generalizing the argument, we can now see that delay is a

general device which permits potentially 'face-threatening' rejections to be forestalled by means of revised proposals, offers and the like. Thus, just as the 'early' production of affiliative actions (e.g. agreements, acceptances, etc.) *maximizes the likelihood of their occurrence* (Pomerantz, 1984), so the delayed production of disaffiliative actions (e.g. disagreements, rejections etc.) *minimizes the likelihood of their occurrence* by permitting them to be forestalled (ibid.). In short, the institutionalized timing features of preference design maximize the tendency for socially solidary actions to take place. The preference system itself is intrinsically 'biased' towards solidary actions.

A final extension to these arguments can be achieved by noting that speakers can 'design in' delay features into their first actions. One way in which this can be done is by adding 'redundant' components − which Davidson terms 'monitor spaces' − to the ends of turn units. One such component which has been prominent in the examples above has been 'or anything'. If we re-examine (25), it can be seen that P's first proposal is, in fact, a compound proposal:

(25) (Davidson, 1984: ST (detail))
    P: Oh I mean uh: you wanna go to the store
    →or anything
       over at the Market Basket
    →or anything?

Here a first proposal is hearably complete at the point at which the word 'store' is uttered and could have been responded to then and there. The addition of 'or anything' thus provides a monitor space in which an early acceptance could have been initiated (in overlap with 'or anything'). With no positive uptake at this point, P builds 'or anything' into a revised proposal referencing the 'Market Basket' in place of the 'store' − this component being hearable as 'or anything over at the Market Basket' with a new completion point on the word 'basket'. Early acceptance of this proposal would then overlap with P's final 'or anything?'. Thus, by the time P hears A's turn beginning with 'Well', she can be sure that rejection is likely because A has already passed over a number of opportunities to accept her variously revised suggestion.

Returning to (20), we can see retrospectively that H's offer is also designed of give the recipient plenty of opportunities to accept and to give himself the opportunity of revision:

(20) (Her:OII:2:4:ST) ((S's wife has just slipped a disc))
   H: And we were <u>w</u>ondering if there's <u>a</u>nything
        we can do
 → to help
   S:⌐Well 'at's⌐
   H:⌊I mean   ⌋can we do any shopping for her
 → or something like tha:t?

Here it can be seen that H's first offer has reached a possible completion point at the word 'do'. The addition of 'to help' provides a monitor space in which S could have taken the option of early acceptance but did not. Thus with no early uptake from S, H can proceed to revise his offer to a more concrete one just as S is beginning to reject it. This use of additional post-positioned turn components is just one of several procedures (see Davidson, 1984) by which first speakers can build monitor spaces into their utterances so as to anticipate, and forestall, rejection.

We have now considered in some detail some ways in which both accounts and time are systematically used, whether consciously or not, as institutionalized resources in the design of preferred and dispreferred actions in ways which maximize the potential occurrence of supportive, solidary social actions. We now complete this discussion by looking briefly at a way in which both elements are combined in a particular class of 'forestalling' sequence – the pre-sequence.

Consider the following:

(26) (Atkinson and Drew, 1979: 253)
   A: Whatcha doin'?
   B: Nothin'
   A: Wanna drink?

(27) (Atkinson and Drew, 1979: 143)
   C: How ya doin'=
       =say wh<u>a</u>t'r you doing?
   R: Well we're going out. Why?

C: Oh, I was just gonna say come out and come over here and talk this evening, but if you're going out you can't very well do that

Plainly the first utterance in each of these sequences is transparently prefatory to something (as it turns out, an invitation in both cases). Equally plainly each is understood as such by the second speaker. Thus, in (26), B's 'nothing' is not to be treated literally but as some kind of 'go ahead', while in (27) R's 'why?' also attends to the prefatory character of C's enquiry.

These two enquiries transparently prefigure some kind of . claim (whether in the form of an invitation or a request) on the time of the recipient and they are directly addressed to the most commonly used account for the refusal of such a claim: namely that the time is already occupied and the speaker is unable to accept an invitation or comply with a request. Pre-sequence objects of this type and their near relatives (e.g. pre-announcements (Terasaki, 1976), joke and story prefaces (Sacks, 1974), pre-introductions, pre-closings (Schegloff and Sacks, 1973) and pre-self-identifications (Schegloff, 1979a) are extremely common in conversation. They constitute a further procedure through which speakers can collaborate in forwarding preferred sequences or actions and avoiding (or aborting) dispreferred ones. As such, an utterance such as 'Are you doing anything tonight?' affords specific advantages both to its producer and to its recipient:

(1) In the event that the recipient already has an activity in hand, this can be stated *in advance* of the invitation/request being made. The intending inviter/requester may thus abort his or her up-coming action and hence avoid any direct threat to the other's 'face'.

(2) In the event that the recipient has no plans, but wishes to avoid receiving an invitation/request, the proposal of some other up-coming activity can be used to forestall the intending inviter/requester without direct damage to the latter's 'face'.

(3) In either event, the person telling about the up-coming activity is enabled to do it in the environment of an

utterance which is, formally at least, a 'request for information' rather than an invitation or request *per se*. Such a person is thus saved from having to engage in, or remedy, face-threatening behaviour.

(4) In the event that the recipient indicates 'no plans', the intending inviter/requester may proceed with greater confidence than before for two reasons. First, a substantial proportion of post-refusal accounts based on references to 'ability' has now been pre-emptively eliminated and, second, because someone who has declined to use a less face-threatening account (i.e. an 'ability' account) in advance of an up-coming invitation/request (a less face-threatening/position) is unlikely to use a more face-threatening account after the event (itself a more face-threatening position).

Here, then, we encounter the pre-sequence object as a further, very commonly used conversational device through which dispreferred, face-threatening actions and sequences can be systematically avoided in interaction. Moreover, it may be added that since pre-sequences are commonly used to this end, a participant's failure to employ one may itself become accountable. The utterance 'May I borrow your car?' which is unprefaced by, for example, 'I was wondering if, by any chance, you weren't using the car tonight' may, unless the circumstances are very special, provoke both sanction and irritated gossip.

By now it should go without saying that the various issues raised above do not begin to exhaust the range of empirical possibilities. For example, a speaker who gives the 'go ahead' in anticipation of an invitation to an enjoyable event may 'suddenly recollect' an obstacle when a less attractive request emerges. Various equivocations may be engineered in the face of pre-sequence objects and the latter may, themselves, vary from the transparent to the opaque (see Drew, 1984a for some more complex examples and issues in relation to pre-sequence objects, and Brown and Levinson, 1978, for a much wider range of issues bearing on turn design). Nonetheless here, in outline at least, we encounter some further resources which contribute towards the maintenance of social solidarity through the ways in which they involve both temporal and accounting considerations.

In this section we have examined some of the ways in which some standard, institutionalized features of utterance and sequence design may be systematically implicated in the maintenance of social solidarity. These characteristic features of preference organization exhibit a systematic 'bias' in favour of conflict avoidance, and their institutionalization collectivizes that bias as a feature of social structure. Only one of several domains in which preference organizations are clearly implicated in conflict avoidance has been touched upon here. But it can be suggested that, minute and short range though these preference constraints may be, their power is substantial because their influence on conduct is so pervasive.

THE AVAILABILITY OF CONTEXT

Towards the beginning of this chapter it was observed that the significance of any speaker's communicative action is doubly contextual. Each action is context-shaped in the ways in which it is designed and understood by reference to the environment of actions in which it participates. And it is context-renewing in the way that each action, in forming a new context to which the next will respond, will inevitably contribute to the environing sequence of actions within which the next will be formed and understood.

Now the issue may properly be raised that the concept of 'context' so far discussed is, by any standards, an exceptionally immediate and local one. The 'contexts' we have discussed thus far have comprised scarcely more than three or four turns at talk. How, it may legitimately be asked, can this highly local sense of context and contextualization enable us to get any purchase on events which are informed by a larger, overarching context such as a social institution? For example, although much has been said about the normative organization of questions and answers, has conversation analysis anything to say when the questions are being asked by managers, doctors, teachers, lawyers and the like? Is there any way in which the local sense of context discussed thus far links with these larger institutional frameworks? What, in short, is the relationship between sequences of talk and institutionalized contexts?

In a paper titled 'Activity types and language', Levinson (1979) makes the appealing proposal that the connection can be established by looking at the ways in which institutionalized 'activity types' constrain the kinds of verbal actions which speakers can perform and guide the interpretations which hearers will make of them. Thus, for example, we can readily understand the following exchange of questions and answers when we know that they took place in a classroom and that the questions were asked by a teacher and answered by school children.

(28) (Levinson, 1979: 384)
    T: What are the names of some trees?
    C_1: There are oaks.
    C_2: Apples!
    T: Apple trees, yes.
    C_3: Yews.
    T: Well done Johnny!
    C_4: Oak trees!
    T: No Sally, Willy's already said that.

Here, to gloss Levinson's remarks, we understand the sequence of questions and answers by reference to their institutional context – a school. Through knowledge of this context, we invoke the kinds of goals and objectives which the participants (especially the teacher) will tend to have, together with our knowledge of the normal ways these goals are pursued – including, of course, various procedures of questioning and answering.

These observations, which are nicely elaborated in Levinson's subsequent discussion, are plainly valid. Nonetheless, a further problem arises as soon as we ask ourselves: *when* is it appropriate to bring these assumptions into play, and on what basis do we do so? In short, how do we know what kind of institutional context is in play here? The orthodox response to this question is to suggest that we (and the speakers) bring knowledge about the institutional context to the talk and that they (and we) use it as a resource in interpreting the talk. Here however it is relevant to notice that the context of interpretation is somehow being treated as *exogenous* to the talk — an external interpretative resource which the speakers (and we) use to understand what is going on.

These proposals, though they are plausible enough, seem to beg the question. For, even though we have a tape-recording labelled 'Botany lesson', we may still reasonably ask whether we can be sure that it is these specific 'institutional' assumptions about activity types which are being made by the speakers, or whether indeed some entirely different set (or indeed no set) are being employed. And our 'overhearer's problem' is matched by an equivalent problem for the speakers — namely how do they know what assumptions to bring into play as the basis on which to interpret the activities of the setting and to design their own actions within it? What, in short, are the guidelines which keep the speakers' (and our) interpretative assumptions on the rails?

This question may, at first, seem as trivial as its answer is obvious. After all, the participants (and we) know that there are varieties of specialist activities and occupations — medicine, education, law, etc. — whose practitioners conduct their business in specially labelled buildings, at specific times of the day, and often 'framed' by access rituals involving a good deal of paraphernalia, pomp and circumstance. Here, surely, are all the guidelines the participants (and we) could possibly need to identify the relevant activity types, bring the relevant interpretative assumptions into play and follow through the course of events with full understanding of what is going on.

And yet a knowledge of the relevant identities, roles and institutions may still be useless (or even downright misleading) in the interpretation of conduct. It is a commonplace that recognizably 'non-pedagogic' interaction may occur in the classroom and, by the same token, that 'pedagogic' interaction may take place outside it – with peers, siblings or grandparents and in front of the TV or over the breakfast table. The first is understood *in spite of* our overarching knowledge of context, the second is grasped *independently* of context. Both can somehow be produced and recognized without any external or independent knowledge of context. Similarly, as the European 'situationists' of the late sixties demonstrated, the panoply of court procedure can easily be turned upside down by a few well-chosen words, notwithstanding the weighty authority of 'context'. 'Cross-examination', moreover, is not unknown outside the courts. Or again, the exchanges which occur in a surgery do not automatically and necessarily assume a 'consultative' character from the moment we walk into the doctor's office. And so *when*, really, and *how* does the 'consultation' recognizably happen?

A solution to these problems can emerge as soon as we abandon our traditional conception of 'context' as something exogenous to interaction or as an external interpretative resource. Instead, we can begin to think of 'context' as something *endogenously* generated within the talk of the participants and, indeed, as something created in and through that talk.

There are plenty of demonstrations that an awareness of context is something which is created through the details of talk. For example, as Atkinson (1982) has observed, it is often possible to recognize the 'institutional' character of sequences of talk without any information beyond the words on the page. Consider the following:

(29) (Levinson, 1979: 380–1)
    A: . . . you have had sexual intercourse on a previous occasion haven't you?
    B: Yes.
    A: On many previous occasions?
    B: Not many.
    A: Several?
    B: Yes.
    A: With several men?
    B: No.
    A: Just one?
    B: Two.
    A: Two. And you are seventeen and a half?
    B: Yes.

Few readers will have been able to resist the conclusion that (29) above is part of the transcript of a rape trial. Many will have correctly inferred that the answers are being produced by the alleged rape victim (B) who is being cross-examined by counsel (A) for the alleged rapist. Somehow this is being inferred endogenously – solely from the resources supplied by the sequence of questions and answers. And so the question arises: what kinds of resources are being drawn upon in this inference and ones like it? And how are they being used, by us and, more importantly, by the parties to the sequences?

In what follows, we will sketch an outline answer to this question, beginning with some uses of questions in ordinary conversation and in pedagogical interaction. As a way into the relevant issues, it is useful to make a preliminary distinction, following Searle, between 'real' questions and 'exam' questions. Here Searle proposes: 'In real questions the speaker wants to know (find out) the answer; in exam questions, the speaker wants to know if the hearer knows' (Searle, 1969: 66). Consider then, the issue of how a recipient might decide whether he has been asked a question of the 'real' or 'exam' variety. We start by instancing some polar types and circumstances.

There will undoubtedly be some circumstances – for example the 'debriefing' of an agent who has 'changed sides' – where the latter may never know which of the questions were 'traps' whose answers were already known in advance. Similarly, when a father asks a son who has newly acquired an atlas for Christmas 'What's the capital of Ecuador?' it may be impossible for the son to determine whether he has been asked a 'real' or an 'exam' question – at least at the moment the question was asked. On the other hand, there are also questions whose design and circumstances may seem to render their status transparent. 'Do you have the time?' is likely, other things being equal, to be understood as a 'real' question (though see Goffman, 1981: 68–70). While, similarly, 'What's the capital of France?' – especially if asked by an adult of, say, a seven year old – is likely to be heard as an 'exam' question. Yet, even here, it must be stressed that these understandings are, properly speaking, 'best guesses' or inferences. The inquiry about the time could be a ploy to initiate a robbery or an introduction, while that about the capital of France just might be an attempt to remedy a temporarily faulty memory.

Between these polar types of complete uncertainty and virtual certainty lie many gradations of doubt and confidence. And this being the case, it might seem that answerers may tend to remain a little 'hazy' about the status of questions they have been asked and for which they have furnished answers. Yet in practice this is rarely the case, and this is so by virtue of the three-part character of the local sequential organization of talk discussed earlier. The following question–answer sequences exhibit one commonly used procedure through which the status of prior questions is clarified.

```
(30) (Rah:I:8:ST)
        V: And she's got the application forms.=
 1 → J: =Ooh:: so when is her interview did she sa⌐:y?
 2 → V:                                            ⌊She
        didn't (.) Well she's gotta send their fo:rm
        back. Sh⌐e doesn't know w⌐hen the ⌐interview is yet
 3 → J:          ⌊O h : : : .      ⌋       ⌊ Oh it's just th
        form,
```

```
(31) (Frankel:TC:1:1:13–14:ST)
 1 → S: ·hh When do you get out. Christmas week or the
        week before Christmas.
        (0.3)
 2 → G: Uh::m two or three days before Ch⌐ristmas,⌐
 3 → S:                                  ⌊O h : , ⌋
```

```
(32) (Rah:B:1:IDJ(12):4:ST)
 1 → J: Okay then I was asking and she says you're
        working tomorrow as well,
 2 → I: Yes I'm supposed to be tomorrow yes,
 3 → J: Oh:::,
```

These three sequences are arranged in an order which corresponds to the degree to which the answer to the question is 'unexpected'. In (30) the answer undercuts the questioner's assumption that the application form for a job has already been sent away and is plainly not expected by the questioner. In (31) the questioner proposes two alternative possibilities as an answer to her question and gets an answer which falls within the parameters of the first of these. Finally, in (32), J's report of another speaker's assertion concerning her co-participant is confirmed by that co-participant (see Pomerantz, 1980, for an account of how such reports come to 'question'). Thus, in (32), the co-participant's confirmation is strongly 'expectable'.

In each of these sequences, we encounter a question–answer–'oh' pattern (arrows 1–3) which is highly recurrent in question–answer sequences. In each case, the third turn 'oh' does not indicate 'surprise' for, although surprise might be relevant in (30), it is certainly not in (31) and (32) and yet 'oh' is used to receipt all three answers. In fact, the 'oh' indicates a 'change of state' of knowledge (Heritage, 1984a). Such an indication is nicely fitted to the question–answer sequences which it completes. In a 'real' question, the questioner proposes to be ignorant about the substance of the question and, as we have seen (pp. 249–51), projects the intended answerer to be knowledgeable about the matter. Thus the provision of an answer should, in such a context, commit the questioner to have undergone a 'change of state' from ignorance to knowledge. The particle 'oh' is a major means of expressing just that. It follows from this that the questioner's 'oh' response – in expressing a change of state of knowledge – serves to confirm, or re-confirm, that the original question was a 'real' one. Once again, then, we find a three-part sequence in which the provision of a third turn unobtrusively consolidates the sense of the first.

These observations can be further strengthened by a consideration of a 'deviant case'. In the following extract, three question–answer–'oh' sequences run to completion in quick succession. Subsequently a fourth such sequence is apparently initiated with the question-intoned utterance 'Nice Jewish bo:y?'

> (33) (HG:II:25:ST) ((Concerning a boyfriend away at university))
> 1 → N: =·hhh Does <u>he</u> have his own apa:rt⌈ment?⌉
> 2 → H: ⌊·hhhh⌋Yea:h,=
> 3 → N: =Oh:
>   (1.0)
> 1 → N: How did you get his <u>number</u>.

```
          (·)
2 → H:  I: (·) called information at San Francisc⌐uh
3 → N:                                        ⌊Oh::::.
          (·)
    N:  Very cleve:r,=
    H:  =Thank you⌐: I– ·hh–·hhhhhhhh   ⌐ h‖=
1 → N:              ⌊What's his last name,⌡
2 → H:  =Uh:: Freedla:nd. ·hh⌐hh
3 → N:                        ⌊Oh⌐:,
    H:                          ⌊(or) Freedlind.=
a → N:  =Nice Jewish bo:y?
          (·)
b → H:| O:f cou:rse,=
c → N:  =Of⌐cou:rse,   ⌐
    H:      ⌊hh-h̄h-hh⌡ hnh·hhhh=
    N:  =Nice Jewish boy who doesn't like to write letters!
```

This final triplet (marked a, b, c on the transcript) although beginning with a question-like turn (arrow a) which offers an inference about the boyfriend's ethnic identity from his surname, does not run off like the previous three. Instead, after the confirming response (arrow b) to the inference, the first speaker echoes the confirmation (arrow c) in such a way as to suggest that her initial 'inference' was not a query, but rather an expression of the obvious. By means of this alternative third turn receipt, an utterance which could have been retrospectively formulated as a question is in fact treated as having been, all along and in the first place, a 'comment'.

In sum, conversationalists have a variety of 'third turn' resources with which to demonstrate that an answer to a question has been 'informative' or 'news' for them. 'Oh' is one such resource, 'really', 'did you', 'God!', 'wow', etc. are other, related resources. There are yet other, more complex and intricate, means of expressing similar orientations. The point to take from this brief discussion is that the questioner's orientation of, to paraphrase Searle, 'wanting to find out something' is, by these various means, preserved and sustained as an intersubjectively confirmed and consolidated orientation in and through these three-part sequences.

Quite a different orientation is displayed in the recurrent

three-part sequences making up 'pedagogical' interaction. Thus in (34), the questioner repeatedly assesses, evaluates or comments on the answers elicited by his questions in a characteristic (arrowed 1–3) question–answer–comment sequence (McHoul, 1978; Mehan, 1979).

```
(34)  (McHoul, forthcoming) (simplified)
  1  →T:  Where else were they taking it before they (1.0)
            started in Western Australia?
            (2.0)
      T:  Mm hm?
            (0.5)
  2  →P₁:  Melbourne?
            (0.5)
  3  →T:  No⌈:::
  2  →P₂:    ⌊°(        )
  3  →T:  No::
            (1.0)
  1  →T:  Where does BHP get its iron ore from?
       ⟋P₃:  ⌈(        )
  2  →P₄:  ⎢(        )
       ⟍P₅:  ⌊(        )
  3  →  T:  Doesn't
  2  →P₆:  (New South Wales)
            · · · · ·
            · · · · ·
  3  →T:  You're guessing
```

It will be apparent from even the most elementary inspection of this sequence that each and every one of the teacher's (arrow 3) responses to the answers to his questions, by accepting or rejecting those answers, proposes independent knowledge of the answer. Each response thereby proposes the prior question to have been an 'exam' question. Furthermore, across a sequence of such question–answer–comment triplets an overwhelmingly 'pedagogical' frame of reference is established. Thus, regardless of whether the above sequence took place in a classroom or not, it is clear that something 'educational' is going on through the stacking up of a series of 'exam' questions. In sum, we scarcely need to see the desks, the blackboard or the other paraphernalia of classroom 'context', because the educational context of this interaction is being renewed with every 'third turn' acceptance or rejection of an answer. By the same token we find that, no matter how objectively 'certain' a particular, a priori contextualized sense for a question may be, the participants nonetheless find themselves employing these 'third turn' resources through which they routinely assure and reassure one another that it is 'this', and not some 'other', sense of context that is operative for the local organization of 'this segment' of interaction.

Now, of course, it is not merely in 'third turns' that participants' orientations to the content and context of institutional activities is displayed as a return to (29) shows.

(29) (Levinson, 1979: 380–1)
    A: . . . you have had sexual intercourse on a previous
       occasion haven't you?
    B: Yes.
    A: On many previous occasions?
    B: Not many.
    A: Several?
    B: Yes.
    A: With several men?
    B: No.
    A: Just one?
    B: Two.
    A: Two. And you are seventeen and a half?
    B: Yes.

The fact that here the questioning is being done neither to 'inform' the questioner (nor, of course, to 'test' the witness's knowledge of her own past experiences) is displayed by the design of the questions. These are hearable neither as 'real' questions or 'exam' questions (Levinson, 1979). Moreover, the fact that these questions are designed to elicit information for the 'bystanding' judge and jury (cf. Goffman, 1981: 133–4) is displayed, *inter alia*, by the questioner's avoidance of any form of third turn receipt item in favour of a move to the next question (cf. Heritage, 1984b). Similarly, that this is a hostile cross-examination rather than a direct examination by friendly counsel is evidenced both by the design of the questions and the witness's less than co-operative responses (cf. Levinson,

1979: 374–5; Atkinson and Drew, 1979: 105–87; Drew, 1984b; Pomerantz and Atkinson, 1984) and, of course, it is also evidenced in the juxtaposition of the counsel's questions which — especially the final one — are plainly designed to build up a portrait which is damaging to the witness (Levinson, 1979: 380–1).

It is thus through the specific, detailed and local design of turns and sequences that 'institutional' contexts are observably and reportably — i.e. accountably — brought into being. They may be created and realized outside of their usual formal locations in classrooms, courtrooms, etc., and, by the same token, they may fail to be realized inside these places. This observation suggests that, notwithstanding the panoply and power of place and role, *it is within these local sequences of talk, and only there, that these institutions are ultimately and accountably talked into being.* And this, in turn, underscores Garfinkel's recommendation that

> any social setting be viewed as self-organizing with respect to the intelligible character of its own appearances. Any setting organizes its activities to make its properties as an organized environment of practical activities detectable, countable, recordable, tell-a-story-aboutable, analysable — in short, *accountable.* Garfinkel, 1967a: 33)

Finally, the considerations of this section show that the details of little, local sequences which at first seemed narrow, insignificant and contextually uninteresting, turn out to be the crucial resources by which larger institutionalized activity frameworks are evoked. Such institutional contexts are created as visible states of affairs on a turn-by-turn basis. It is ultimately through such means that 'institutions' exist as accountable organizations of social actions.

CONCLUSION

Although this has been a lengthy chapter and an extensive effort has been made to illustrate the kind of research work represented by conversation analysis, we have in fact scarcely grazed the surface of its orientations and achievements. In essence, the omissions of this chapter are twofold. First, there are whole domains of research which have been overlooked. These include the organization of turn-taking, the management of repair, the analysis of topic organization, the integration of vocal and non-vocal activities which, together with numerous sub-areas, now have extensive literatures (see Heritage, 1984c, for details). Second, while the relevance of conversation analytic findings to a number of topics — the maintenance of intersubjective understanding, the maintenance of social solidarity and the endogenous constitution of 'context' — has been briefly discussed, it should not be concluded that conversation analysis is specially devised or directed to deal with these matters. On the contrary, other studies could have been cited which are geared to quite different objectives, for example the analysis of how speakers manage particular interactional roles or project specific identities, or of how orators mobilize crowd support for their claims, or again how conversationalists go about the task of communicating personal troubles to one another. There is, then, no fixed agenda intrinsic to conversation analysis, any more than there is for ethnomethodology or, indeed, the discipline of sociology as a whole. Rather, conversation analysis represents a general approach to the analysis of social action which can be applied to an extremely varied array of topics and problems.

The central achievement of conversation analysis has been its wholesale advance in the detailed analysis of the organization of social action. This advance has created anxieties in some quarters. In particular, it has been suggested by commentators of a humanist persuasion that conversation analysis represents a betrayal of the principles of *verstehende* sociology in favour of a new behaviourism which is every bit as mechanistic and deterministic as its psychological predecessor. Such fears are entirely groundless. Conversation analysis in fact represents a vast extension — in both scope and detail — of the basic theorem of accountable action presented in chapter 5. That theorem, it will be recalled, was non-deterministic. According to that theorem actors may, or may not, act in accordance with the normatively organized constraints which bear upon them — subject only to the condition that 'deviant' actions may ultimately be recognizable, accountable and sanctionable as such.

The organization of talk thus participates in a dialectical relationship between agency and structure in social life and in a cognitive-moral way. Without a detailed texture of institutionalized methods of talking to orient to, social actors would inevitably lose their cognitive bearings. Under such circumstances, they would become incapable both of interpreting the actions of co-participants and of formulating their own particular courses of action. A texture of institutionalized methods of talking is thus essential if actors are to make continuous sense of their environments of action. Moreover, a range of moral considerations may be superimposed on these cognitive ones. For in the absence of a detailed institutionalization of methods of talking, actors could not be held morally accountable for their actions, and moral anomie would necessarily compound its cognitive counterpart. In the end, therefore, what is at stake is the existence of a form of social organization which is so strong and detailed as to render choices among courses of action both conceivable and possible. It is the specification of this social organization, with all its nuances, ramifications and cultural variations, which conversation analysis is essentially about.

CHAPTER 9

Epilogue: An Uncompleted Quest

In exactly the ways that a setting is organized, it consists *of members' methods for making evident that setting's ways as clear, coherent, planful, consistent, chosen, knowable, uniform, reproducible connections, i.e. rational connections.*

Garfinkel, *Studies in Ethnomethodology*

In the final chapter of this book we turn to the most recent phase of Garfinkel's programme of research: the 'studies of work'. These studies were first introduced at the Ninth World Congress of Sociology at Uppsala, Sweden, in 1978 and a number of publications have subsequently appeared (Garfinkel, Lynch and Livingston, 1981; Lynch, 1982; Lynch, Livingston and Garfinkel, 1983). The latter have been concerned with aspects of natural scientific activity, but a series of forthcoming volumes (Garfinkel, forthcoming; Lynch, forthcoming) will deal with a broader range of work domains including law, medicine, art and mathematics. The discussion of the present chapter cannot properly or usefully anticipate these concrete studies but will be limited to a treatment of the programme of work outlined in the published papers.

At its most basic, the studies-of-work programme is directed to analysing the specific, concrete material practices which compose the moment-to-moment, day-by-day work of occupational life. These practices are treated as *endogenous* to the work domains in which they occur and which they constitute. Access to these practices is gained through the fact that in a variety of ways – some tacit, some partially formulated – they are produced and recognized by the parties to work environments as locally accountable competences in working activities. The competences which enter, for example, into such activities as playing jazz piano (Sudnow, 1978), or using 'chalk and talk' to engage in mathematical reasoning (Livingston, 1978, 1982), or establishing that a set of electron micrographs are free of artefacts (Lynch, 1979, forthcoming) are in the first instance produced and recognised *in situ*. They are locally accountable competences whose practice makes up a course of working activity which may, additionally, be impregnated with a range of related concerns and preoccupations. The task of the studies-of-work programme is to develop descriptions of these competences as they manifest themselves in specific courses of conduct which are accountable as distinctive occupational work.

BACKGROUND

In a number of respects, the studies-of-work programme can be viewed as an extension of research themes developed by Garfinkel and his associates during the sixties. Zimmerman's work on bureaucratic procedures in a social welfare agency (1969a, 1969b), Wieder's study of a half-way house for paroled narcotics offenders (1974), Bittner's analyses of police conduct (1967a, 1967b) and Cicourel's research on police contacts with juvenile offenders (1968) and student counselling (Cicourel and Kitsuse, 1963) were all concerned with documenting the mundane activities composing the organizational domains they studied, though in several cases this theme was over-whelmed by a concern with the ways in which 'normalizing' occupational practices influenced the construction of official statistics. Two of Garfinkel's papers from this period – his analysis of occupational practices at a suicide-prevention centre (Garfinkel, 1967i; 1967a: 11–18) and of clinic records (Garfinkel, 1967f) – are also focused on the contingencies of specific work activities.

In his study of the Los Angeles Suicide Prevention Center, Garfinkel noted relatively general features of its staff members' preoccupations and practices. Thrown of necessity into the midst of the particular and concrete remains of equivocal deaths, their day's work consisted of assembling 'a profession-ally defensible and thereby . . . a *recognizably* rational account of how the society worked to produce those remains' (Garfinkel,

1967a: 17). To achieve this end, SPC staff drew upon a great range of recipe knowledge which was drawn upon *ad hoc* to meet the contingencies of each case. In pursuing their investigations as a daily task, the staff recognized that their inquiries were

> intimately connected to the terms of employment, to various internal and external chains of reportage, supervision, and review, and to similar organizationally supplied 'priorities of relevances' for assessments of what 'realistically', 'practically' or 'reasonably' needed to be done and could be done, how quickly, with what resources, seeing whom, talking about what, for how long, and so on. Such considerations furnished 'We did what we could, and for all reasonable interests here is what we came out with' its features of organizationally appropriate sense, fact, impersonality, anonymity of authorship, purpose, reproducibility – i.e. of a *properly* and *visibly* rational account of the inquiry. (ibid. 13)

Finally, Garfinkel noted that the SPC officers conducted their work in the knowledge that their cases were never absolutely closed or beyond revision by the courts or through internal review. Thus

> inquirers wanted very much to be able to assure that they could come out at the end with an account of how the person died that would permit the coroner and his staff to withstand claims arguing that the account was incomplete or that the death happened differently. (ibid. 15–16)

Moreover the staff were aware that their reports had a chronically 'open' character in that upon any occasion of their use

> it can remain to be seen what can be done with them, or what they will have come to, or what remains done 'for the time being' pending the ways in which the environment of that decision may organize itself to 'reopen the case', or 'issue a complaint', or 'find an issue' and so on. (ibid. 17)

These possibilities formed a permanent background against which the SPC officers' accounts of death were formulated and to which their accounts were oriented.

The 'defensive' concern with the accountability of accounts also constitutes a substantive theme of Garfinkel's discussion of case records in a psychiatric clinic, reported in his ' "Good" organizational reasons for "bad" clinic records' (Garfinkel, 1967f). His starting point is the 'normal, natural troubles' which social science researchers routinely encounter in dealing with clinic records as scientific data and which centre on the records' incompleteness and lack of clarity. The problematic status of such records has a number of basic explanations. The cost of record keeping is considerable. It is difficult to justify the 'core' status of any particular corpus of information. It is difficult to motivate clinic personnel to maintain detailed records when the latter may be viewed as irrelevant, intrusive or problematic 'given the unpredictable character of the occasions under which the record may be used as part of an ongoing system of supervision and review' (ibid. 194). Finally, there is the range of problems which arise from the use of standardized forms as a reporting medium which hinge on the disparity between the fixed terminology of the forms and the variety of events to be brought under their jurisdiction.

But these standard sources of troubles, Garfinkel proposes, do not go to the heart of the difficulties which social scientists encounter when they seek to use records for research purposes. Social scientific uses involve treating the records as *actuarial* in character – as listing, with whatever deficiencies, a sequence of transactions between clinicians and patients. But, Garfinkel proposes, the records are not maintained with such actuarial objectives in view. Rather, they are designed so as to testify to the fulfilment of a *therapeutic contract* with medico-legal obligations between clinician and patient: 'the contents of clinic folders are assembled with regard for the possibility that the relationship may have to be portrayed as having been in accord with expectations of sanctionable performances by clinicians and patients' (ibid. 199). The possibility that the records were being used to supply indices of a therapeutic contract explained some of the puzzles and paradoxes which are routinely encountered by researchers:

When any case folder was read as an actuarial record its contents fell so short of adequacy as to leave us puzzled as to why 'poor records' as poor as these should nevertheless be so assiduously kept. On the other hand, when folder documents were regarded as unformulated terms of a potential therapeutic contract, i.e. as documents assembled in the folder in open anticipation of some occasion when the terms of a therapeutic contract might have to be formulated from them, the assiduousness with which folders were kept, even though their contents were extremely uneven in quantity and quality, began to 'make sense'. (ibid. 200)

Garfinkel elaborates these observations by drawing attention to the highly elliptical character of the observations contained in the record.

As expressions, the remarks that make up these documents have overwhelmingly the characteristic that their sense cannot be decided by a reader without his necessarily knowing or assuming something about a typical biography and typical purposes of the user of the expressions, about typical circumstances under which such remarks are written, about a typical previous course of transactions between the writers and the patient, or about a typical relationship of actual or potential interaction between *the writers and the reader.* Thus *the folder contents much less than revealing an order of interaction, presuppose an understanding of that order for a correct reading.* (ibid. 201)

Thus, while their elliptical character precludes the treatment of the records as actuarial documents, it permits them to be interrogated by those 'who know how to read them'. And this restriction to 'competent readers' may have a particular value for the preparers and users of the records.

Folder contents are assembled against the contingent need, by some clinic member, to construct a potential or past course of transactions between the clinic and the patient as a 'case' . . . frequently in the interests of justifying an actual or potential course of actions between clinic persons and patients. (ibid. 203)

In this context, the use of elliptical observations, the fact that they cannot be coherently interpreted without reference to the organized ways of the clinic and its personnel, and that their interpretation routinely requires the supplying of contexts in which the remarks can be treated as indexing legitimate courses of conduct, taken together, result in a situation in which 'speaking euphemistically, between clinic persons and their clients, and between the clinic and its environing groups, the exchange of information is something less than a free market.' (ibid. 197)

Although the studies reviewed above take concrete work domains as a primary anchorage point, their substantive focus is less on the details of particular work practices than on the abiding preoccupations of the practitioners with the temporality and accountability of their tasks. The studies-of-work programme, by contrast, raises the prospect of a direct analytic engagement with the specifics of concrete work practices which is unprecedented in its detail and precision. And this, in turn, foreshadows the development of an observationally founded science of mundane work activity.

THE PROBLEM OF AN OBSERVATIONAL SCIENCE AND ITS MISSING LITERATURE

Garfinkel introduces the studies-of-work programme by raising the question of a missing social science literature (Garfinkel, 1978; Garfinkel, Lynch and Livington, 1981: 132–3). In this context, he draws attention to the following paradoxical feature of social scientific studies of occupations. While a large number of studies of occupations command our attention and interest either because of the intrinsic significance of the occupation in question (e.g. surgery) or because of its 'exotic' character (e.g. the jazz musician), these studies tend to be 'about', rather than 'of', the occupation in question (ibid.). The studies tend to generate full and detailed descriptions of such matters as the income, social networks and role relations among the participants, but they are largely silent about the matters which make these occupations significant in the first place, namely that they involve the conduct of surgical procedures or the playing of jazz music.

At the very heart of the social science literature on occupations, therefore, we encounter a descriptive gap which Garfinkel often epitomizes by recounting Shils's complaint to Strodtbeck:

In 1954 Fred Strodtbeck was hired by the University of Chicago Law School to analyse tape-recordings of jury deliberations obtained from a bugged jury room. Edward Shils was on the committee that hired him. When Strodtbeck proposed to administer Bales Interaction Process Analysis categories, Shils complained: 'By using Bales Interaction Process Analysis I'm sure we'll learn what about a jury's deliberations makes them a small group. But we want to know what about their deliberations makes them a jury.' (ibid. 133)

The gap in the social science literature on occupations consists of all the missing descriptions of what occupational activities consist of and all the missing analyses of how the practitioners manage the tasks which, for them, are matters of serious and pressing significance. The gap becomes glaringly visible as soon as we ask such questions as: how is an accountably adequate surgical incision produced and recognized? Or, how is a stream of sounds produced and recognized as the playing of jazz music? Or, how is the utterance of a juror the recognizably judicious outcome of 'talking in a juror's fashion'? (cf. Garfinkel, 1967d). Merely to ask these questions is to expose the ways in which standard social scientific techniques are profoundly insensitive to what Garfinkel refers to as the 'quiddity' or 'just whatness' of occupational practices. And it is just these features of occupations which are systematically absent from the social science literature.

One result of this gap is that occupational practitioners frequently fail to recognize themselves or their daily concerns in social scientific accounts (Garfinkel, 1978) and for this reason, and just as frequently, they find the latter to be uninteresting, misleading or plain exasperating (ibid.). Aspects of these sentiments are expressed by the distinguished bio-chemist, Jonas Salk in his introduction to Latour and Woolgar's *Laboratory Life*:

> Scientists often have an aversion to what non-scientists say about science . . . Social studies of science and philosophy of science tend to be abstract or to deal with well-known historical events or remote examples that bear no relationship to what occurs daily at the laboratory bench or in the interactions between scientists in the pursuit of their goals . . . In the name of 'science policy', studies of scientific activity by economists

and sociologists are often concerned with numbers of publications and with duplication of effort. While such examinations are of some value, they leave much to be desired because, in part, the statistical tools are crude and these exercises are often aimed at controlling productivity and creativity. Most importantly, *they are not concerned with the substance of scientific thought and scientific work*. For these reasons, scientists are not drawn to read what outsiders have to say about science and much prefer the views of scientists about scientific endeavours. (Latour and Woolgar, 1979: 11) (emphasis added)

While it may be disconcerting to find that occupational practitioners may find their daily activities better represented in, for example, narrative fiction than in social scientific reports, the social sciences have their defences. Thus it may be held that policy studies should legitimately restrict their focus to matters directly related to costs and benefits, or that social studies of occupations cannot afford to become bogged down with the minutiae of occupational activities and practices. Or again, it may be held that there are no obvious gains to be had from engaging in the detailed description of occupational practices and preoccupations. For these and other reasons, direct investigations into the details of occupational worlds are normally deferred until 'some other time'. As Garfinkel et al. put it in an ironic reference to Shils's complaint:

The social sciences are unresponsive to Shils's complaint. Technical methods for turning Shils's complaint into an agenda of researchable phenomena are not available to the social sciences. Strodtbeck replied and Shils agreed: Shils was asking the wrong question! (Garfinkel et al. 1981: 133)

Now it is not simply a matter for regret or disappointment that social scientists have, for one reason or another, failed to depict the core practices of the occupational worlds which they have studied. Rather the observation raises further serious questions and difficulties. What, after all, *is* being studied with the use of social scientific methods? And what relation does this subject matter have to the occupational worlds under investigation? The answer appears to be that, *somehow*, the lived realities of occupational life are transmuted into objects suitable for treatment within the accounting practices of professional social science. The accountable organizational objects and events of an occupational domain are thus, through some process of translation, re-presented as the accountable organizational objects of social science research and theorizing. But, in the absence of detailed knowledge of occupations as domains of accountable activities, the translations bear an unknown relationship to the domains of activity they intendedly depict.

These abstract methodological remarks have more concrete corollaries. Few natural observational records of occupational activities are available for social scientific inspection and, as a result, social studies of occupations effectively lack a natural observational base. No manuals of procedure are available which describe how social scientific concepts can be 'operationally' applied to naturally occurring occupational conduct. Nor is there a stable 'lore' of tried and trusted procedures through which, for example, taped records of occupational transactions can be brought to routine social scientific description. And, lacking any stable observational base, it is clear – to recall Sacks's (1984a) observations – that social scientific studies of occupations are not informative about actual events in the straightforward ways that even the most primitive of classificatory sciences are. No student of occupations can go to a record of events and confirm or challenge the assertions of another observer. In short, the social sciences 'are talking sciences, and achieve in texts, not elsewhere, the observability and practical objectivity of their phenomena' (Garfinkel et al., 1981: 133). The studies-of-work programme thus pointedly raises the question of whether, and in what ways, the social sciences can be simple observational sciences capable of depicting the mundane details of ordinary human activities with the same measure of precision and having similar mechanisms for resolving disputed claims as were achieved, for example, by the naturalists of the nineteenth century.

The detailed description of mundane actions and of the competences which inform them involves tasks whose dimensions and scope have yet to be fully determined and grasped. Some of the tasks of analysis are adumbrated, though scarcely developed in a naturalistic direction, in the writings of Heidegger and Merleau-Ponty (e.g. Heidegger, 1967; Merleau-

Ponty, 1968) which have served as orienting resources for some studies (cf. Lynch, Livingston and Garfinkel, 1983). The 'boundaries' of specific, located ordinary actions, their 'units' or 'segments', the determination of adequacy in their description or representation – all of these questions and many more pose problems which cannot be resolved 'in principle' but which require solution in the context of practical engagement with descriptive tasks. For many areas, though certainly not all, recordings of conduct can help, but not necessarily or invariably. There are scarcely any straightforward methodological pathways which presently inform the descriptive enterprise.

The studies-of-work programme addresses these issues by proposing to treat as relevant materials for analysis all exhibits of activity which are recognized as belonging to a domain of action by the participants to that domain. These materials are subjected to a rigorous naturalistic description in which the focus is on the production, management and recognition of specific, material competences as they are exhibited in real time and in settings in which their employment is recognizably consequential. Ordinary activities are thus examined for the ways in which they exhibit accountably competent work practice as viewed *by practitioners*. Competences are exclusively treated 'from within' – within scenes of commonplace work activity and by mundanely competent practitioners – for competent occupational practice is recognizably produced only within such scenes and by such persons and not elsewhere. Occupations are thus understood, not as the products of normative socialization, unstated conventions, beliefs or tacit assumptions (cf. Lynch et al., 1983: 208) but, primordially, as self-organizing domains of recognizably competent work practices which 'compose themselves through vernacular conversations and the ordinariness of embodied disciplinary activities' (ibid.). And work competences are found, not in the privacy of individual consciousness, but as publicly observable courses of specific, local and temporally organized conduct. Accordingly, in the studies of work

> there is a unique preoccupation with local production and with the worldly observability of reasoning. This means that

> reasoning is displayed in the midst of orders of intersubjectively
> accountable details: the order of spoken utterances by different
> parties in conversation, the compositional order of manipulated
> materials at the laboratory bench, or the transitive order of
> written materials on a page of text. (ibid. 206)

Thus, just as conversation analysts have approached the intelligible character of interaction by examining the local and sequenced nature of the parties' contributions to particular passages of talk, so too in the studies of work, researchers have sought to treat mundane occupational practices and events by reference to their essentially temporal organizational features.

Since the publication of a substantial number of studies of work is pending at the present time, no attempt will be made here at a pre-emptive description of the leading themes and findings of this latest phase of research by Garfinkel and his 'second generation' of graduate students. The reader is immediately referred, however, to a number of suggestive studies which have already been published. Sudnow's (1978) analysis of his own apprenticeship as a jazz musician contains an outstanding depiction of the changing ways in which hand and mind engage with a terrain which physically exists as a piano keyboard, but which is constituted and reconstituted in and through the changing manual competences with which the keyboard is addressed. Lynch's (1979, forthcoming) discussions of the role of artefact accounts in laboratory science is a pioneering study which, together with Gilbert and Mulkay's (1984) research on scientists' accounts, stresses the openness of scientific practitioners to 'the contingent ties between human actions and their objectified results' (Lynch, 1982: 511). Finally Garfinkel et al.'s (1981) study of the discovery of an optical pulsar opens up an entirely new approach to the origins of cultural objects. It does so by focusing on the ways in which a discovered natural object of scientific inquiry is developed as the product of temporally situated courses of practical actions in which an 'instrumentally available', though vaguely known, object is disengaged from the immediate practical conditions of its availability and attached to nature as 'a relatively finished object'.

None of these studies make for easy reading – not least because of the inherent difficulties of describing scenes of practical activity in an adequate fashion. But the revolutionary potential of their analyses should not be underestimated. For the first time, specific settings of concrete work activities are being examined so as to disclose the detailed, reticulated textures of practices through which culturally transcendent objects are created as their project and as their embodied, yet disengageable outcome.

CONCLUSION

In a recent study of Parsons, Steven Savage has observed that he 'sought to answer questions where others have not even seen the possibility of a question' (Savage, 1981: 235). No remark could be a more apt characterization of Parsons's famous student. Garfinkel has had a long and consistently innovative career which has embraced studies of many recondite topics. His most significant innovations, however, have concerned not the exotic but the routine. His achievement has been to maintain a consistent and productive focus on facts of social life which are so obvious, so mundane and so deeply part of the background of our lives that a special effort of the imagination is required to notice them, let alone perceive their significance. His explorations of elementary properties of practical actions have issued in a profound reorientation of the theory of action which still awaits the full recognition and assimilation which will be crucial for a wide range of developments in theoretical and empirical research in the social sciences.

Any serious attempt to grasp the nature of Garfinkel's contribution to contemporary social science must begin by considering the ways in which he systematically transformed the theory of action developed by Parsons. The fundamental problem of social science for Parsons was to explain the persistence and reproduction of institutionalized patterns of social relations. At the level of action, Parsons treated the problem as essentially a motivational one. The stability of social institutions is threatened by the irreducible egoism of individuals whose motivations must somehow be harnessed to the workings of social structures. The solution to this motivational 'problem of order', he proposed, flows from the fact that cultural norms are internalized within actors during the course of socialization and these norms subsequently shape both their desires and the courses of action which they adopt to attain their ends. The major result of this process is that individuals want to act in ways which maintain institutionalized patterns of action.

Garfinkel's response to this analysis was to accept that the persistence and reproduction of social relations is the fundamental problem of social science. But, he proposed, any solution to this problem requires an analysis of how the actors come to share a common appraisal of their empirical circumstances and, ultimately, a common world. This cognitive 'problem of order', he argued, is analytically prior to its Parsonian motivational counterpart because the actors must be able to view the world in the same terms if they are to be able to co-ordinate their activities in relation to one another. At the end of the day, neither co-operation nor conflict can be managed by actors who cannot engage in co-ordinated activity.

In developing his approach to this problem, Garfinkel did not take up the question-begging Parsonian proposal that institutionalized norms guarantee an intersubjective cognitive order. Instead, drawing upon the work of Husserl and Schutz, he began from the notion that intersubjective sense is the product of an active process which proceeds within a framework of taken-for-granted assumptions which Schutz had described under the heading of the attitude of everyday life. Within this framework, sense-making activities consist of the endogenous assimilation of a range of particular situated actions and events to some underlying theme or organization for the situation as a whole in a process which Garfinkel, following Mannheim, termed the documentary method of interpretation.

Much of Garfinkel's early work consisted of attempts to explore the parameters of this process, and the results of these explorations were both surprising and paradoxical. Specifically, he found that some established sense for a domain of activity could be maintained even in the face of grossly 'discrepant' information. Here actors remained committed to a particular trusted view of the situation and accomodated 'discrepancies' to this view by manipulating background assumptions in terms of which the information itself was to be understood. In this research, Garfinkel found that a huge array of unstated presuppositions and assumptions could be mobilized *ad hoc*, with the effect of preserving some original viewpoint against destruction.

In the experimental procedures which he had employed to yield these results, Garfinkel had expected to achieve massive disruptions in the subjects' perceptions and cognitions and he was undoubtedly surprised by the extent to which, through their accomodative work, the subjects were able to 'normalize' the situation and remain undisturbed. Yet a related set of procedures involving the disruption of small-scale real life interactions yielded an opposite pattern. As Garfinkel put it:

> It was unnerving to find the seemingly endless variety of events that lent themselves to the production of really nasty surprises. These events ranged from those that, according to sociological commonsense, were 'critical', like standing very, very close to a person while otherwise maintaining an innocuous conversation, to others that according to sociological commonsense were 'trivial', like saying 'hello' at the termination of a conversation. Both procedures elicited anxiety, indignation, strong feelings on the part of experimenter and subject alike of humiliation and regret, demands by the subjects for explanation and so on. (Garfinkel, 1963: 198)

A solution to this paradox lies in the *methodic* character of sense-making practices. For as long as the participants in a scene can remain assured that their ordinary trusted methods of common-sense reasoning were adequate to their tasks, they continued to employ them with varying degrees of cognitive discomfort. As soon as the applicability of the methods themselves was threatened, anger and bewilderment immediately made their appearance. The effect of these experiments was to show that, while a shared cognitive order is ultimately based on shared and trusted methods of understanding, the use of these methods is the object of extremely powerful normative sanctions. Thus although, in Garfinkel's analysis, the cognitive and normative dimensions of action are not linked after the fashion proposed by Parsons, they are nonetheless strongly interrelated through the variety of ways in which each actor's implementation of these methods is treated as morally accountable.

These theoretical and empirical studies of the 1950s and early 1960s have foreshadowed and strongly influenced the growing consensus within the social sciences on the need for a new theoretical framework for the analysis of action. This movement of thought, like Garfinkel's work itself, has emerged in a wide-ranging reaction to the normative determinism of the post-war Parsonian synthesis and is expressed in the general view that any new analytic framework for the study of action must not violate fundamental aspects of ordinary human experience. Such a framework must find a place for the basic experience of human agency and transcend the sterile confrontation between 'consensus' and 'conflict' theories (Dawe, 1978; Giddens, 1978; Harre and Secord, 1972). Moreover it must locate a theoretical stance which lies beyond not only traditional determinisms which imply unrealistic levels of predictability in the social world, but also the Pirandello-esque worlds of 'anything goes' interpretivism which end up threatening the very possibility of a stable social world (Atkinson, 1981).

The positive outcome of these imperatives has been a stress on the cognitive bases of action which goes well beyond routine references to the actor's 'definition of the situation'. Influenced by parallel developments in social psychology and cognitive science, there has been a substantial movement towards script- and schema-based analyses of social activity. This cognitive approach to action is also linked with what Knorr-Cetina (1981: 6) has recently termed 'methodological situationism', in which actions are treated not simply as the products of individual dispositions nor of external constraints, but as reciprocally organized within a setting in which the actors' cognitive frameworks are instantiated as patterned interaction.

These positive developments of the last decade show considerable promise. Nonetheless, it is a very substantial step from these relatively programmatic positions to concrete analyses of the organization of social action. The gap between cognition and action is a complex one. Moreover, there is an ever-present danger that oversimplified attempts to bridge this gap will result in the creation of a new form of *cognitive* 'judgemental dope'. A 'scripted' analysis of action in which the actors' actions are treated as determined by hierarchies of pre-ordained cognitive schemata is just as capable of ignoring the common-sense rationalities of judgement (cf. Garfinkel, 1967: 68) as its sociological and psychological forerunners. Such an analysis would profoundly threaten the theoretical gains of the past twenty years. It is at this point, where an analysis of cognition must be integrated with an analysis of action, that Garfinkel's true stature as an originator manifests itself most clearly and it is here that his essential theoretical message must not be lost from sight.

Garfinkel bridges the gap between cognition and action by stressing that action is through and through a *temporal* affair which is *reflexively accountable*. Each actor inhabits a setting of action which is unfolding on a moment-by-moment basis in and as a temporal succession of actions. Each 'next' action, in occurring in temporal juxtaposition to the sequence of actions comprising a setting, constitutes both an 'incarnate' commentary on and an intervention in the setting in which it occurs. Actions-as-constitutive-of-their-settings and settings-as-constitutive-of-their-actions are two halves of a simultaneous equation which the actors are continually solving through a mass of *methodic* procedures. It is through these methods, brought to bear on a temporal succession of actions, that actors are continually able to establish the 'state of play' between them, to grasp the nature of the circumstances in which they are currently placed and, not least, to assess the moral character, dispositions and identities of those with whom they are dealing.

In short, it is through the application of methods of practical reasoning to a temporal succession of activities that all aspects of social action are rendered accountable. The ancient adage that people are known by their deeds is thus at best a half truth. It would be more accurate to say that it is through, and only through, the reflexive accountability of its constituent deeds that every aspect of a situation of action, its participants, their rationalities and their motives can be known. It is this insight into the ineluctable, incarnate accountability of action which lies at the core of Garfinkel's cognitive revolution in sociology. And it is this same insight which has motivated contemporary research into the immense variety of methods which underly the chronic and multifarious intelligibility of action. Without the assimilation of this fundamental principle, with all its complex ramifications, the cognitive revolution in sociology will give rise to stillborn progeny – 'judgemental dopes' incapable of analysing their circumstances, incapable of agency and incapable of holding others morally accountable for their actions.

This analysis of cognition and action, which has received considerable empirical exemplification within conversation analysis, has transformed the analysis of the role of normative conventions in social organization which was consolidated in the Parsonian syntheses of 1937 and 1951. For it is the methodic intelligibility of their actions which provides an environment of 'considerations' to which individual actors may orient in the design of their actions. Here the actors' primary concern may be with what is, in its double sense, the accountability of what they do. Compliance with the normative requirements of a setting may thus be most realistically treated not as the unreflecting product of the prior internalization of norms, but as contingent upon a reflexive awareness of how alternative courses of action will be analysed and interpreted. This treatment has the important consequence that the constraining power of normative conventions can be construed as, at most, a 'tendency to bind' rather than as a matter of the normative determination of action. Additionally, this constraining power can be treated as variously and varyingly infused with considerations of self-presentation and self-interest. Finally, this treatment does not require the analyst to intellectualize the actors by imputing an explicit knowledge of norms to them, or to suggest that the actors have self-conscious knowledge of the normative principles to which their mundane actions may be oriented. While such principles may analysably underly the actors' actions, they may manifest themselves from the actors' point of view only as 'practical considerations' in the design of actions. By and large the actors are, as Garfinkel puts it, 'not interested' in the methodic bases of their actions and this comment extends to the normative aspects of these methods.

In a further extension of these conclusions, Garfinkel has developed a radical analysis of natural language use. Here two major and related points need to be stressed. First, Garfinkel has consistently rejected prevailing views of language which are dominated by conceptions of its representative function. This is partly because, like Wittgenstein, he has sought to focus attention on the variety and variability of the ways in which language makes contact with the world. This variability is a characteristic feature even of occasions in which language is being used in an intendedly representative way. For even here, Garfinkel argues, the meaning of the words is not ordained by some pre-existing agreement on correspondences between words and objects. Instead, it remains to be actively and constructively made out. And part of this interpretative process will involve the recognition that the words were intended to be understood *as* representative – and as representative in some particular way. Both recognitions will themselves be methodically achieved.

Second and relatedly, Garfinkel has consistently emphasized the ways in which all forms of natural language accounts, including those which are intendedly representative of some state of affairs, are themselves active interventions within the fields of events in which they occur and which they may partially bring to formulation. This is a phenomenon which speakers tacitly recognize in their understandings of utterances, but is relatively unacknowledged in contemporary analyses of language. All uses of language, including the most mundane of descriptions, are routinely – if tacitly – understood as *actions* which are grasped through an understanding of the purposes and intentions of speakers. As Garfinkel pointedly observes, the understanding of speech consists of understanding 'how the parties spoke'. Speaking is a major domain of social action and is not to be treated as something separate from social action or as organized by a separate set of methods. Far from being a rigid framework for the transmission of representations between actors, language is an elastic medium for the performance of actions, and the understanding of utterances must necessarily involve the same range of methodic contextual considerations as the understanding of any other form of action.

These core themes of Garfinkel's work are vividly exempli-fied in the detailed analyses of interaction which are currently being developed by conversation analysts and in the various studies of institutional and occupational activities inspired by his initiatives. Both areas of study are marked by the anti-essentialism which is a hallmark of ethnomethodological work and by an awareness of the internal complexity of the constituent activities through which social institutions are produced and reproduced. It is the complexity and multiplicity of these interlocking social practices which, together with the ways in which institutionalized accounting frameworks are their unseen presupposition and product, give social structures of everyday activities their underlying stability and resistance to change.

At the end of his dissertation, Garfinkel observed that 'we conclude on the note that there are more questions to be asked than answers. In attempting to redeem one promisory note we have had to give ten in its place.' This comment is not inapposite to the contemporary state of ethnomethodology. In the course of his career Garfinkel has repeatedly questioned established understandings of social processes, raising new issues to be considered and opening up new domains for investigation. The common theme of these enterprises has been his attempt to come more directly into contact with the raw data of human experience and conduct by stripping away the innumerable theoretical and methodological barriers which imperceptibly interpose themselves between observers and the organizationally significant features of social activity. If it is to succeed, such an enterprise must inevitably involve a willingness to issue, and accept, promisory notes, but it would be misleading to regard the matter as resting there. The research of the last twenty years or so has resulted in the creation of the sociological equivalent of the microscope. The use of this instrument is yielding glimpses of previously unimaginable levels of social organization in human conduct and it is clear that major findings at the molecular and sub-molecular levels of social structure are there to be made. The problems involved at this level of investigation are undoubtedly very complex, but there need be little cause for anxiety on this score when there is so much that is fascinating and significant about human conduct to be discovered on the way to their solution. The instrument has been built: the challenge is to start working with it.

Appendix: Glossary of Transcript Symbols

(Condensed from Jefferson, 1984a)

[A single left bracket indicates the point of overlap onset.

]   A single right bracket indicates the point at which an utterance or utterance-part terminates *vis-à-vis* another.

=   Equal signs, one at the end of one line and one at the beginning of a next, indicate no 'gap' between the two lines.

[]   A combined left/right bracket indicates simultaneous onset of the bracketed utterances.

It is also used as a substitute for *equal signs* to indicate no 'gap' between two utterances. This relationship may be shown as:

E: Yah,=

L: =Tuh hell with im.

or as:

E: Yah,[

L: [Tuh hell with im.

(0.0)   Numbers in parentheses indicate elapsed time in silence by tenths of seconds. For example (1.3) is one and three-tenths seconds.

(.)   A dot in parentheses indicates a tiny 'gap' within or between utterances. It is probably no more than one-tenth of a second.

—   Underscoring indicates some form of stress, via pitch and/or amplitude. A short underscore indicates lighter stress than does a long underscore.

::   Colons indicate prolongation of the immediately prior sound. The length of the colon row indicates length of the prolongation.

:+___ Combinations of stress and prolongation markers indicate intonation contours. If the underscore occurs on a letter before a colon, it 'punches up' the letter; i.e. indicates an 'up → down' contour. If the underscore occurs on a colon after a letter, it 'punches up' the colon; i.e. indicates a 'down → up' contour.

In the following utterance there are two pitch-shifts, the first, the 'venee:r', an 'up → down' shift, the second, in 'thou:gh', a 'down → up'.

J: it's only venee:r thou:gh,

↑ ↓ Arrows indicate shifts into higher or lower pitch than would be indicated by just the combined stress/prolongation markers.

?, Punctuation markers are used to indicate intonation. The combined question mark/comma (?,) indicates a stronger rise than a comma but weaker than a question mark.

These markers massively occur at appropriate syntactical points, but occasionally there are such displays as:

C: Oh I'd say he's about what.five three enna ha:lf?arentchu Robert,

And occasionally, at a point where a punctuation marker would be appropriate, there isn't one. The absence of an 'utterance-final' punctuation marker indicates some sort of 'indeterminate' contour.

WORD Upper case indicates especially loud sounds relative to the surrounding talk.

° The degree sign is used as a 'softener'.

Utterances or utterance parts bracketted by degree signs are relatively quieter than the surrounding talk.

word A sub-scribed dot is frequently used as a 'hardener'. In this capacity it can indicate, e.g. an especially dentalized 't'. Usually when it occurs under a 'd' it indicates that the 'd' sounds more like a 't'. And, for example, under a possibly ambiguous 'g', it indicates a hard 'g'. Under a possibly ambiguous 'th', it indicates a hard 'th'.

‹ A pre-positioned left carat indicates a hurried start. A common locus of this phenomenon is 'self repair'. For example:

C: Monday nights we play, (0.3) ‹I mean we go to ceramics,
J: y'see it's diffrent f'me:.‹eh f'(.) the othuh boy:s

A post-positioned left carat indicates a sudden stop.

— A dash indicates a cut-off.

› ‹ Right/left carats bracketting an utterance or utterance-part indicate speeding up.

hhh	A dot-prefixed row of h's indicates an inbreath. Without the dot the h's indicate an outbreath.
wohhrd	A row of h's within a word indicates breathiness.
(h)	A parenthesized 'h' indicates plosiveness. This can be associated with laughter, crying, breathlessness, etc.
wghord	A 'gh' within a word indicates gutteralness.
( )	Empty parentheses indicate the transcriber's inability to hear what was said. The length of the parenthesized space indicates the length of the untranscribed talk.
	In the speaker-designation column, the empty parentheses indicate inability to identify a speaker.
(word)	Parenthesized words are especially dubious hearings or speaker-identifications.
(( ))	Doubled parentheses contain transcribers' descriptions rather than, or in addition to, transcriptions.
(NB:II:1)	Codes that identify fragments being quoted designate parts of the author's tape collections, or cite a published source for the datum in question. All names of the speakers have been changed.

Bibliography

Abel, T. 1948: The operation called *Verstehen*. *American Journal of Sociology*, 54, pp. 211–18.

Alexander, J. forthcoming: The 'individualist dilemma' in phenomenology and interactionism: towards a synthesis with the classical tradition. In S. N. Eisenstadt and H. J. Helle (eds), *Revisions and Relations of Macro- and Micro-Sociological Paradigms*, New York, Sage.

Apel, K.-O. 1967: *Analytic Philosophy of Language and the 'Geisteswissenschaften'*. Foundations of Language supplementary series, vol. 5, Dordrecht, Reidel.

Apel. K.-O. 1972: The *a priori* of communication and the foundation of the humanities. *Man and World*, 5, pp. 1–37.

Asch, S. E. 1951: Effects of group pressure on the modification and distortion of judgements. In H. Guetzkow (ed.), *Groups, Leadership and Men*, Pittsburgh, Carnegie Press, pp. 177–90.

Atkinson, J. M. 1971: Societal reactions to deviance: the role of coroners' definitions. In S. Cohen (ed.), *Images of Deviance*, Harmondsworth, Penguin, pp. 165–91.

Atkinson, J. M. 1978: *Discovering Suicide: Studies in the Social Organization of Sudden Death*, London, Macmillan.

Atkinson, J. M. 1981: Ethnomethodological approaches to sociolegal studies. In A. Podgorecki and C. J. Whelan (eds) *Sociological Approaches to Law*, London, Croom Helm, pp. 201–23.

Atkinson, J. M. 1982: Understanding formality: notes on the categorization and production of 'formal' interaction. *British Journal of Sociology*, 33, pp. 86–117.

Atkinson, J. M. and Drew, P. 1979: *Order in Court: the Organization of Verbal Interaction in Judicial Settings*, London, Macmillan.

Atkinson, J. M. and Heritage, J. C. 1984: *Structures of Social Action: Studies in Conversation Analysis*, Cambridge, Cambridge University Press.

Attewell, P. 1974: Ethnomethodology since Garfinkel. *Theory and Society*, 1, pp. 179–210.

Baker, G. P. 1981: Following Wittgenstein: some signposts for *Philosophical Investigations*, paras. 143–242. In C. M. Leich and S. H. Holtzman (eds), *Wittgenstein: to Follow a Rule*, London, Routledge and Kegan Paul.

Baker, G. P. and Hacker, P. M. S. 1980: *Wittgenstein: Understanding and Meaning*, Oxford, Basil Blackwell.

Barnes, B. 1981: On the conventional character of knowledge and cognition. *Philosophy of the Social Sciences*, 11, pp. 303–33.

Barnes, B. 1982a: *T. S. Kuhn and Social Science*, London, Macmillan.

Barnes, B. 1982b: On the extension of concepts and the growth of knowledge. *Sociological Review*, 30, pp. 23–44.

Barnes, B. and Law, J. 1976: Whatever should be done with indexical expressions? *Theory and Society*, 3, pp. 223–37.

Berger, P. and Luckmann, T. 1967: *The Social Construction of Reality*, London, Allen Lane.

Bershady, H. 1973: *Ideology and Social Knowledge*, Oxford, Basil Blackwell.

Bittner, E. 1965: The concept of organization. *Social Research*, 32, pp. 230–55.

Bittner, E. 1967a: Police discretion in emergency apprehension of mentally ill persons. *Social Problems*, 14, pp. 278–92.

Bittner, E. 1967b: The police on skid-row: a study of peace keeping. *American Sociological Review*, 32, pp. 699–715.

Bloor, D. 1976: *Knowledge and Social Imagery*, London, Routledge & Kegan Paul.

Bloor, D. 1978: Polyhedra and the abominations of Leviticus. *British Journal for the History of Science*, 11, pp. 245–72.

Bloor, D. 1981: The strengths of the strong programme. *Philosophy of the Social Sciences*, 11, pp. 199–213.

Blumer, H. 1969: *Symbolic Interactionism: Perspective and Method*, Englewood Cliffs, NJ, Prentice-Hall.

Brown, P. and Levinson, S. 1978: Universals in language usage: politeness phenomena. In E. Goody (ed.) *Questions and Politeness: Strategies in Social Interaction*, Cambridge, Cambridge University Press, pp. 56–289

Bruner, J. 1974: *Beyond the Information Given*, London, Allen & Unwin.

Bruner, J. 1975a: From communication to language: a psychological perspective. *Cognition*, 3, pp. 225–87.

Bruner, J. 1975b: The ontogenesis of speech acts. *Journal of Child Language*, 2, pp. 1–19.

Bruner, J. 1976: On prelinguistic prerequisites of speech. In R. N. Campbell and P. T. Smith (eds), *Recent Advances in the Psychology of Language: Language Development and Mother–Child Interaction*, London, Plenum Press, pp. 199–214.

Bruner, J. 1977: Early social interaction and language acquisition. In H. R. Schaffer (ed.), *Studies in Mother–Infant Interaction*, London, Academic Press, 271–89.

Bruner, J. 1984: *Child's Talk: Learning to Use Language*, Oxford, Oxford University Press.

Bruner, J., Goodnow, J. and Austin, G. A. 1956: *A Study of Thinking*, New York, Wiley.

Bruner, J. and Postman, N. 1949: On the perception of incongruity: a paradigm. *Journal of Personality*, 18, pp. 206–23.

Button, G. and Casey, N. 1982: Topic nomination and topic pursuit. Mimeo, Plymouth Polytechnic.

Button, G. and Casey, N. 1984: Generating topic: the use of topic initial elicitors. In Atkinson and Heritage 1984, pp. 167–90.

Cavell, S. 1961: *The Claim to Rationality*. Unpublished Ph.D. dissertation, Harvard University.

Cavell, S. 1962: The availability of Wittgenstein's later philosophy. *The Philosophical Review*, 71, pp. 67–93.

Cavell, S. 1979: *The Claim of Reason*, Oxford, Oxford University Press.

Chomsky, N. 1957: *Syntactic Structures*, The Hague, Mouton.

Chomsky, N. 1965: *Aspects of the Theory of Syntax*, Cambridge, Mass., MIT Press.

Cicourel, A. V. 1964: *Method and Measurement in Sociology*, New York, Free Press.

Cicourel, A. V. 1968: *The Social Organization of Juvenile Justice*, New York, Wiley.

Cicourel, A. V. 1973: *Cognitive Sociology*, Harmondsworth, Penguin.

Cicourel, A. V. 1974: *Theory and Method in a Study of Argentine Fertility*, New York, Wiley.

Cicourel, A. V., et al. 1974: *Language Use and School Performance*, New York, Academic Press.

Cicourel, A. V. and Kitsuse, J. I. 1963: *The Educational Decision Makers*, New York, Bobbs Merrill.

Collett, P. (ed.) 1975: *Social Rules and Social Behaviour*, Oxford, Basil Blackwell.

Collins, H. M. 1975: The seven sexes: a study in the sociology of a phenomenon, or the replication of experiments in physics. *Sociology*, 9, pp. 205–24.

Collins, H. M. 1981: Son of seven sexes: the social destruction of a phenomenon. *Social Studies of Science*, 11, pp. 33–62.

Collins, H. M. and Pinch, T. 1982: *Frames of Meaning: the Social Construction of Extraordinary Science*, London, Routledge & Kegan Paul.

Coulter, J. 1971: Decontextualized meanings: current approaches to to *verstehende* investigations. *Sociological Review*, 19 (New Series), pp. 301–33.

Coulter, J. 1973: Language and the conceptualization of meaning. *Sociology*, 7, pp. 173–89.

Coulter, J. 1975a: Perceptual accounts and interpretive assymetries. *Sociology*, 9, pp. 385–96.

Coulter, J. 1975b: *The Operations of Mental Health Personnel.* Unpublished Ph.D. dissertation, University of Manchester.

Davidson, J. 1984: Subsequent versions of invitations, offers, requests and proposals dealing with potential or actual rejection. In Atkinson and Heritage 1984, pp. 102–28.

Dawe, A. 1970: The two sociologies. *British Journal of Sociology*, 21, pp. 207–18.

Dawe, A. 1978: Theories of social action. In T. Bottomore and R. Nisbet (eds), *A History of Sociological Analysis*, London, Heinemann, pp. 362–417.

Denzin, N. 1971: Symbolic interactionism and ethnomethodology. In Douglas 1971, pp. 259–84.

Douglas, J. 1967: *The Social Meanings of Suicide*, Princeton, Princeton University Press.

Douglas, J. (ed.) 1971: *Understanding Everyday Life*, London, Routledge & Kegan Paul.

Drew, P. 1978: Accusations: the occasioned use of members' knowledge of 'religious geography' in describing events. *Sociology*, 12, pp. 1–22.

Drew, P. 1984a: Speakers' 'reportings' in invitation sequences. In Atkinson and Heritage 1984, pp. 129–51.

Drew, P. 1984b: Analyzing the use of language in courtroom interaction. In T. van Dijk (ed.), *A Handbook of Discourse Analysis: Vol. 3, Genres of Discourse*, New York, Academic Press.

Durkheim, E. 1952: *Suicide: A Study in Sociology* (trans. J. A. Spaulding and G. Simpson), London, Routledge & Kegan Paul. (Originally published in 1897.)

Durkheim, E. 1982: *The Rules of Sociological Method* (trans. W. D. Halls), London, Macmillan. (Originally published in 1895.)

Durkheim, E. and Mauss, M. 1963: *Primitive Classification* (trans. R. Needham), London, Cohen and West. (Originally published in 1903.)

Engels, F. 1968: The origin of the family, private property and the state. In K. Marx and F. Engels, *Selected Works*, London, Lawrence and Wishart.

Ervin-Tripp, S. and Mitchell-Kernan, C. (eds), 1977: *Child Discourse*, New York, Academic Press.

Evans-Pritchard, E. E. 1937: *Witchcraft, Oracles and Magic among the*

Azande, Oxford, Oxford University Press.

Farber, M. 1943: *The Foundation of Phenomenology*, Cambridge, Mass., Harvard University Press.

Foote, N. 1951: Identification as a basis for a theory of motivation. *American Sociological Review*, 16, pp. 14–21.

Friedman, N. 1967: *The Social Nature of Psychological Research*, New York, Basic Books.

Garfinkel, H. 1949: Research note on inter- and intra-racial homicides. *Social Forces*, 27, pp. 370–81.

Garfinkel, H. 1952: *The Perception of the Other: a Study in Social Order.* Unpublished Ph.D. dissertation, Harvard University.

Garfinkel, H. 1956a: Conditions of successful degradation ceremonies. *American Journal of Sociology*, 61, pp. 240–4.

Garfinkel, H. 1956b: Some sociological concepts and methods for psychiatrists. *Psychiatric Research Reports*, 6, pp. 181–95.

Garfinkel, H. 1959: Aspects of the problem of commonsense knowledge of social structures. *Transactions of the Fourth World Congress of Sociology*, 4, pp. 51–65.

Garfinkel, H. 1963: A conception of, and experiments with, 'trust' as a condition of stable concerted actions. In O. J. Harvey (ed.), *Motivation and Social Interaction*, New York, Ronald Press, pp. 187–238.

Garfinkel, H. 1967: *Studies in Ethnomethodology*, Englewood Cliffs, NJ, Prentice-Hall. Paperback edition, 1984: *Studies in Ethnomethodology*, Polity Press, Cambridge.

Garfinkel, H. 1967a: What is ethnomethodology? In Garfinkel 1967, pp. 1–34.

Garfinkel, H. 1967b: Studies of the routine grounds of everyday activities. In Garfinkel 1967, pp. 35–75. (Reprinted with revisions from *Social Problems*, 11, 225–50.)

Garfinkel, H. 1967c: Commonsense knowledge of social structures: the documentary method of interpretation in lay and professional fact finding. In Garfinkel 1967, pp. 76–103. (Originally published in J. M. Sher (ed.) *Theories of the Mind*. New York: Free Press, 1962.)

Garfinkel, H. 1967d: Some rules of correct decision making that jurors respect. In Garfinkel 1967, pp. 104–115.

Garfinkel, H. 1967e: Passing and the managed achievement of sexual status in an intersexed person, part 1. In Garfinkel 1967, pp. 116–185.

Garfinkel, H. 1967f: 'Good' organizational reasons for 'bad' clinic records. In Garfinkel 1967, pp. 186–207.

Garfinkel, H. 1967g: Methodological adequacy in the quantitative study of selection criteria and selection practices in psychiatric outpatient clinics. In Garfinkel 1967, pp. 208–61.

Garfinkel, H. 1967h: The rational properties of commonsense and scientific activities. In Garfinkel 1967, pp. 262–84. (Reprinted from *Behavioural Science*, 5, 72–83.)

Garfinkel, H. 1967i: Practical sociological reasoning: some features in the work of the Los Angeles Suicide Prevention Center. In E. S. Schneidman (ed.), *Essays in Self-Destruction*, New York, International Science Press, pp. 171–87.

Garfinkel, H. 1968: oral contributions in R. J. Hill and K. S. Crittenden (eds), *Proceedings of the Purdue Symposium on Ethnomethodology*, Institute Monograph Series, no. 1, Institute for the Study of Social Change, Purdue University.

Garfinkel, H. 1974: On the origins of the term 'ethnomethodology'. In R. Turner (ed.), *Ethnomethodology*, Harmondsworth, Penguin, pp. 15–18. (Abstracted from Hill and Crittenden (eds), *Proceedings of the Purdue Symposium on Ethnomethodology*, Institute Monograph Series, no. 1, Institute for the Study of Social Change, Purdue University, 1968, pp. 5–11.)

Garfinkel, H. 1978: Introduction to the session on ethnomethodology, studies of work, Ninth World Congress of Sociology, Uppsala, Sweden.

Garfinkel, H. forthcoming: *A Manual for the Study of Naturally Organized Ordinary Activities* (3 volumes), London, Routledge & Kegan Paul.

Garfinkel, H., Lynch, M. and Livingston, E. 1981: The work of a discovering science construed with materials from the optically discovered pulsar. *Philosophy of the Social Sciences*, 11, pp. 131–58.

Garfinkel, H. and Sacks, H. 1970: On formal structures of practical actions. In J. C. McKinney and E. A. Tiryakian (eds), *Theoretical Sociology*, New York, Appleton Century Crofts, pp. 338–66.

Giddens, A. 1979: *Central Problems in Social Theory*, London, Macmillan.

Gilbert, G. N. and Abell, P. (eds) 1983: *Accounts and Action*, Farnborough, Gower.

Gilbert, G. N. and Mulkay, M. 1980: Contexts of scientific discourse: social accounting in experimental papers. In K. Knorr *et al.* (eds), *The Social Process of Scientific Investigation*, Dordrecht, Reidel, pp. 269–284.

Gilbert, G. N. and Mulkay, M. 1982a: Warranting scientific belief. *Social Studies of Science*, 12, pp. 363–408.

Gilbert, G. N. and Mulkay, M. 1982b: Experiments are the key: scientists' and historians' history-making. Mimeo, Universities of Surrey and York. (To appear in *Isis* in 1984.)

Gilbert, G. N. and Mulkay, M. 1984: *Opening Pandora's Box: an Analysis of Scientists' Discourse*, Cambridge, Cambridge University Press.

Goffman, E. 1955: On face-work: an analysis of ritual elements in social interaction. *Psychiatry*, 18, pp. 213–31.

Goffman, E. 1956: The nature of deference and demeanor. *American Anthropologist*, 58, pp. 473–502.

Goffman, E. 1963: *Behaviour in Public Places*, New York, Free Press.

Goffman, E. 1971: *Relations in Public*, New York, Basic Books.

Goffman, E. 1981: *Forms of Talk*, Oxford, Basil Blackwell.

Goldthorpe, J. H. 1973: A revolution in sociology? *Sociology*, 7, pp. 449–62.

Goodwin, C. 1979a: The interactive construction of a sentence in natural conversation. In Psathas 1979, pp. 97–121.

Goodwin, C. 1979b: review of S. Duncan Jr. and D. W. Fiske, *Face to Face Interaction: Research, Methods and Theory*. *Language in Society*, 8, pp. 439–44.

Goodwin, C. 1981: *Conversational Organization: Interaction Between Speakers and Hearers*, New York, Academic Press.

Goodwin, C. and Goodwin, M. H. 1982: Concurrent operations on talk: notes on the interactive organization of assessments. Paper presented at the 77th Annual Meeting of the American Sociological Association, San Francisco, California.

Grathoff, R. 1978: *The Theory of Social Action: the Correspondence of Alfred Schutz and Talcott Parsons*, Bloomington, Indiana University Press.

Gregory, R. 1974a: Perceptions as hypotheses. In S. C. Brown (ed.), *Philosophy of Psychology*, London, Macmillan, pp. 195–210.

Gregory, R. 1974b: *Concepts and Mechanisms of Perception*, London, Duckworth.

Grice, H. P. 1975: Logic and conversation. In P. Cole and J. L. Morgan (eds), *Syntax and Semantics 3: Speech Acts*, New York, Academic Press, pp. 41–58.

Gurwitsch, A. 1964: *The Field of Consciousness*, Duquesne, Duquesne University Press.

Gurwitsch, A. 1966: *Phenomenology and Psychology*, Evanston, Ill., Northwestern University Press.

Halbwachs, M. 1978: *The Causes of Suicide*, (trans. H. Goldblatt), London, Routledge & Kegan Paul. (Originally published in 1930.)

Harre, R. and Secord, P. F. 1972: *The Explanation of Social Behaviour*, Oxford, Basil Blackwell.

Harris, R. 1980: *The Language Makers*, London, Duckworth.

Hart, H. L. A. 1961: *The Concept of Law*, Oxford, Oxford University Press.

Heath, C. C. forthcoming: *The Partnership: Essays in the Social Organization of Speech and Body Movement in the Medical Consultation*, Cambridge, Cambridge University Press.

Heidegger, M. 1967: *What is a Thing?* Chicago, Henry Regnery.

Heritage, J. C. 1978: Aspects of the flexibilities of natural language use. *Sociology*, 12, pp. 79–103.

Heritage, J. C. 1983: Accounts in action. In Gilbert and Abell 1983, pp. 117–31.

Heritage, J. C. 1984a: A change of state token and aspects of its sequential placement. In Atkinson and Heritage 1984, pp. 299–345.

Heritage, J. C. 1984b: Analysing news interviews: aspects of the production of talk for an overhearing audience. In T. van Dijk (ed.), *Handbook of Discourse Analysis, Vol. 3: Genres of Discourse*, New York, Academic Press.

Heritage, J. C. 1984c: Recent developments in conversation analysis. Warwick Working Papers in Sociology No. 1, Department of Sociology, University of Warwick.

Hesse, M. B. 1974: *The Structure of Scientific Inference*, London, Macmillan.

Hesse, M. B. 1980: The strong thesis of sociology of science. In M. B. Hesse, *Revolution and Reconstructions in Science*, Hassocks, Harvester Press, pp. 29–60.

Hindess, B. 1973: *The Use of Official Statistics in Sociology*, London, Macmillan.

Hollis, M. 1977: *Models of Man: Philosophical Thoughts on Social Action*, Cambridge, Cambridge University Press.

Homan, R. 1981: Crises in the definition of reality. *Sociology*, 15, pp. 210–24.

Husserl, E. 1970a: *Logical Investigations* (trans. J. N. Findlay), New York, |Humanities |Press). (Originally published in 1901.) |

Husserl, E. 1970b: *The Crisis of European Sciences and Transcendental Phenomenology: an Introduction to Phenomenological Philosophy* (trans. David Carr), Evanston, Ill., Northwestern University Press. (Originally published in 1938.)

Husserl, E. 1973: *Experience and Judgement* (trans. J. S. Churchill and K. Ameriks),| Evanston, Ill., Northwestern University Press. (Originally published in 1939.)

James, W. 1950: *Principles of Psychology* (2 vols.), New York, Dover Publications.

Jefferson, G. 1979: At first I thought . . . Unpublished lecture presented at the University of Warwick.

Jefferson, G. 1980a: *Final Report to the [British] SSRC on the Analysis of Conversations in which 'Troubles' and 'Anxieties' are Expressed* (no. HR 4805).

Jefferson, G. 1980b: On 'trouble-premonitory' response to inquiry. *Sociological Inquiry*, 50, pp. 153–85.

Jefferson, G. 1981a: The abominable 'Ne?': a working paper exploring the phenomenon of post-response pursuit of response. University of Manchester, Department of Sociology, Occasional Paper no. 6.

Jefferson, G. 1981b: 'Caveat speaker': a preliminary exploration of shift implicative recipiency in the articulation of topic. Report to the (British) SSRC.

Jefferson, G. 1983: On exposed and embedded correction in conversation. *Studium Linguistik*, 14, pp. 58–68.

Jefferson, G. 1984a: Caricature versus detail: on capturing the particulars of pronunciation in transcripts of conversational data. *Tilburg Papers on Language and Literature No. 31*, University of Tilburg, Netherlands.

Jefferson, G. 1984b: On stepwise transition from talk about a trouble to inappropriately next-positioned matters. In Atkinson and Heritage, 1984, pp. 191–222.

Kendon, A. 1979: Some theoretical and methodological aspects of the use of film in the study of social interaction. In G. P. Ginsburg (ed.), *Emerging Strategies in Social Psychological Research*, New York, Wiley, pp. 67–91.

Kendon, A. 1982: The organization of behaviour in face-to-face interaction: observations on the development of a methodology. In K. R. Scherer and P. Ekman (eds), *Handbook of Methods in Nonverbal Behaviour Research*, Cambridge, Cambridge University Press, pp. 440–505.

Knorr-Cetina, K. 1981: The micro-sociological challenge of macro-sociology: towards a reconstruction of social theory and methodology. In K. Knorr-Cetina and A. V. Cicourel (eds), *Advances in Social Theory and Methodology: Toward an Integration of Micro- and Macro-Sociologies*, London, Routledge & Kegan Paul, pp. 1–47.

Knorr-Cetina, K. and Mulkay, M. (eds), 1983: *Science Observed*, London, Sage.

Kripke, S. 1981: Wittgenstein on rules and private language. In I. Block (ed.), *Perspectives on the Philosophy of Wittgenstein*, Oxford, Basil Blackwell, pp. 238–312.

Kuhn, A. and Wolpe, A. 1978: *Feminism and Materialism: Women and Modes of Production*, London, Routledge & Kegan Paul.

Kuhn, T. S. 1970: *The Structure of Scientific Revolutions* (2nd edn), Chicago, University of Chicago Press.

Kuhn, T. S. 1977: Second thoughts on paradigms. In T. S. Kuhn, *The Essential Tension*, Chicago, University of Chicago Press, pp. 293–319.

Labov, W. 1972: Rules for ritual insults. In Sudnow 1972, pp. 120–69.

Labov, W. and Fanshel, D. 1977: *Therapeutic Discourse: Psychotherapy as Conversation*, New York, Academic Press.

Laing, R. D. 1965: *The Divided Self*, Harmondsworth, Penguin.

Latour, B. and Woolgar, S. 1979: *Laboratory Life: the Social Construction of Scientific Facts*, London, Sage.

Levinson, S. C. 1979: Activity types and language. *Linguistics*, 17, pp. 356–99.

Levinson, S. C. 1981a: The essential inadequacies of speech act models of dialogue. In H. Parret, M. Sbisa and J. Verschueren (eds), *Possibilities and Limitations of Pragmatics*, Amsterdam, Benjamins, pp. 473–92.

Levinson, S. C. 1981b: Some pre-observations on the modelling of dialogue. *Discourse Processes*, 4, pp. 93–110.

Levinson, S. C. 1983: *Pragmatics*, Cambridge, Cambridge University Press.

Livingston, E. 1978: Mathematicians' work. Paper presented at the session on ethnomethodology, studies of work, Ninth World Congress of Sociology, Uppsala, Sweden.

Livingston, E. 1982: *An Ethnomethodological Investigation of the Foundations of Mathematics*. Unpublished Ph.D. dissertation, University of California at Los Angeles.

Lynch, M. 1979: *Art and Artefact in Laboratory Science: a Study of Shop Work and Shop Talk in a Research Laboratory*. Unpublished Ph.D. dissertation, University of California at Irvine.

Lynch, M. 1982: Technical work and critical inquiry: investigations in a scientific laboratory. *Social Studies of Science*, 12, pp. 499–534.

Lynch, M. forthcoming: *Art and Artefacts in Laboratory Science*, London, Routledge & Kegan Paul.

Lynch, M., Livingston, E. and Garfinkel, H. 1983: Temporal order in laboratory work. In Knorr-Cetina and Mulkay 1983, pp. 205–38.

McBarnet, D. 1981: *Conviction*, London, Macmillan.

McCarthy, P. and Walsh, D. 1966: Suicide in Dublin. *British Medical Journal*, 1, pp. 1393–6.

McHoul, A. 1978: The organization of turns at formal talk in the classroom. *Language in Society*, 7, pp. 183–213.

McHoul, A. forthcoming: Notes on the organization of repair in classroom talk. In J. N. Schenkein (ed.), *Studies in the Organization of Conversational Interaction, Volume II*, New York, Academic Press.

McHugh, P. 1968: *Defining the Situation*, New York, Bobbs Merrill.

Marr, D. 1982: *Vision*, San Francisco, Freeman.

Marx, K. and Engels, F. 1965: *The German Ideology*, London, Lawrence and Wishart.

Mead, G. H. 1934: *Mind, Self and Society*, Chicago, University of Chicago Press.

Mead, G. H. 1938: *The Philosophy of the Act*, Chicago, University of Chicago Press.

Mehan, H. 1979: *Learning Lessons: Social Organization in the Classroom*, Cambridge, Mass., Harvard University Press.

Mennell, S. 1976: Ethnomethodology and the new *methodenstreit*. In D. C. Thorns (ed.), *New Directions in Sociology*, Newton Abbot, David and Charles.

Merleau-Ponty, M. 1962: *Phenomenology of Perception*, (trans. G. Smith), London, Routledge & Kegan Paul.

Merleau-Ponty, M. 1964: *The Primacy of Perception and Other Essays*, James Edie (ed.), Evanston, Ill., Northwestern University Press.

Merleau-Ponty, M. 1968: *The Visible and the Invisible* (trans. A. Lingis), Evanston, Ill., Northwestern University Press.

Merritt, M. 1976: On questions following answers (in service encounters). *Language in Society*, 5, pp. 315–57.

Mills, C. W. 1940: Situated actions and vocabularies of motives. *American Journal of Sociology*, 5, pp. 904–13.

Mulkay, M. 1981: Action and belief or scientific discourse?: a possible way of ending intellectual vassalage in social studies of science. *Philosophy of the Social Sciences*, 11, pp. 163–71.

Mulkay, M. and Gilbert, G. N. 1981: The truth will out: a device which scientists use to resolve potential contradictions between interpretative repertoires. Mimeo. Universities of Surrey and York. (Appears as chapter 5 of Gilbert and Mulkay, 1984.)

Mulkay, M. and Gilbert, G. N. 1982a: Accounting for error. *Sociology*, 16, pp. 165–83.

Mulkay, M. and Gilbert, G. N. 1982b: What is the ultimate question? *Social Studies of Science*, 12, pp. 309–19.

Mulkay, M. and Gilbert, G. N. 1982c: Joking apart: some recommendations concerning the analysis of scientific culture. *Social Studies of Science*, 12, pp. 585–613.

Mulkay, M. and Gilbert, G. N. 1983: Scientists' theory talk. *Canadian Journal of Sociology*, 8, pp. 179–197.

Mulkay, M., Potter, J. and Yearley, S. 1983: Why an analysis of scientific discourse is needed. In Knorr-Cetina and Mulkay 1983, pp. 171–204.

Natanson, M. 1956: *The Social Dynamics of George Herbert Mead*, Washington, Public Affairs Press.

Neumann, J. van and Morgenstern, O. 1952: *Theory of Games and Economic Behaviour* (2nd edn), Princeton, Princeton University Press.

Ochs, E. and Schieffelin, B. 1979: *Developmental Pragmatics*, New York: Academic Press.

O'Keefe, D. J. 1979: Ethnomethodology. *Journal for the Theory of Social Behaviour*, 9, pp. 187–219.

Parsons, T. 1936: review of Alexander von Schelting, *Max Weber's Wissenschaftslehre. American Sociological Review*, 1, pp. 675–81.

Parsons, T. 1937: *The Structure of Social Action*, New York, McGraw-Hill. (Page references are from the 1963 Free Press edition.)

Parsons, T. 1940: An analytical approach to social stratification. *American Journal of Sociology*, 45, pp. 841–62.

Parsons, T. 1942: Age and sex in the social structure of the United States. *American Sociological Review*, 7, pp. 604–16.

Parsons, T. 1943: The kinship system of the contemporary United States. *American Anthropologist*, 45, pp. 22–38.

Parsons, T. 1951: *The Social System*, New York, Free Press.

Parsons, T. 1954: A revised analytical approach to the theory of social stratification. In T. Parsons, *Essays in Sociological Theory* (revised edn), New York, Free Press.

Parsons, T. 1970: On building social system theory. *Daedalus*, 99, pp. 826–75.

Parsons, T. et al. 1951: *Towards a General Theory of Action*, Cambridge, Mass., Harvard University Press. (Page references are from the 1962 Harper Torchbook edition.)

Phillips, J. 1978: Some problems in locating practices. *Sociology*, 12, pp. 56–77.

Pitkin, H. F. 1972: *Wittgenstein and Justice*, Berkeley, University of California Press.

Pollner, M. 1974: Mundane reasoning. *Philosophy of the Social Sciences*, 4, pp. 35–54.

Pollner, M. 1975: 'The very coinage of your brain': the anatomy of reality disjunctures. *Philosophy of the Social Sciences*, 5, pp. 411–30.

Pomerantz, A. M. 1975: *Second Assessments: a Study of Some Features of Agreements/Disagreements*. Unpublished Ph.D. dissertation, University of California at Irvine.

Pomerantz, A. M. 1978a: Compliment responses: notes on the co-operation of multiple constraints. In Schenkein 1978, pp. 79–112.

Pomerantz, A. M. 1978b: Attributions of responsibility: blamings. *Sociology*, 12, pp. 115–21.

Pomerantz, A. M. 1980: Telling my side: 'limited access' as a 'fishing' device. *Sociological Inquiry*, 50, pp. 186–98.

Pomerantz, A. M. 1981: Speakers' claims as a feature of describing: a study of 'presenting the evidence for'. Paper presented at the 76th Annual Meetings of the American Sociological Association, Toronto, Canada.

Pomerantz, A. M. 1984: Agreeing and disagreeing with assessments. In Atkinson and Heritage 1984, pp. 57–101.

Pomerantz, A. M. and Atkinson, J. M. 1984: Ethnomethodology, conversation analysis and the study of courtroom behaviour. In D. J. Muller, D. E. Blackman and A. J. Chapman (eds), *Topics in Psychology and Law*, Chichester, Wiley, pp. 283–97.

Pope, W. 1976: *Durkheim's Suicide*, Chicago, University of Chicago Press.

Procter, I. 1978: Parsons' early voluntarism. *Sociological Inquiry*, 48, pp. 37–48.

Procter, I. 1980: Voluntarism and structural-functionalism in Parsons's early work. *Human Studies*, 3, pp. 331–46.

Psathas, G. (ed.) 1979: *Everyday Language: Studies in Ethnomethodology*, New York, Irvington Press.

Reiss, A. J. 1967: The social integration of queers and peers. In J. H. Gagnon and W. Simon (eds), *Sexual Deviance*, New York, Harper and Row.

Richards, J. L. 1979: The reception of a mathematical theory: non-euclidean geometry in England 1868–1883. In B. Barnes and S. Shapin (eds), *Natural Order: Historical Studies of Scientific Culture*, London, Sage, pp. 143–66.

Richards, M. P. M. 1971: Social interaction in the first weeks of human life. *Psychiat. Neurol. Neurochir.*, 14, pp. 35–42.

Richards, M. P. M. 1974: First steps in becoming social. In M. P. M. Richards (ed.), *The Integration of a Child into the Social World*, Cambridge, Cambridge University Press, pp. 83–97.

Rosch, E. 1975: Universals and cultural specifics in human categorization. In R. Brislin, S. Bochner and W. Lonner (eds), *Cross-Cultural Perspectives on Learning*, New York, Halstead Press, pp. 177–206.

Rosch, E. 1977: Human categorization. In N. Warren (ed.), *Advances in Cross-Cultural Psychology*, London, Academic Press, pp. 1–49.

Rosch, E. 1978: Principles of categorization. In E. Rosch and B. Lloyd (eds), *Cognition and Categorization*, Hillsdale, NJ, Erlbaum, pp. 27–48.

Rosch, E. and Mervis, C. B. 1975: Family resemblances: studies in the internal structure of categories. *Cognitive Psychology*, 7, pp. 573–605.

Rosch, E., Simpson, C. and Miller, R. J. 1976: Structural bases of typicality effects. *Journal of Experimental Psychology: Human Perception and Performance*, 2, 491–502.

Rosenthal, R. 1966: *Experimenter Effects in Behavioural Research*, New York, Appleton Century Crofts.

Sacks, H. 1963: Sociological description. *Berkeley Journal of Sociology*, 8, pp. 1–16.

Sacks, H. 1964–72: Unpublished transcribed lectures, University of California at Irvine. (Transcribed and indexed, G. Jefferson.)

Sacks, H. 1972a: An initial investigation of the usability of conversational data for doing sociology. In Sudnow 1972, pp, 31–74.

Sacks, H. 1972b: On the analysability of stories by children. In J. J. Gumperz and D. Hymes (eds), *Directions in Sociolinguistics*, New York, Holt, Rinehart and Winston, pp. 325–45.

Sacks, H. 1974: An analysis of the course of a joke's telling in conversation. In R. Bauman and J. Sherzer (eds) *Explorations in the Ethnography of Speaking*, Cambridge, Cambridge University Press, pp. 337–53.

Sacks, H. 1984a: Methodological remarks. In Atkinson and Heritage 1984, pp. 21–27.

Sacks, H. 1984b: On doing 'being ordinary'. In Atkinson and Heritage 1984, pp. 413–29.

Sacks, H., Schegloff, E. A. and Jefferson, G. 1974: A simplest systematics for the organization of turn-taking for conversation. *Language*, 50, pp. 696–735.

Savage, S. 1981: *The Theories of Talcott Parsons*, London, Macmillan.

Schegloff, E. A. 1968: Sequencing in conversational openings. *American Anthropologist*, 70, pp. 1075–95.

Schegloff, E. A. 1972: Notes on conversational practice: formulating place. In Sudnow 1972, pp. 75–119.

Schegloff, E. A. 1979a: Identification and recognition in telephone conversation openings. In Psathas 1979, pp. 23–78.

Schegloff, E. A. 1979b: The relevance of repair to syntax-for-conversation. In T. Givon (ed.), *Syntax and Semantics 12: Discourse and Syntax*, New York, Academic Press, pp. 261–88.

Schegloff, E. A. 1979c: Repair after next turn.]Unpublished paper presented at the *Conference on Practical Reasoning and Discourse Processes*, St Hugh's College, Oxford.

Schegloff, E. A. 1980: Preliminaries to preliminaries: can I ask you a question? *Sociological Inquiry*, 50, pp. 104–52.

Schegloff, E. A. 1984: On some questions and ambiguities in conversation. In Atkinson and Heritage 1984, pp. 28–52.

Schegloff, E. A., Jefferson, G. and Sacks, H.. 1977: The preference for self-correction in the organization of repair in conversation. *Language*, 53, pp. 361–82.

Schegloff, E. A. and Sacks, H. 1973: Opening up closings. *Semiotica*, 7, pp. 289–327.

Schelling, T. C. 1960: *The Strategy of Conflict*, Oxford, Oxford University Press.

Schenkein, J. N. 1978: *Studies in the Organization of Conversational Interaction*, New York, Academic Press.

Schutz, A. 1962: *Collected Papers*, volume 1, The Hague, Martinus Nijhoff.

Schutz, A. 1962a: Commonsense and scientific interpretations of human action. In Schutz 1962, pp. 3–47.

Schutz, A. 1962b: Concept and theory formation in the social sciences. In Schutz 1962, pp. 48–66.

Schutz, A. 1962c: Choosing among projects of action. In Schutz 1962, pp. 67–98.

Schutz, A. 1962d: Some leading concepts of phenomenology. In Schutz 1962, pp. 99–117.

Schutz, A. 1962e: On multiple realities. In Schutz 1962, pp. 207–59.

Schutz, A. 1962f: Symbol, reality and society. In Schutz 1962, pp. 287–356.

Schutz, A. 1964: *Collected Papers*, volume 2, The Hague, Martinus Nijhoff.

Schutz, A. 1964a: The social world and the theory of social action. In Schutz 1964, pp. 3–19.

Schutz, A. 1964b: The dimensions of the social world. In Schutz 1964, pp. 20–63.

Schutz, A. 1964c: The problem of rationality in the social world. In A. Schutz 1964, pp. 64–90.

Schutz, A. 1964d: Don Quixote and the problem of reality. In Schutz 1964, pp. 135–58.

Schutz, A. 1966: *Collected Papers*, volume 3, The Hague, Martinus Nijhoff.

Schutz, A. 1966a: The problem of transcendental intersubjectivity in Husserl. In Schutz 1966, pp. 51–83.

Schutz, A. 1966b: Type and eidos in Husserl's late philosophy. In Schutz 1966, pp. 92–115.

Schutz, A. 1967: *The Phenomenology of the Social World* (trans. G. Walsh and F. Lehnert), Evanston, Ill., Northwestern University Press. (Originally published in 1932.)

Schutz, A. 1970: *Reflections on the Problem of Relevance*, New Haven, Yale University Press.

Schutz, A. and Luckmann, T. 1974: *The Structures of the Life World*, London, Heinemann.

Schwabe, A. D., Solomon, D. H., Stoller, R. J. and Burnham, J. P. 1962: Pubertal feminization in a genetic male with testicular atrophy and normal urinary gonadotropin. *Journal of Clinical Endocrinology and Metabolism*, 8, pp. 839–45.

Scott, J. F. 1963: The changing foundations of the Parsonian action scheme. *American Sociological Review*, 28, pp. 716–35.

Searle, J. 1969: *Speech Acts*, Cambridge, Cambridge University Press.

Sharrock, W. 1974: On owning knowledge. In R. Turner (ed.),

Ethnomethodology, Harmondsworth, Penguin, pp. 45–53.

Simmel, G. 1971: The transcendent character of life. In D. N. Levine (ed.), *Georg Simmel on Individuality and Social Forms*, Chicago, Chicago University Press, pp. 353–74.

Skinner, Q. 1978: *The Foundations of Modern Political Thought, vol. 1: The Rennaisance*, Cambridge, Cambridge University Press.

Smith, D. 1978: K is mentally ill: the anatomy of a factual account. *Sociology*, 12, pp. 23–53.

Snow, C. E. and Ferguson, C. A. (eds) 1977: *Talking to Children*, Cambridge, Cambridge University Press.

Stengel, E. and Farberow, N. L. 1967: Certification of suicide around the world. In N. L. Farberow (ed.), *Proceedings of the Fourth International Conference for Suicide Prevention*, Los Angeles, Delmar Publishing Co.

Stoller, R. J. 1968: *Sex and Gender*, London, The Hogarth Press.

Stoller, R. J. 1975: *The Trans-sexual Experiment*, London, The Hogarth Press.

Stoller, R. J., Garfinkel, H. and Rosen, A. C. 1960: Passing and the maintenance of sexual identification in an intersexed patient. *Archives for General Psychiatry*, 2, pp. 379–84.

Stoller, R. J., Garfinkel, H. and Rosen, A. C. 1962: Psychiatric management of intersexed patients. *California Journal of Medicine*, 96, pp. 30–4.

Sudnow, D. 1965: Normal crimes. *Social Problems*, 12, pp. 255–76.

Sudnow, D. (ed.) 1972: *Studies in Social Interaction*, New York, Free Press.

Sudnow, D. 1978: *Ways of the Hand*, Cambridge, Mass., Harvard University Press.

Terasaki, A. K. 1976: Pre-announcement sequences in conversation. Social sciences working paper no. 99, Irvine, University of California.

Turner, J. H. and Beeghley, L. 1974: Current folklore in the criticism of Parsonian action theory. *Sociological Inquiry*, 44, pp. 47–55.

Turner, R. 1971: Words, utterances and activities. In Douglas 1971, pp. 169–87.

Tylor, S. 1969: *Cognitive Anthropology*, New York, Holt, Rinehart and Winston.

Watson, D. R. 1978: Categorization, authorization and blame negotiation in conversation. *Sociology*, 12, pp. 105–13.

Weber, M. 1949: *The Methodology of the Social Sciences* (trans. E. Shils and H. Finch), New York, Free Press.

Weber, M. 1968: *Economy and Society*, volume 1 (ed. G. Roth and C. Wittich), New York, Bedminster Press.

Wieder, D. L. 1974: *Language and Social Reality*, The Hague, Mouton.

Wilson, B. (ed.) 1970: *Rationality*, Oxford, Basil Blackwell.

Wilson, T. P. 1971: Normative and interpretive paradigms in sociology. In Douglas 1971, pp. 57–79.

Winch, P. 1958: *The Idea of a Social Science*, London, Routledge & Kegan Paul.

Wittgenstein, L. 1958: *Philosophical Investigations* (2nd edn), Oxford, Basil Blackwell.

Wittgenstein, L. 1969: *The Blue and Brown Books* (2nd edn), Oxford, Basil Blackwell.

Wootton, A. 1981: The management of grantings and rejections by parents in request sequences. *Semiotica*, 37, pp. 59–89.

Wrong, D. H. 1961: The oversocialized conception of man in modern sociology. *American Sociological Review*, 26, pp. 183–93.

Zimmerman, D. 1969a: Record keeping and the intake process in a public welfare agency. In S. Wheeler (ed.), *On Record: Files and Dossiers in American Life*, New York, Sage, pp. 319–54.

Zimmerman, D. 1969b: Tasks and troubles: the practical bases of work activities in a public assistance agency. In D. H. Hansen (ed.), *Explorations in Sociology and Counselling*, New York, Houghton Mifflin.

Zimmerman, D. 1971: The practicalities of rule use. In Douglas 1971, pp. 221–38.

Zimmerman, D. and Pollner, M. 1971: The everyday world as a phenomenon. In Douglas 1971, pp. 80–103.

Zimmerman, D. and West, C. 1975: Sex roles, interruptions and silences in conversation. In B. Thorne and N. Henley (eds), *Language and Sex: Difference and Dominance*, Rowley, Mass., Newbury House, pp. 105–29.

INDEX